The Bomb in My Garden

The Bomb in
My Garden

The Secrets of Saddam's
Nuclear Mastermind

MAHDI OBEIDI AND KURT PITZER

WILEY

John Wiley & Sons, Inc.

Published by John Wiley & Sons, Inc., Hoboken, New Jersey
Published simultaneously in Canada

Design and composition by Navta Associates, Inc.

For general information about our other products and services, please contact our Customer Care Department within the United States at (800) 762-2974, outside the United States at (317) 572-3993 or fax (317) 572-4002.

Wiley also publishes its books in a variety of electronic formats. Some content that appears in print may not be available in electronic books. For more information about Wiley products, visit our web site at www.wiley.com.

Library of Congress Cataloging-in-Publication Data:

Obeidi, Mahdi, 1944–
    The bomb in my garden : the secrets of Saddam's nuclear mastermind / by Mahdi Obeidi and Kurt Pitzer.
        p.   cm.
    Includes index.
    ISBN 0-471-67965-8
 1. Nuclear weapons—Iraq. 2. Obeidi, Mahdi, 1944– 3. Nuclear physicists—Iraq—Biography. 4. Nuclear nonproliferation I. Pitzer, Kurt. II. Title.
    UA853.I75O24   2004
    956.7044'092—dc22

2004015415

Printed in the United States of America

10 9 8 7 6 5 4 3 2 1

This book is dedicated to Layla, Isra'a, Zaid, Amne, and Ayat Obeidi—for enduring years of hardship with strength and love.

CONTENTS

PREFACE

On February 5, 2003, as American troops massed in Kuwait to prepare for the invasion of Iraq, my family and I sat in our living room in Baghdad to watch U.S. Secretary of State Colin Powell's presentation to the United Nations Security Council, in which he was to give evidence that Iraq was still developing weapons of mass destruction. We had postponed our evening meal to watch the speech live from New York, where it was morning. The five of us crowded anxiously around our wide-screen television set I had rigged to an illegal satellite dish on our roof. We were acutely aware that the threat of war hung in the balance and that this was a critical moment in the histories of both Iraq and the United States.

We tuned in to the Arabic-language news channel Al-Jazeera for the benefit of my wife and children, but having been educated in the United States and Britain I could understand the original words in English beneath the translation. Powell, wearing an elegant diplomat's suit, sat behind the wooden desk in the UN chamber and began presenting evidence on an overhead monitor.

His arguments sounded cool-headed and rational, with none of the flowery jargon typical of speeches in Saddam's Iraq, and his tone appealed to the scientist in me. When he came to the nuclear issue, I sat on the edge of the sofa and leaned forward to catch every word. As the creator and director of Saddam's former nuclear centrifuge program, I was one of a very few people who knew the truth about the some of the allegations he would make.

The United States, he said, suspected that Iraq planned to manufacture high-quality magnets for use in centrifuges that would enrich uranium for nuclear weapons. For weeks UN weapons inspectors had been asking about an Iraqi magnet factory, which was still in the conceptual stage. I had overseen the financial plans for the facility, and had recently helped try to convince weapons inspectors that it was designed to manufacture magnets for peaceful purposes—and not centrifuges.

Powell's second point was one to which the UN inspectors had given special emphasis. Iraq had ordered thousands of high-grade aluminum tubes to be used for artillery rockets, which allegedly could also be used in a centrifuge program. Pictures of the confiscated tubes flashed on a screen for the Security Council and the rest of the world to see. Weapons inspectors in Iraq asked about these tubes repeatedly. We even tried to explain our case to a separate team from South Africa's former nuclear program. I knew these tubes were not intended for centrifuges. Aluminum is a much lower-grade material than the carbon fiber or top-quality steel we had worked with more than twelve years earlier. Also, the diameter of the tubes in question was about half the diameter of those we had used throughout our centrifuge program. From an engineering standpoint, their specifications would have required us to start almost from scratch. I thought back to our struggles to acquire tubes appropriate for centrifuges during the late 1980s and, knowing what I did, how unreasonable it was to think that these aluminum tubes could be part of a revived Iraqi nuclear weapons program.

But Powell sounded so sure of himself that I felt almost tempted to believe his credible-sounding arguments. Sitting there on my sofa, I asked myself the same question that had bothered me ever since the UN inspectors had come to Iraq with fresh accusations several months earlier: Could Saddam have restarted a nuclear program and kept me out of the loop? Were the inspectors about to discover a centrifuge facility that had been hidden from me? No, I realized again, it simply wasn't possible. I had built the centrifuge program from the ground up, and I saw it dismantled by the UN weapons inspectors after the 1991 Gulf War. I had been the linchpin of Saddam's effort to conceal it from inspectors, who had destroyed much of our equipment in Iraq and carted off the rest during the 1990s. By the end of that decade the only elements of the nuclear centrifuge program still hidden—the complete set of designs and a few prototype components—were buried in our garden just a few feet from our living room, unbeknownst even to my family, let alone the rest of the world. Saddam simply couldn't have reconstituted this program without my participation, or at least my knowledge.

After dinner my family and I went outside to sit in our garden, where we felt that we were farther from Saddam's bugging devices and therefore freer to speak our minds. War seemed unavoidable now. Iraq's insistence that the country had no weapons of mass destruction fell on deaf ears. Saddam had always hungered for a nuclear bomb, and few in the West could believe that he was not secretly trying to develop one. He had continued to break international rules, building missiles with ranges that slightly exceeded limits set by the UN and unmanned aircraft that could travel deep into neighboring countries. Now the mistrust between Saddam and, especially, the United States and Great Britain, had led to a point of no return. Although we could be punished with death for saying so, my wife and children and I were sure that Saddam's track record doomed Iraq to invasion.

In many ways Saddam was himself a weapon of mass destruction. He had invaded two neighboring countries, killed thousands of Iraqis and Iranians with chemical weapons, tortured and terrorized his own people, and buried many of his victims in mass graves. For years his erratic behavior had proven just how delusional and sinister he was. The idea that he might one day surprise the world with a nuclear bomb was a powerful nightmare.

I knew Saddam's entire regime was based on deception. I also knew how close he had come to actually getting the bomb; I had been caught in the very center of this story. During the late 1980s, spurred on by his threats and bullying tactics, I went undercover to many institutions and companies in the United States and Europe that possessed the intricate knowledge we needed to build centrifuges. I exploited a sprawling international black market for materials and technical assistance, successfully disguising our project by scattering our efforts around the globe. By the outbreak of the 1991 Gulf War, we had succeeded in a key step toward enriching uranium for an Iraqi nuclear bomb. The world came frighteningly close to finding out what Saddam might do with one.

During the 1990s, Saddam hid my identity from UN weapons inspectors for as long as possible, presumably in the belief that it would be easier to restart the centrifuge program if my role was not compromised. By the end of the decade, however, the Iraqi nuclear program was little more than a memory. As the world speculated about whether Saddam was reconstituting his nuclear and other unconventional weapons programs in the years leading up to the 2003 invasion, my role as one of the directors of Iraq's military-industrial apparatus gave me a bird's-eye view inside the dictatorship. I testified only once before weapons inspectors after they reentered Iraq in 2002 in the prelude to the war. My family and I barely survived the battle that ensued. In the postwar chaos and uncertainty, not knowing at first whether I was on the "deck of cards" list of most-wanted Iraqis, I made the risky decision to unearth the nuclear secrets buried in my garden and turn them over to American investigators. They were the most telling weapons of mass destruction secrets the Americans found in Iraq in the months after the war.

In writing this book, I hope to give the first account of Saddam's nuclear saga right up through the war's aftermath. In many ways this is a cautionary tale about how nuclear weapons are produced in secret. Assembling a nuclear bomb is tricky, but relatively easy compared to developing the material for it. The difficult part, as every scientist in every covert nuclear program in the world knows, is getting enough weapons-grade material for an explosive chain reaction. For a country trying to hide its nuclear ambitions, the centrifuge is the preferred method of enriching uranium because it requires the least amount of space and power consumption and is therefore the easiest to conceal.

The story of how Iraq mastered centrifuge technology in just over three years—and then how we tried to hide the key elements of the program from the international community—is not just a piece of history. I believe that a careful analysis of how this is done can be critically important as the world tries to stop the spread of the ultimate weapon of mass destruction.

The danger of nuclear proliferation will haunt mankind for many lifetimes to come. And the fear expressed by Powell and others that someone such as Saddam could provide terrorists with weapons of mass destruction, or the means to produce them, is very real. The idea of terrorists armed with chemical or biological weapons is scary indeed; the nuclear bomb, however, is still humanity's worst nightmare. It is the only weapon capable of killing hundreds of thousands of civilians.

I write my tale hoping that it brings readers closer to the truth. There was no active nuclear weapons program before the invasion of Iraq. However, Saddam certainly had the capabilities and, it must be presumed, the intention to restart it someday when the world was no longer watching him so closely. As long as tyrants like Saddam are willing to intimidate frightened scientists into doing their bidding, the threat of covert nuclear programs will continue. I hope that my story can help the public understand how such dangerous programs are developed so that they can be stopped wherever possible.

CHAPTER 1

The Bomb in My Garden

I emerged from my daughter's home the morning of April 10, 2003, to find the city of Baghdad in a state of total anarchy. Two days of ferocious battle during the American invasion had left carnage and confusion in its wake. Intermittent gunfire and explosions echoed through the city. Columns of smoke from burning government buildings rose into the sky across the horizon. The smell of sulfur and toxic gases released from the fires permeated the warm morning air. A sense of jittery calm settled on the residential streets of my daughter's neighborhood.

A few neighbors crept out of their homes to look at the two houses down the block that had been destroyed by American artillery two nights earlier. The structures lay half in rubble. A small crowd stood shaking their heads over the tragedy, but no one seemed to know whether anyone had been killed in these homes. On the street corner, the charred remains of two Iraqi military trucks stood like twisted sculptures of war, their frames blown apart and partly melted. Nearby, a group of teenage boys bent over the severed arm of an Iraqi soldier lying in the gutter.

The body to which it should have been attached was nowhere to be seen.

One of my daughter's neighbors, a middle-aged man I didn't recognize, came to me and asked after the welfare of my family.

"We are all alive and safe, thanks be to God," I said. "And yours?"

He was extremely agitated and said he was not sure. Telephone service was cut throughout Iraq, and he had no news of his eldest son's family, who lived in the northeastern section of the city. He was desperate to drive across town to find them.

"Do you think it is safe to make the journey?" he asked.

"I don't know," I said. "Things seem very unstable, but perhaps if you proceed cautiously, it will be fine. I hope to take my family back to our own home, too."

Leaving my wife and daughters in the house, my son Zaid and I drove west toward the al-Ghazaliya quarter to see whether our house had survived the combat that had engulfed our neighborhood. As we approached the commercial area around the University District, the roads were so littered with wreckage and destroyed vehicles it was difficult to navigate. The pop of gunfire echoed off the walls, and I could feel the adrenaline rising in my neck. Traffic lights were dead, along with the city's electricity, and drivers recklessly careened toward each other, ignoring rules of the road and eyeing each other with apprehension.

I looked out the passenger window in shock at the obscenity of the wreckage. Next to a white minivan with bullet holes in its windshield lay the bodies of two men in bloodstained white robes, their faces black and swollen with death. Zaid swerved around the corpse of a donkey that had fallen in the road, pockmarked with shrapnel wounds. Its four legs, stiff with rigor mortis, pointed at the passing cars as though accusing them of the outrage.

Reaching the commercial district, we now saw plenty of ordinary citizens in the road. Scores of men scurried across the street carrying looted furniture on their heads and electrical appliances under their arms. They looked wild, as if delirious. Young men disappeared inside the smashed-in storefront of a computer shop and came out with armloads of equipment and anything else of value. Several cars drove past with trunks open and bulging with stolen goods. A few blocks further along, the owner of a bicycle shop stood guard outside his property armed with a rifle. On side streets I noticed residents setting up roadblocks to the entrances to their neighborhoods using chunks of debris, palm fronds, and broken bottles.

"What is this?" I said to Zaid. "What is happening to these men?"

I was momentarily overcome with shame. As an Iraqi who is proud of his people, I could not believe this behavior. Baghdad was a place of civilized people, not looters. It was as though the sudden removal of the Saddam regime had induced a temporary madness.

We drove down Al-Nafaq, the tunnel road that led to one of the large intersections of Baghdad. A giant mural of Saddam Hussein stood in the middle of the traffic circle. As we drew closer, I could see a group of men dressed in black and heavily armed with automatic weapons and rocket-propelled grenade launchers: members of the Fedayeen Saddam, the fiercely loyal personal militia of the president. I stared at them in disbelief. It seemed impossible that Fedayeen fighters could be at this intersection. The Americans had swept through the district during the invasion and couldn't be far away.

The Fedayeen had spread out across the roundabout and were using their weapons to wave traffic around the circle. Their faces looked hard but weary from days of heavy fighting. Two of the militiamen leaned against the portrait of Saddam as though in the absence of the president to protect, they would make their last stand defending only his image.

Zaid and I sped three quarters of the way around the traffic circle and onto the entrance to the Abu Ghraib Expressway, leading to our neighborhood. As soon as we made the turn, my heart froze. Less than two hundred meters away, a column of American armored vehicles was headed directly for us, taking up all three lanes in the wrong direction. We were trapped.

I glanced through the rear window. I was certain that any moment the Fedayeen fighters would hear the approaching convoy and we would be caught in crossfire. Zaid and I looked desperately for an exit from Abu Ghraib Street as the American column grew closer. Their cannons pointed directly at us. We were seconds away from annihilation.

"Over there!" I shouted.

Zaid veered off an exit to our right onto a small byroad parallel to the main street. Seconds later the tanks roared past us, and the shooting began. The first heavy round shuddered through the air, followed by staccato machine-gun rounds. A grenade exploded somewhere behind our car as the Fedayeen Saddam fighters returned fire. Terrified that we would be hit by stray bullets, we turned onto a residential side street, drove a hundred meters, and parked. Only a half mile from the battle, we heard the constant spray of gunfire with only short pauses in between. It seemed too close, so we drove another hundred meters down the road.

For fifteen minutes the air was torn apart by the cracking sound of gunfire. I imagined the Iraqi fighters scrambling for cover, hopelessly outmatched by the American armor. Finally, the shooting came in spasms. Then we heard mostly silence, broken by infrequent bursts.

"It is getting less now," I told Zaid. "Let's move on."

As we turned onto the byroad, I looked back and saw many American vehicles parked at the intersection, but no soldiers. The Americans must have pursued Saddam's militiamen into the surrounding streets. Later we were told that eleven Fedayeen militiamen had been killed there.

Further west, the Abu Ghraib Expressway was eerily deserted. Normally, it was one of the busiest roads in Baghdad. Now it felt dead, as though the Americans had turned it into a ghost highway.

On the road to our house, spent bullet shells and debris littered the pavement like gravel, proof that our quarter had seen heavy fighting. When we arrived at our security gate, we could see that our five-bedroom house was intact. I unlocked the front door and Zaid and I went room to room, methodically checking for signs of damage. A water glass lay shattered on the kitchen floor, presumably having fallen due to the force of nearby explosions. One window was cracked. Otherwise our home seemed unscathed.

I stepped out into our walled garden, which had been my place of refuge during the years I spent as Saddam Hussein's nuclear mastermind. I am probably overzealous in my gardening, which I approach with a typical engineer's eye for the straight line and the perfect detail. I surveyed the yard for flaws. The date palm next to the fence looked fine. A single young mango still hung from the little mango tree, and I expected it would ripen within about three months. I lingered over the lime tree, whose sapling I had bought years ago from a hothouse in Holland while searching for the secrets of uranium enrichment during the 1980s. The tiny citrus flowers had survived the war and would soon become fruit. The Indian berry vines, grafted from cuttings I had gathered on a trip to Bombay, were in good shape. Around our kidney-shaped lawn, the gardenias were in full bloom.

The dichondra grass, with its delicate round leaves, was already drying out in the hot Iraqi sun and badly needed watering. I noticed several places along its border where the lawn had overgrown my careful hedging. A few pieces of debris littered the lawn, including a cone-shaped gray object about a foot long, which I didn't recognize at first.

I turned the corner into the side yard and saw that something was amiss with the metal rack where I kept my gardening tools. It leaned sideways and its tin roof had collapsed and curled around something. Coming nearer, I was stunned as I realized that an unexploded missile poked through both sides of the destroyed shelving. Could that be? Yes, there was no doubt. Thin, but more than two meters in length, it would have been taller than I am if stood upright. I calculated the base as roughly 25 centimeters in diameter. It was whitish in color. I noticed the fins halfway along its sides had chipped off. The front end was blunt, as if the nose cone had come off.

I knew right away that it was an American bomb, because it was completely unlike anything in the Iraqi arsenal. I didn't know much about American missiles, but with my many years directing Iraq's nuclear program, and then as one of the directors of Saddam's military-industrial complex, I was very familiar with rocketry in general. Its length suggested it had been launched from the air. A bomb of this size would obliterate everything within at least a fifty-yard radius, probably much more, including my entire house and garden. I quickly discarded the notion that it had been aimed at my home. The Americans had no reason to target the home of a scientist, and even if they had, I doubted they would have known where I lived. The bomb must have been aimed at a nearby Iraqi military position.

Its front end had come to rest just a few feet from the wall of my daughters' bedroom. I shuddered as I tried to calculate the mathematical percentages of the two factors that had favored our survival. The split-second decision I had made on April 8 to spend the night of battle away from home had been nearly fifty-fifty. I didn't know the probability of a missile failing to explode on impact, but figured it was low. If both factors had gone the other way, though, we would have been obliterated in a millisecond. Suddenly it dawned on me: the object on my lawn was very likely its fuse.

I stood looking at the missile for a few moments before I was struck by the incredible irony of the situation. Less than twenty feet away, in the ground beneath a lotus tree next to my rose garden, lay a green fifty-gallon drum that I had buried in 1992. It contained the remnants of Iraq's nuclear program.

Inside was the complete set of extremely detailed plans and design drawings needed to manufacture centrifuges. More than two hundred booklets served as instruction manuals for building every piece of the centrifuge and how to assemble them. Some of the parts are so difficult to manufacture that the specifications for them are among the world's most classified information. The documents provided the specifications, tolerances, and dimensions for each part, along with the detailed designs for manufacturing them.

Also buried in the drum were prototypes of four of the most highly advanced centrifuge components. These metal pieces, small enough to fit in a suitcase, don't seem dangerous to look at, but they are incredibly complex. Manufacturing them requires elaborate calculations of geometry, advanced metallurgy, and knowledge of stress and tolerances beyond the capabilities of most nations. I spent millions of dollars, traveled thousands of miles, and negotiated a hair-raising series of international deals in order to learn the secrets of their manufacture.

One of the four most intricate parts is the ball bearing on which the centrifuge rotor sits. Nearly small enough to conceal in your hand, the bearing is possibly its most important piece and requires mathematical precision to an infinitesimal degree. Roughly the shape of a toy spinning top, the shiny metallic ball bearing balances the centrifuge rotor tube as it spins at speeds greater than 60,000 rpm. At the bottom tip of the bearing a tiny round bead, four millimeters in diameter and etched with microscopic grooves, gives the whole centrifuge grab and play. Even the pattern of the microscopic grooves is a highly classified secret.

The second prototype I had buried was the centrifuge motor. Made of gleaming aluminum and about the size of a round loaf of bread, it contains an interdependent series of magnets and coils that drive the centrifuge. The centrifuge rotor hangs inside a hole in its center, and the magnets create an electromagnetic field so powerful that it spins the centrifuge without ever touching it. To a scientist, it is a beautiful piece of work.

The magnetic upper bearing was another marvel of science. Two segmented aluminum-nickel-cobalt magnet discs, roughly the size of checkers pieces, are connected by wispy threads of steel. Sitting at the top of the centrifuge, these magnets hold the rotor in place in a vacuum as it spins at supersonic speeds.

The fourth component—a thin, gunmetal-colored disk about six inches in diameter and two inches in height—looked deceptively ordinary to the untrained eye. Called a bellows, its purpose is to connect centrifuge tubes end to end, to create a longer centrifuge of approximately three meters in length. This longer version can enrich uranium substantially faster than ordinary two-foot-long centrifuges, thereby increasing bomb-making capacity considerably. The dimensions of a crimp—a microscopic ridge in its midsection where the centrifuge tubes meet at the point of greatest stress— required something called hairy mathematics. At the time, even the Japanese had failed to design such a bellows.

These drawings, documents, and prototypes represented the accumulated knowledge of the Iraqi nuclear centrifuge program. They were not actual weapons of mass destruction, but they were probably the most valuable building blocks for WMD that Iraq ever possessed. Saddam's son Qusay had ordered me to keep them safe from UN weapons inspectors in 1992, and the Iraqi government concocted a story that they had been destroyed by the security services. Although the weapons inspectors were extremely skeptical, this was the story we had maintained despite continual pressure. By 1998, they were Iraq's sole remaining nuclear secrets. It is difficult to overestimate their importance or the danger they potentially posed to the international community. In the wrong hands they could have enabled Saddam or anyone else to quickly initiate a deadly nuclear weapons program.

Had the American bomb exploded, the force of it might well have unearthed the plastic drum. As I calculated the distance between the missile and the lotus tree, I imagined Iraq's precious nuclear documents fluttering out of the bomb crater and carried away in the wind, or the prototype centrifuge parts being examined amid the rubble by scavengers who had no concept of their worth or their purpose. But the bomb had not exploded, and the drum lay undisturbed under the lotus tree.

Its contents had afforded me little peace for more than a decade. As the keeper of Saddam's most precious nuclear asset, I was tethered to the regime and constantly under surveillance. I assumed the Iraqi intelligence service, the Mukhabarat, was watching my every move. Even when gardening, I was always mindful of what lay just underfoot. Now that American forces controlled Iraq, I knew these buried secrets would perhaps shape my family's destiny.

When United Nations weapons inspectors entered Iraq in the fall of 2002 to search for Saddam's weapons of mass destruction, their attention quickly turned to the importance of interviewing Iraqi scientists. In November, UN inspectors demanded that some scientists be allowed to leave Iraq along with their families so that they could speak freely, without risking retribution. A friend had given me a copy of a *Washington Post* article he had downloaded from the Internet that listed me as one of the top five scientists that inspectors hoped to interview outside Iraq. I read it again and again. I wondered whether my family and I might be whisked out of Iraq so that I could testify to the truth about what Saddam was and was not hiding.

This idea was soon cut short by Saddam's officials. In early February 2003, a month and a half before the war, I was called to a security meeting of the Military Industrialization Commission (MIC), in which I was the only scientist present. Deputy Prime Minister Abdul Tawab Mullah Hwaish presided over the meeting. As the head of MIC, Abdul Tawab was my boss and the man who kept me under implicit surveillance. He was a stout man who relished his powerful position and liked to shout and fire his pistol into the air during pro-Saddam rallies. With his thick brush of a mustache and in the olive green military uniform favored by all of Saddam's flatterers, it was clear how much Abdul Tawab wanted to emulate the president. Yet all he had been able to copy effectively was Saddam's ruthlessness. Abdul Tawab was well known for imprisoning military contractors who missed delivery deadlines, some of whom died in prison, and for putting scientists and engineers in confinement. He was really little more than a bully, pounding tables into splinters with his fists when he didn't get his way and shouting expletives at terrified military engineers and project leaders.

Abdul Tawab lacked the oddly graceful tyranny of his mentor. Saddam Hussein's culture of intimidation was almost mystical. Saddam made people think of him as a god, with godlike powers. Mullahs were required to praise his name before prayers, in the same breath as the name of Allah. Saddam never lost his temper, at least in public. He didn't need to. He had people like Abdul Tawab to do this for him.

Abdul Tawab called the meeting to order. After an elaborate speech about the enemies of Iraq and the duty of Iraqis and all

Arabs to resist, he excoriated the West for demanding access to the nation's weapons sites.

"There is much talk about the ultimatums of President Bush and the United Nations weapons inspectors," he said. "They are creating a pretext for war, and they want to use our honorable scientists as tools for their hostile intentions. Is there anyone here who cares to comment?"

Abdul Tawab did not look at me, and one of his deputies rose to speak.

"Some of the scientists might be eager to leave the country," the deputy said, as though making a prearranged speech. The other MIC officials shook their heads and a few clucked their tongues. "Perhaps a few of the scientists would even like to defect."

Abdul Tawab held up his hand to cut him short. He turned to me and looked me in the eye menacingly for a few heartbeats. "Let the scientists leave Iraq to meet the inspectors," he said. Then he grimaced and drew a finger across his throat. "Their families will stay here."

I trembled. Rarely were threats in Iraq so overt and so public. For decades we had endured threats that were merely implied. This is part of the Arabic way of communicating: to say something without really saying it, using subtlety to convey one's intentions. Saddam and his men were cordial but chilling, masters of deadly insinuation. With a single glance, they could freeze your blood. But Abdul Tawab's gesture was crude and unmistakable, almost stage-managed. I wondered if it had been planned beforehand.

It is difficult to describe the sense of total fear we lived under. I censored myself at work and at home because I knew my family wasn't safe. Even with the person I am closest to in the world, my wife of thirty-four years, I didn't have the courage to express my true feelings. We knew our telephone was most likely tapped, and we feared that microphones were hidden in our car or in household items such as a vase, a lamp, or the television. We trained ourselves to guard every word we said, no matter how private. My most painful regret is how my highly classified work affected my family. They lived in terror that any night I might not come home, that I might have been imprisoned or tortured. When I came home late, it was to worried faces expressing relief.

Whenever our friends and relatives came to visit us, I noticed they were especially cautious with what they said. They were well aware that my home was almost certainly under surveillance. If a conversation touched on something even vaguely political, we instinctively used hand signals and walked out into our garden, where we felt safer from the electronic ears of the regime. This was especially true during the last weeks of Saddam's rule.

A month before the war started, we had a big family gathering in the house of one of my distant cousins. As we sat down to a sumptuous meal at a large table, the conversation turned to the American military buildup. We felt freer to express ourselves in a relative's house than we would have in my own home. Like most Iraqis, every member of my family wanted to see Saddam deposed, but we were of differing opinions about whether that would happen. Voices were raised. One group said that war was inevitable and that Saddam was finished. They were jokingly called "the hawks," after the American officials of the same opinion. At the time in Iraq, we could have been executed for saying so. Another group argued that there would be no war and Saddam would continue to rule. We called this group "the doves." Then there was a lone dissenter: a cousin of mine who predicted that the Americans would wage war on Iraq, but Saddam would survive and outlive the hostilities. I guffawed and said, "You're neither a hawk nor a dove—you're a crow!" To which everyone laughed.

Then a silence fell over the table, and terror rose in each of us. Everyone realized that we had crossed into dangerous territory. I could see my family members' eyes darting nervously around the room looking for hidden microphones. Not another word was said about the matter.

As the aircraft carriers steamed toward the Gulf and U.S. president George Bush and British prime minister Tony Blair made increasingly warlike statements to the world, the people of Baghdad began to prepare for war with resignation, but also with dignity. We had been through this before, and we knew what we must do. Long lines for gasoline formed at every station, as drivers prepared for shortages, but this was done in an orderly fashion. The main frustrations were with costs: the jump in prices of canned foods, bottled water, and generators, as people prepared to bunker themselves in their homes. Like many families, mine reluctantly decided to buy a Kalashnikov rifle in case law and order broke down.

The world watched tens of thousands of U.S. troops setting up offensive positions near the Iraqi border in Kuwait. What they couldn't see were the strange things happening at the highest levels of Saddam's government. In the upper echelons of power, the grip of the regime tightened even further. Casual conversations turned formal, with insincere but loudly proclaimed expressions of patriotism. A delusional sense of reality spread throughout the government. Unlike the citizens of Iraq, the government seemed totally unprepared for war.

On March 19, the first day of air strikes on Baghdad, I followed instructions to report to MIC headquarters as usual. The bombing had started before dawn and then stopped, and an anticipatory lull had fallen over the city. When I arrived, fearful that I was driving into a bombing zone, a frightened-looking official told me to report instead to a kindergarten in the middle-class Jumhuriya district, which was being turned into makeshift offices for MIC directors and our senior staff. Other government agencies were evacuating to similar locations, he said. Overnight, the regime went underground, in the hope that U.S. pilots would be reluctant to bomb schools.

I reached the kindergarten in the midmorning to find a traffic jam of black Mercedes sedans and other expensive cars favored by top Iraqi officials clogging the residential alleys around the school. Classes had been suspended, and the neighborhood children were under orders to stay at home, but many had come out to look excitedly at the luxury cars suddenly filling the narrow streets. Curious residents of the three- and four-story apartments in the neighborhood peered out of their windows to watch the spectacle. I made a quick tally around the kindergarten and counted more than fifty cars used by MIC officials. I realized that such a clot of official cars might easily be spotted by American surveillance planes, which now completely dominated the skies over Baghdad.

Inside the kindergarten Baathist officers hurried about, assigning classrooms to the various MIC departments. A chaotic meeting of directors was already underway in one of them. There had been no contingency plan for the American invasion, and it was unclear who was to be in charge. Two ranking officials, Brigadier Walid Muslih, the head of the technical department, and Raja al-Khazraji, the director general of management, shouted orders and classroom assignments as several dozen of us crowded around. I raised my hand and offered a suggestion.

"There are more than fifty of our cars parked in the immediate vicinity," I said. "This could be dangerous in view of the surveillance by American aircraft. Shouldn't we move to disperse them?"

This apparently hadn't dawned on any of my colleagues, and suddenly fear filled the room as they recognized the implications. Raja al-Khazraji barked at our drivers to scatter our cars throughout a wider area.

We were divided into emergency units, to organize short-term support for the war and weapons procurements. In one of the classrooms, I noticed a picture of Saddam Hussein posing with his late son-in-law, Hussein Kamel, who had been my boss during the years we spent developing nuclear weapons during the 1980s. We sat on miniature chairs, trying to fit our knees under tables meant for six-year-olds. Alphabet lessons could still be seen on the chalkboards. Outside our windows, swing sets and children's play equipment seemed to offer our only defense against a possible American attack. The scene might have been funny had it not been so terrifying. Next to the kindergarten, a shipping container had been half buried in the ground with a staircase leading down into the metal hull to create a makeshift bunker where we could hide in case of a bombing strike.

I sat in on one group instructed to pressure manufacturers of rocket-propelled grenade launchers to reduce production times from months to weeks. The idea was based on the absurd assumption that armament factories could still function normally.

"What is the purpose of these RPGs?" I asked, without mentioning the well-known fact that even after manufacture, it would take weeks for the parts to be assembled into a usable weapon.

"To strengthen the army, of course!" a deputy cried.

After that first meeting, I tried to avoid staying at the makeshift headquarters for more than fifteen minutes at a time. I assigned myself "surveillance" missions to visit my science and engineering colleagues, who had been ordered to stay in other bunkers. With this trumped-up assignment, I was able to spend much of the first part of the war driving on the relatively safe streets of Baghdad, away from government buildings that were obvious bombing targets. I tried to avoid exposure and spent as much time as possible at home with my family.

The sense of total denial among government officials continued to the end, however, along with the pressure to obey ridiculous commands. On April 7, 2003, as American troops reached the very outskirts of Baghdad, I was ordered to report by 9 P.M. to the kindergarten bunker once again. My family had begged me not to go. They knew that driving across town that evening could be suicidal. The Americans were using very good intelligence to bomb official gatherings. I insisted it was more dangerous for all of us if I stayed home. The area inside Baghdad was still Saddam's Iraq and disobeying an order carried an instant death penalty.

Electricity was cut throughout the city. Buildings appeared in silhouette against the nightmarish orange glow, illuminated by fires and flashes of explosives. I drove with only my parking lights on, hoping to avoid becoming a target for the American planes. I could hear them cutting through the skies overhead.

At the kindergarten bunker, small groups of scientists, technicians, and Baath Party officials eyed each other anxiously; none of us knew why we had been called there. Somewhere above our heads a generator rattled, powering the two bare light bulbs that cast dim shadows on the cheap conference table where our fate would be made clear. We could be jailed or executed if Saddam or his henchmen had decided we were to blame for Iraq's poor performance in the war. Or perhaps we would be ordered to embark on some grand engineering feat they had dreamed up as a last-ditch attempt to hold the coalition forces at bay. Maybe the purpose for the meeting was to keep watch on everyone, to make sure we hadn't defected.

"For what purpose?" I wondered. "Can't they read the writing on the wall?"

It reminded me of scenes from *Gone with the Wind*, in which the southerners clung to their doomed lifestyle, ignoring the advancing Union forces that were about to sweep it into history. In Iraq, the peculiar mind-set of the whole regime was symbolized by Saddam's order that key buildings be covered with mud and oil fires set around the city, in the belief that smoke would fool American pilots. The Americans could easily navigate through the smoke, but no one was brave enough to tell Saddam. In the end the smoke did more harm to Iraqi antiaircraft efforts. But because Saddam said so, everyone had convinced themselves that "if we can't see the American planes, then they can't see us," like the old folktale folly of the ostrich burying its head in the sand in order to hide.

Officials gathered in small clusters, speaking in low voices. I briefly joined one group, where a Baathist official was holding the party line, maintaining the denial. He described in detail the battle for the international airport, which he said was littered with bodies of American soldiers. The men around him nodded their heads, although I was sure they all knew this wasn't true. Another official noted proudly that Saddam himself had used the bunker we were in the previous night for a cabinet meeting. I overheard him describe the president flying into a rage at the unexplained absence of Abdul Tawab. Threatening to kill him if he had defected or tried to flee, Saddam had sent a search party to find his deputy vice president. Abdul Tawab had not fled or defected, however. He was at the head of the table preparing to lead the meeting. Despite all the speculation about the president's possible death or severe injury, Saddam was still in control.

I could see that Abdul Tawab had lost none of his theatrical menace. He slammed his fists on the table and called the meeting to order.

"I can see victory ahead as clearly as I see all of you in front of me," he said with bravado, apparently having convinced himself that this was a jolly moment, despite the thud of bombs outside and the fact that we were bunkered in an emergency meeting. "After we have slaughtered the Americans and driven them from our land, I promise to throw a big party."

He glanced over at the only woman in the room, a conservative manager named Ms. Jabriya, who had complained about entertainment at past official functions, and laughed.

"And there will be plenty of gypsies dancing, despite the objections of the lady present."

Abdul Tawab brought up the only piece of business on the eleventh-hour agenda: a request from the Iraqi army to devise a concrete beam across a highway as an obstacle to advancing American troops. A concrete beam! How telling that the men behind Iraq's military-industrial complex were reduced to the desperate level of putting up such a crude defense of the city. It was so ridiculous I almost laughed. I didn't know the exact capabilities of the U.S. military, but I had an intimate knowledge of the Iraqi forces. I had overseen the construction of facilities to produce artillery pieces, tanks, and rockets based on antiquated Russian models that were a pathetic match for the sophisticated weaponry of the Americans. I knew that the Iraqi military was like a stick of butter waiting for a warm knife. And now the army wanted us to build them a roadblock to hold the American and British forces back.

"The Americans are making whole buildings disappear with great precision," I couldn't help saying. "Do any of you really believe a concrete beam will be of any use?"

The response was silence and blank stares from those around the table. I realized with a shudder that I had mentioned the unspeakable: that the Americans would invade Baghdad very soon, and it was pointless for these men to resist. I mentally replayed my remark, hoping I hadn't sounded too pleased at my conclusion.

Under the tense circumstances, objecting to any order could be considered treason. No one challenged me, though. Perhaps they were thinking the same thing. Rather than confronting the silliness of the request, a committee was formed to design the beam.

After the meeting, we were forbidden to leave the kindergarten grounds and ordered into different security posts. I spent the night within sight of the bunker entrance, in a parked car with a Baathist partisan who kept a Kalashnikov rifle on his knees. For hours we sat listening to the bombs and artillery raining down on Baghdad, petrified that if the Americans were accurately able to track the movements of Saddam's government, our bunker would be a prime target. I worried about my wife and my grown children. Every time I heard an explosion in the distance, I pleaded silently: "Please let them be okay. Please let them survive." My worst fear was that while I sat in this car waiting for a missile intended for Saddam, my family might be in danger.

As dawn broke, I raced back home through nearly deserted streets. Above the lush palm trees and sand-colored buildings, much of the sky was black from Saddam's futile smoke screen. I saw a few Republican Guard artillery pieces and tanks hidden among the trees of public parks. My suspicion was that the smoke would not hinder the American pilots and that this Iraqi military hardware would soon be bombed. I arrived home to find my wife and children frightened but alive. We wept with relief at seeing each other, and after we embraced, I vowed not to leave them again.

My son Zaid had stayed awake all night patrolling the perimeter of our house, and he said that during the night he had heard, just beyond the wall of our garden, the voices of Fedayeen fighters setting up a position under an overpass of the Abu Ghraib Expressway, which is the major western entrance into Baghdad. He said he had heard shooting close by, minutes ago. I went to the garden wall to listen for myself. I could hear many low voices speaking in Arabic but with accents from Egypt, Syria, and elsewhere. Foreign mercenaries. I figured they had come to Iraq to fight to the end, and that they were the type who would rather die than flee.

In our living room I held an urgent meeting with my wife, Layla, my two teenage daughters, and Zaid, to discuss evacuating our home, because it seemed likely that battle was literally at our doorstep. Zaid and I decided to make a reconnaissance drive around the streets of our quarter. The alleyways around our house were deserted, and the front gates of our neighbors' compounds were all shut tight. Despite the troops gathering outside our garden wall, stillness had descended on the neighborhood. The streets seemed like a sanctuary of refuge rather than a virtual battle zone.

Zaid and I were about to return home after a final loop when we came upon an Iraqi checkpoint. A Republican Guard officer brandished his Kalashnikov rifle. He was in his twenties, with fair skin and a well-trimmed mustache, wearing the red beret favored by Saddam's elite troops. He seemed very tense. He lowered his face to our car window and looked at us with suspicion.

"Peace be upon you," he said. "Who are you, and what are you doing here?"

"Our home is here in this neighborhood," I said, pointing in the direction of our house. "Do you think it is wise to stay in the area?"

"It is your prerogative," the young officer said, "but this neighborhood is now the front line. The Americans are very close by. They are closing in, and the battle is near. I suggest you evacuate."

The officer's expression was grim, and it struck me that the inevitability of defeat might finally be dawning on Iraqi officers. A day earlier, admitting this would have been tantamount to subversion, but now this young officer's face told a different story. I realized our family needed to act quickly.

Zaid drove nearly a mile on a narrow byroad of the Abu Ghraib Expressway, searching for a place where the road widened and we could turn around. As we approached a clearing, we saw smoke rising from the highway overhead. Then, through the smoke, we spotted a smoldering American tank that had obviously been hit during a recent firefight. I couldn't see any American soldiers, but I realized we were truly on the front line and in the lull of a battle.

"Let's get back to the house," I urged Zaid, as he spun our car around.

As Zaid executed a two-point turn, I heard several sharp hissing sounds outside our car, followed by the crack of weapons fire. We were under sniper attack from American gunmen.

We both ducked our heads to the dashboard as Zaid pushed the accelerator to the floor and we sped along the byroad. We heard the hiss of bullets just missing our car. Seconds later, when we arrived home, we leapt out and bundled Layla and the girls into the back seat and made a hurried decision to drive to the home of my eldest daughter, Isra'a, who lived about fifteen minutes away in the Yarmouk area of south Baghdad.

Once at my daughter's, we felt only slightly safer. Ahmed, my son-in-law, said that the night before, American bombs had sounded dangerously close to their home too. We arranged the furniture in a ring in the living room in case the windows or the walls blew in. It made a flimsy barricade of protection for the nine of us, including my five-year-old grandson and my three-year-old granddaughter. We duct-taped all the windows with an X, leaving a few open to prevent a pressure explosion, which occurs when an explosive shock wave in a closed space blows out windows and throws people and furniture around the room. The thud of faraway artillery drew nearer, until the crack of exploding rockets became deafening. We had avoided one battlefield to find ourselves in the middle of another.

We huddled in the center of the living room as U.S. and Iraqi troops battled around the presidential palace nearby. The sharp smell of gunpowder and burning buildings stung our noses and coated the insides of our mouths. To me that will forever be the taste of war. I thought my heart would burst as I saw the terror on the faces of my family. My grandchildren wailed uncontrollably. I kept whispering to them, "Don't worry, darlings, the bombs are aimed at the soldiers and not at us. We will be just fine." But I wasn't sure at all. We all said a few silent prayers to Allah, begging to be spared.

Late in the morning, there was about a half-hour pause in the bombardment, though I could hear gunfire and tank rounds in the middle distance. I thought the worst might be over and that we had been spared. I told my grandchildren, who still wore their pajamas from the night before, to try to sleep in our laps, hoping that this might help them feel safer from the nightmare around us. Then the air seemed to literally explode. Incoming artillery rounds whistled and boomed on all sides. Fighter jets came screaming over our neighborhood dropping cluster bombs that shook the walls. I heard something that made my blood run cold: the sound of Iraqi soldiers shouting to each other in the streets south of my daughter's home. We were truly in the middle of a battle. Then we heard the sound of the engines of military vehicles and more shouting.

The thunderclap and the sound of our windows shattering came at the same moment. I may have lost consciousness for a few seconds before another rocket landed in the garden of the neighboring house, jolting us from the floor like a split-second earthquake. Moments later a third explosion rocked the air on the other side of the house. I leapt up shouting, "Zaid, Ahmed, get everyone! Let's go! Let's go!" I was sure that if we didn't move we would die sitting in the living room. The women were screaming as we picked up the grandchildren and ran for the back door. I noticed that neither grandchild was crying. They just stared at nothing with their mouths open, shell-shocked.

We scrambled into our two cars as the sky flashed around us. We were racing, but time seemed to slow down as though I was caught in a terrible dream. As we pulled onto the street leading toward the town center, we passed an Iraqi soldier on the ground. His body was cut in half, with his legs scattered near the upper part of him. His eyes were open. One arm was missing from his torso, but the other arm seemed to be reaching out to us. Even now I can't get the image out of my mind. Sometimes at night the vision of that soldier comes back to me. As he stares through our windshield, I see his lips move, forming the words, "Help me." I hope this is only a trick of memory.

My gut told me we should not go home again. I told Zaid to head for the house of my brother-in-law, Ali, across town in north-eastern Baghdad. We sped north on Damascus Street past the bombed Saddam Tower, navigating on pure adrenaline. The sky continued to pop with deafening cracks, like some new kind of lightning storm that sends out concussive waves. I was afraid we would be incinerated on the streets. Zaid wove between abandoned Iraqi cars and military vehicles. I kept glancing over my shoulder to check that my son-in-law, my daughter, and my grandchildren were still driving behind us in their Toyota. My wife and younger daughters held on to each other wordlessly in the rear seat. I reached back and held their hands.

When we reached the Al Ahrar Bridge over the Tigris River, I saw a line of cars ahead of us, and we found ourselves in a small traffic jam of other Baghdadis fleeing eastward. The Republican Guard had set up checkpoints on either side of the bridge and were forcing civilians to drive onto the sidewalk to go around them. At the bridge entrance, two young soldiers barely noticed us. They looked frightened, and I could tell they were forced to be there under threat of death from their commanders. I hoped they would be able to flee.

When we arrived my brother-in-law rushed to embrace us. "Thanks be to God!" he cried. "I was sure you had all been killed!"

As the American troops fought their way into Baghdad, we stayed at his home for several hours, long enough for a lunchtime meal. We were all tired of eating canned meat and rice and potatoes. My brother slaughtered one of his few remaining sheep, and the women set about making a traditional feast of Iraqi *pacha*: a gravy of bread, meat, and spices known as *tishrib* and white and red rice. Our small celebration was cut short, however, when the terrible sound of bombs and artillery shells began to approach Ali's home as well, and the chairs began to shake beneath us. Afraid that we would be caught in a third battle zone, I made a decision.

"We will go back to Isra'a's home," I announced, unsure if this was the right move for our safety. At this point one place in Baghdad seemed as unsafe as any other. But in a way it felt safer to be moving. We set off on another tense journey through the wartime streets. The bombing seemed more infrequent now as we wound our way through side streets to reach my daughter's home.

Like any family anticipating a disaster, we had stocked up on supplies. Isra'a and Ahmed had a generator, and Zaid and I had recently installed a satellite dish on their roof. Throughout the night we watched live footage broadcast by BBC and Al Jazeera of the invasion happening around us. The fighting still shook the ground, even though by now it was taking place miles away. Some of the family dozed off during the early morning, but I sat riveted by scenes of the fall of our city.

After daybreak on April 9, with the sound of heavy fighting still pounding Baghdad, we saw images of American tanks on the city's southern bridges over the Tigris. That afternoon we saw something we could never have imagined. Thousands of our fellow Baghdadis mobbed the famous Firdos Square. Many used sledgehammers to chip away at the base of a statue of Saddam, cheered on by the crowd. We sat pointing at the TV with our hands over our mouths in disbelief.

"Look at that," Ahmed said. "They are chopping at his feet, and no police are stopping them!"

It was an image I knew was being watched around the world. A U.S. armored personnel carrier rolled into the square to help them, with a chain tied around Saddam's neck, to pull the statue over.

"He's going to fall!" my wife gasped.

Saddam's figure tottered, fell face forward to the ground, and was instantly set upon by Iraqis beating his likeness with sticks, their shoes, and anything else they could find. I couldn't believe my eyes. It was as though I were watching the death of the tyrant himself. There fell the man who, for more than twenty years, had kept me and my fellow scientists physically and mentally on a string around his finger and my family under a shadow of fear. There fell the man for whom, years earlier, I had tried to produce enough enriched uranium for a nuclear weapon. There went the statue of a man who used fear to make scientists lie and deceive. He was pulled down by his neck.

A tyrant bends every aspect of his subjects' behavior to his rule. My family and I had survived the worst of it, thanks to my position. We had lived on shaky ground, second-guessing our most intimate whispers, since before most of my children were even born. Saddam had literally ruled our lives. In that instant the fear that my family and I had lived through did not disappear, and in some respects it probably never will, but its grip loosened ever so slightly. The fall of that one statue seemed to set free an emotion that I don't have a name for. Although the war was still raging and uncertain, we cheered openly and embraced each other. We looked at one another in disbelief, shaking our heads and grinning with the first sense that a long nightmare might be about to end.

The following day, as I stared in bewilderment at the American bomb in our garden, my elation evaporated. My mind turned to the nuclear secrets buried a few feet from where I stood. They would be of major importance to everyone with an interest in what had been Iraq's programs to develop weapons of mass destruction. I could see many dangers still ahead and potential consequences, none of which were yet fully formed in my mind. It was as though the documents and components were ticking underneath the soil like a time bomb. Only one thing was clear: what I did with Iraq's remaining centrifuge secrets would most likely determine the fate of me and my family forever.

The first item on my agenda, however, was to remove the unexploded American bomb from our garden, so my family could return home. For more than a week after I discovered it, I made repeated attempts to find American soldiers to take it away. At first, I felt nervous about the idea of speaking to them. I walked out to the main road near our home, which is next to the highway that leads westward through the desert to Jordan. An American M1 Abrams tank stood guard on the overpass, which days earlier had seen heavy fighting with the Fedayeen Saddam and the Republican Guard. They were the first American soldiers I had seen. They looked quite young, and somewhat at a loss as to how to respond to the crowd of Iraqis gathered around their tank shouting things such as, "Hello, mister! Saddam bad. Thank you!"

I approached the tank and waited among the crowd until one of the soldiers noticed me. Then I called up to him, trying to sound jovial and relaxed.

"I hope you're enjoying our fine Iraqi weather," I said. "Is it a perhaps a bit hot for you?"

He looked startled at the sight of an Iraqi man speaking in fluent English.

"Where do you come from?" I asked.

"Arkansas, sir," he said. His lower lip bulged with a wad of chewing tobacco, so his words came out slightly garbled. He spat into the lower half of a plastic water bottle.

"I have visited your lovely state," I said. "It was many years ago on a camping trip, when I was a student at the Colorado School of Mines. Have you heard of it?"

"No, sir."

"Well, you are very welcome in Iraq," I said. "I was hoping to ask a favor. There is one of your unexploded missiles in my backyard. Do you think it would be possible to find someone to remove it?"

The soldier gave me a blank look.

"I have orders not to leave my position, sir," he said.

He directed me to a U.S. Army camp being erected in a field about a mile from my home. Zaid parked nearby and I stood at the gate hoping that by wearing slacks pressed with my wife's battery-operated iron and a freshly laundered sport shirt, I appeared different from the rest of the crowd. When I saw a young man with two stripes on his uniform, I spoke up.

"Excuse me, sir, I was hoping to report a missile in my backyard," I said. "To whom should I speak?"

"Come back later," he said. "We're just getting set up here."

I returned the next day and was told at the gate to speak to a Lieutenant Copley. I waited three hours, and when Copley arrived, obviously preoccupied, he asked me to meet him the following day.

"At what time should I come?" I asked.

"About three," he said.

I arrived at three the following day and approached a young sergeant who manned the gate.

"You're not supposed to stand here!" he shouted.

"But I have a meeting with Lieutenant Copley," I said. "It's about an unexploded missile, you see."

"Out!" he shouted, motioning for me to remove myself. I was surprised at his brusqueness. Just then the gate opened and a convoy of military vehicles entered the camp from the street, sending a thick cloud of dust over me and Zaid.

"Stand back!" the sergeant shouted, too late to save my freshly laundered clothes from a coat of Iraqi dust.

A few days later I stopped to speak to an army unit parked by a roadside in our neighborhood. I was pleased when the soldiers told me they were engineers. Their commanding officer, Captain Butler, was a handsome young African American man with a friendly manner.

"As engineers, what sort of work are you doing here in Iraq?" I asked.

"Right now, we're mostly detonating unexploded ordnance," he said. "But we'll be doing reconstruction projects as soon as this mission is accomplished. Our mandate is to try to make Iraq a better place."

I liked Captain Butler from the moment I met him. He showed me a misshapen cylinder of metal and explained that it was part of an American cluster bomb that his unit had found in the neighborhood. They had made a controlled explosion to render it useless. When I told him about the unexploded bomb in my garden, hundreds of times the size of his cluster bomb, he seemed genuinely alarmed and promised to come to my home within a couple of hours.

Captain Butler came that afternoon as promised, with five soldiers from his engineers unit. I led them into my garden, and when he saw the dimensions of the thing, he let out a whistle and said he would have to come back the next day with a bigger truck. He returned the next morning with twenty soldiers and a large flatbed vehicle. I took them around to the side of my house and showed them the missile, and they looked at each other nervously and ordered me to stand back as they cut my metal gardening rack apart and gingerly removed it. As most of the soldiers stood back, shouting at their commander to be careful, Captain Butler and two of his men hoisted it on their shoulders and carried it to an armored vehicle to be carted away for controlled detonation. I had reason to believe that if the missile had not exploded on impact, it was unlikely to detonate now on the shoulders of these young American soldiers. After they strapped the missile on their truck, I led Captain Butler back to my yard.

I am proud of my garden, and I showed Captain Butler my prized gardenias and fruit trees, which he was kind enough to admire. A few feet away, the branches of the lotus tree shaded the spot where Iraq's nuclear know-how still lay buried. During my years pruning roses and gardening with the plastic drum just underfoot, I had been struck by another irony of the situation that I had not been aware of when I chose this place. In the Koran the lotus, or *lote*, represents the boundary between mortal knowledge and God, the border between what is known and what cannot be known. It symbolizes the furthest edge of human pursuit, beyond which there is only divine judgment. I had a fleeting urge to tell Captain Butler about this story. He seemed like a nimble-minded young man who would appreciate the subtle layers of meaning behind it. But the secret was too dangerous to reveal in this setting. Instead, I led Captain Butler away from the lotus tree to the edge of my lawn, where the gray, cone-shaped object had come to rest on the dichondra grass.

"I believe this might be the fuse of the bomb," I said, picking it up. I showed him the chipped edges and suggested that this piece had been at the nose of the missile but had dislodged on impact and been hurled to its current position.

"The fuses of your missiles are normally at the front end, isn't that correct?" I asked. "Perhaps this is why the bomb failed to explode."

Captain Butler agreed that this was a likely explanation, but he gave me a strange look.

"How do you know all this?" he asked incredulously.

I shrugged, knowing that to say more could invite awkward questions.

"I'm an engineer," I said, without elaborating. "Just like you."

CHAPTER 2

Early Ambitions

Of course, I was not just an engineer like Captain Butler. I figured that we shared a love of science and, by virtue of our positions within military systems, both of us were bound to follow orders. But the comparison more or less ended there. Captain Butler would never understand what it was like to live under total secrecy, trying to meet absurd deadlines and following orders backed by the threat of execution. At least I hoped he would not, for his sake.

But when I looked into Captain Butler's eyes I saw something familiar from my almost forgotten boyhood: a spark of idealism that glows inside young people determined to make the world a better place. I myself had grown up with lofty aspirations, to help my country advance and prosper for the benefit of the Iraqi people. As a young man I never dreamed that my fate would be to develop nuclear weapons for a dangerously erratic dictator.

I was born in 1944 to middle-class parents of mixed Shi'ite and Sunni backgrounds on a plantation in the rural Zafaraniya area, about ten miles south of Baghdad. Ours was a medium-sized piece of land of roughly a square mile in area, crosshatched with orange and apple trees, between a dusty road and the Tigris River. My parents were financially comfortable, such that they owned one of the first cars in our small village, yet not so wealthy to become caught up in politics or the increasingly tumultuous situation in the nearby capital. I spent my early years playing among the fruit trees with my older brother Hadi and my four younger sisters, surrounded by peasants and seasonal workers. Even today, the scent of an orange transports me back to childhood.

My father was a quick-tempered and determined man who taught me the value of perseverance, which was a trait I would call on throughout my life. My enduring memory of him is of the day after he broke his arm falling from a ladder in our orchards, before I was old enough for school. The night before, the doctor had come to our house, set my father's arm in a cast, and told him to rest until he was healed. My father barely grimaced and shook his head impatiently at the suggestion. The next morning, shrugging off the physical pain, he set off into the orchards again with me tagging along; he was carrying a shovel over one shoulder with one arm, while his other arm remained in a sling.

My mother was both a pious Muslim and a superstitious woman who believed her dreams spoke of the future, especially when she dreamed about her family members. She told me many times that I would one day go to America, which eventually came true. Once I went with her to visit my uncle on an errand to warn him that she had dreamed he would lose his life the next day unless he stayed at home. He laughed and ignored her entreaties and left the house the next morning. Within minutes of walking out his front door, he was shot dead in the street. His murder was never solved.

When I was three years old, I fell into a reservoir in our orange grove and nearly drowned. Some of the workers had seen me fall in and rushed over to fish my unconscious body out of the water. Although I was saved from drowning, I became very sick. My abdomen swelled, and the doctors told my parents I had severe liver damage and that I would probably not survive. After weeks of attempted treatments, they finally told my mother it was useless to continue bringing me to their hospital. My family despaired and prepared for my death. That night, my mother later told me, she dreamed that a cousin would visit us the next day with news of a Christian doctor who was treating a neighbor woman. According to her dream, this doctor could cure me. In the morning, everything transpired just as she had dreamt it. Our cousin arrived and recommended a doctor who gave me a different type of medicine, and within a week I was cured.

Although I was too young to view my mother's prophetic powers with a critical eye, I knew that she believed in them, and her sense of spirituality helped to shape my childhood. Later in life, as a practical-minded scientist, I often thought about her premonitions with a sense of wonder. My mother believed that my sickness caused me to become a quiet and hardworking boy. She also told me many times that my near-death experience proved that God had saved me for some important work.

In primary school I settled down to my lessons with the concentration of a much older student. My teachers noticed my special interest and skill in mathematics, and by age fourteen I was offered a place in a more prestigious high school in the Karada neighborhood of Baghdad. The next year, my parents helped me buy an old Volkswagen Beetle to make the trip from our farmhouse into the city. I spent hours driving that old car through the palm and citrus groves that lined the Tigris River, and because it needed constant repair, I began to take an interest in machines and how they operate.

By the time I reached high school, I was becoming aware of the growing turmoil that, beyond the confines of our family's fruit plantation, had been brewing for years. Iraq's first decades as a nation had been rocky. After the collapse of the Ottoman Empire during World War I, British troops occupied the territories that became Iraq and set up a provisional government controlled from London. This did not sit well with many Iraqis, who repeatedly protested in the streets. Opposition clerics issued fatwas against

Iraqis participating in the occupation government. Finally, in 1920, Sunni and Shi'ite insurgents declared common cause against the British and rose up in armed revolt. British troops eventually quelled the uprising, at the cost of the lives of hundreds of British soldiers and thousands of Iraqis. Soon afterward, the British established a monarchy to lead a new Iraqi government, with the newly crowned King Amir Faisal on the throne. The monarchy experimented with democratic reforms, including attempts to extend freedoms to the press and political parties. But protests by Iraqis who saw the government as a pawn of Western powers interested only in Iraq's oil resulted in crackdowns and violent clashes in the streets. The monarchy appointed a series of harsh prime ministers, the most powerful of which was the feared Nuri al-Said, a personal friend of T. E. Lawrence (Lawrence of Arabia).

I was on summer vacation from high school on July 14, 1958, when the radio broadcast news of a bloody coup d'état. The night before, taking the monarchy completely by surprise, Iraqi army units under the command of Colonel Abd al-Salam 'Arif and Brigadier Abd al-Karim Qasim slipped into Baghdad and occupied all the important government buildings and ministries. Army units surrounded the royal palace and bombarded it until the royal guard surrendered. Within minutes, they had rounded up the young grandson of the late King Faisal I, his crown prince, and the rest of the royal family, including the palace cooks, teachers, and other staff, and shot them on the palace grounds. Nuri al-Said managed to escape from his house disguised as a woman. But the next morning he was recognized, caught, and executed in the street. A crowd, incited by the coup plotters, dragged his corpse behind a motorcycle, then dismembered it, and put its limbs on display.

Brigadier Qasim appointed himself prime minister, and although he promised democratic change, he and his military government continued the repressive ways of the monarchy. Qasim banned political parties and frequently imposed martial law. The events of these years foreshadowed the violence that would plague Iraq in the decades to come. As Iraqis struggled for a sense of identity after centuries of foreign rule, a new opposition group called the Baath Party began to attract an underground following with its calls for Arab unity and national pride.

In October 1959, as I began my sophomore year in high school, members of the Iraqi Baath Party hatched an unsuccessful assassination plot against Qasim. One of the would-be killers was a twenty-two-year-old from the Tikrit area named Saddam Hussein, who managed to escape the country and survive Qasim's revenge.

The development that directly affected my life was the growing world demand for oil. The formation of the Organization of Petroleum Exporting Countries (OPEC) in 1960 meant that Iraq and other Arab states were gaining greater control not only of oil prices but also of oil production on their lands. With the second-largest oil reserves on earth, Iraq had increased production fourfold during the 1950s. There was only one problem: Iraq lacked the skilled personnel to operate a large-scale local oil industry. To meet this urgent need, the government began sending hundreds of its top math and science students abroad to study at the finest Western scientific institutions.

As my high school graduation approached, I began to consider my future and how to fulfill my mother's prediction that I would do important work. The decision was made for me. One day, the head-master called me into his office with exciting news: the Ministry of Education was offering me a scholarship for a five-year program at the Colorado School of Mines in the United States. I was ecstatic. I raced home to tell my mother and father, who embraced me and told me how proud they were. I was the first member of our imme-diate family to study outside of Iraq.

In June 1962, at the age of eighteen, I journeyed alone to Washington, D.C., for a summer course in English before my college classes began. I lived in a tiny, grim apartment near Dupont Circle, and suddenly, after a sheltered childhood surrounded by my family, I felt very alone in the American capital. On my third day I wept with homesickness. Eventually, however, my temporary home began to fascinate me. Iraq was still a very poor country when I left, with shabby buildings and potholed roads. Washington D.C. seemed like a fantasyland. I spent my free time walking around the city center and marveling at the grandeur of the White House, the Smithsonian Institution, and the monuments. I remember one afternoon standing under the dome of the Jefferson Memorial and reading Jefferson's words inscribed on the inside of the cupola: "I have sworn upon the altar of God eternal hostility against every form of tyranny over the mind of man." These words resonated with me in a way that would probably escape someone who had not been raised in a repressive country. Ever since the overthrow of the monarchy, tyranny had been the rule in Iraq. We were careful about what we said even in high school. And in ways that I could not foresee at the time, the stranglehold of tyranny would only tighten in Iraq during the coming decades, bending to its will the best minds of the nation, including my own.

My five-year sojourn at the Colorado School of Mines was the most carefree time of my life. The college, nestled in the former gold-mining town of Golden, Colorado, at the foot of the Rocky Mountains, was one of the most prestigious mining and engineering schools in the world. I was amazed by the directness of Americans, and the way their social interaction is based on trust and straight-forwardness. My dormitory roommate, David, was an avid mountain climber with whom I spent many weekends hiking in the Rockies. As we drove his dilapidated Mercedes up toward the breathtaking peaks above our school, he was always amused by my strange expressions translated from Arabic. As I became more comfortable speaking English, I was able to entertain David and other classmates with descriptions of my homeland. I told them of the Bedouin camel herders in the deserts of Mesopotamia and about my tribe, the Obeidis, descendants of the Queen of Sheba's ancient clan of Yemeni Arabs, some of whom migrated north thousands of years ago and became regional rulers near what is now Baghdad.

During my five years of college I did not return home, and Iraq seemed very remote to me. I spent vacations traveling around the United States with friends or taking summer courses. In my sophomore year I began dating an education and philosophy student from the University of Denver named Phyllis Mulhausen. Phyllis was a soft-spoken redhead who helped keep me focused on my studies. We spent many long hours together, eating cakes at a local café and talking about the differences in our cultures. Her parents invited me for dinner at least once a week, and I soon began to feel as though I were a part of her family. Before I graduated in 1967, Phyllis and I were talking about getting married, but in the end she chose to stay in America and I wanted to return to Iraq. It was a turning point at which an Iraqi friend, Hamid al-Hakeem, went the other direction. Hamid and I had been very close throughout our years at the School of Mines, and toward the end we often talked about returning to Iraq together. Just before our departure date, however, Hamid called me to say he planned to stay in the United States. He later married a courtroom stenographer named Patricia and took an oil exploration job with Arco in Houston. Because of those youthful decisions—his to stay, and mine to return to Iraq—our paths diverged to the widest degree imaginable.

When my parents opened their door and welcomed their homecoming son, they saw a young man flushed with a new graduate's optimism and sense of purpose. Iraq was on the threshold of an industrial revolution and, I believed, ready to create a self-sufficient oil industry that would improve the quality of life for all Iraqis. With my new master's degree in petroleum-refining engineering, I felt I could help my country bloom. Iraqis had been unnecessarily impoverished for too long, considering the richness of the land's resources and a history of innovation that stretched back to man's earliest endeavors. The basin of Mesopotamia, after all, was where civilization began. Twelve thousand years ago, humans invented a system of agricultural irrigation not far from the orchards where my parents raised me. Ancient Mesopotamian people invented writing, worked out a system for telling time, and developed a useful invention called the wheel. For thousands of years, the forebears of Iraqis wrote much of the world's greatest poetry, histories, and sagas. Upon my return I entertained the hope that Iraq might once again become a leading civilization in the world.

In my absence, however, political instability had continued. A coup d'état in 1963 brought the Baath Party briefly to power, but a countercoup by military officers ejected the Baathists less than a year later. After an unsuccessful attempt to retake power, Baath Party leader Ahmad Hasan al-Bakr, his young relative Saddam Hussein, and other members of the party were thrown into prison. Saddam remained behind bars until 1966, cementing relationships with fellow inmates who joined him and others in the 1968 coup that established Baathist rule.

Apart from the political turmoil, some things in Iraq were beginning to change for the better. The government allocated more funds for schools and hospitals, especially around Baghdad, where the signs of progress multiplied. My life in those years seemed ideal. I met a beautiful woman named Layla, who became my soul mate, and I married her two years later.

The Ministry of Oil assigned me to the Daura oil refinery near Baghdad. I took pride in my work, and soon afterward the director general of the region assigned me to work as a troubleshooter for problems in the refineries throughout Iraq. By 1972 I was one of Iraq's most experienced refinery engineers. When the Ministry of Oil offered me a grant to pursue a Ph.D. program in materials engineering at University College of Swansea in Wales, Layla and I jumped at the chance to live and study abroad.

Near the end of my three-year doctorate program in the United Kingdom, I befriended a fellow Iraqi doctoral student at Swansea who had worked at the Iraqi Atomic Energy Commission (IAEC). I was only vaguely aware that Iraq had a nuclear energy program, which my new friend said was in its infancy. He described it as a fascinating place to work, offering the opportunity to do research, unlike the Ministry of Oil, where I had essentially been involved only in production.

The idea that Iraq, a developing country, was stepping into the nuclear age had an intoxicating appeal to me. Nuclear research was at the absolute forefront of science, and it had a whiff of the future, with applications in agriculture and food preservation, medical research and the treatment of cancer and heart disease, and, of course, the production of atomic energy. I felt that, even more than in the oil industry, I could help my country blossom through atomic research. When Layla and I returned to Iraq in 1975, I applied to the IAEC and was asked to present a lecture about my work in materials engineering. After an hour, they were impressed enough to hire me on the spot.

My doctoral studies applied directly to a problem that had bedeviled a 2-megawatt nuclear reactor Iraq had purchased from Russia in the mid-1960s. Used for research in physics and medicine, this small reactor was prone to corrosion in its aluminum shell and in the block that held the radioactive fuel. If the aluminum became corroded, fuel might leak out of the core and release radioactive gases into the atmosphere. When I joined the IAEC, my first mandate was to ensure the safety of the reactor.

I participated in the upgrade of the reactor to a newer 5-megawatt version at the Nuclear Research Center at Tuwaitha, about ten miles southeast of Baghdad, not far from the orchards where I spent my childhood. Housed in a large hall underneath a dome, the reactor block sat in a cylindrical pit about fifteen feet in diameter and about twenty-four feet deep, filled with water. I remember the first time I descended a ladder to the bottom of the empty pool, I was awed by the amount of space required to cool such a small reactor.

At the time, Iraq was negotiating with France to purchase a larger research reactor with 40 megawatts of power, which would help the IAEC gain a greater understanding of nuclear physics and engineering. This was an essential step toward the eventual goal of purchasing a full-scale, 600-megawatt nuclear reactor to generate power.

The IAEC put me in charge of materials research and, in 1976, sent me to apprentice for four months in the Italian nuclear program, financed partly by a grant from the United Nations, which hoped to ensure the safety of reactors purchased by developing countries. The Italians were very kind and allowed me almost unrestricted access to their facilities and reactor designs. I met brilliant fellow engineers who helped me design experiments to learn how different materials react in the harsh environment of a power reactor. We simulated conditions of up to 360 degrees centigrade and pressures of more than 100 atmospheres (or 100 times the pressure of the air at sea level), and I found the steep learning curve exhilarating. After four months, I had formed solid relationships with a few Italian engineers and grasped many of the finer points of reactor engineering and experiment design.

To understand how nuclear reactors work, and how they relate to nuclear weapons, one must start with a basic understanding of what happens at the atomic level. All matter is made of atoms, at the center of which are dense nuclei made up of particles called protons and neutrons held together by powerful nuclear forces. If this nucleus can be split apart through bombardment at the subatomic level, these gluelike forces release energy. A nuclear reactor works like a pinball machine, firing free-floating neutrons at the nuclei of certain volatile atoms in an attempt to split them and release massive amounts of stored energy, in a process called irradiation.

Most elements on the periodic table are impervious to such bombardment. But the heaviest element in nature, uranium, contains an extremely unstable isotope called uranium-235. Natural uranium contains less than 1 percent uranium-235 and is not susceptible to irradiation because of the density of its stable cousin, uranium-238. To achieve the nuclear fission that releases energy, uranium must be enriched. Most nuclear reactors that generate power run on uranium fuel that is between 2 and 4 percent uranium-235. This allows the atoms to split at a manageable rate so that the energy can be harnessed for electricity.

Something quite different happens in a nuclear bomb. The same uranium neutrons that do the work of producing energy and serving medicine and agriculture become lethal when uranium is enriched to more than 90 percent U-235. More than fifteen kilograms of such highly enriched uranium becomes a powder keg, in which neutrons smash into neighboring nuclei at an exponential rate. The chain reaction instantly spirals out of control and results in a cataclysmic nuclear explosion.

A nation with a nuclear reactor can use it to develop nuclear weapons in two ways. First, some of the enriched uranium used for reactor fuel might be set aside for further enrichment to weapons-grade using a variety of methods. Even more worrisome, however, is the fact that a nuclear reactor can be used as a tool to produce plutonium. Plutonium is an unnatural element synthesized in a reactor by wrapping the uranium fuel cells with blankets containing U-238 during irradiation. In this process, instead of splitting atoms, the neutron bullets bond with nuclei to form unstable plutonium, Pu-239, which may then be chemically separated in a reprocessing plant. Plutonium is far more radioactive than enriched uranium and extremely dangerous to those who handle it, though less of it is required for a weapon. The bomb dropped on Nagasaki in 1945 contained about thirteen pounds of plutonium, and modern plutonium weapons use even smaller amounts.

A nuclear reactor is like a knife—it is a necessary utensil for cutting bread, but it can also be used to cut a throat. Any nation may legally purchase a nuclear reactor and, since there are many peaceful uses for atomic energy, it is difficult to deny this technology to even the most dangerous-seeming regime. Because of this, a number of developing countries have turned to the plutonium option in attempts to develop nuclear weapons covertly, in addition to applying the centrifuge technique to produce enriched uranium. India used a reactor acquired from Canada in the 1950s to produce plutonium for the bombs it tested in 1998. Israel, the only nuclear-armed nation in the Middle East, began producing plutonium shortly after its nuclear plant at Dimona went operational in 1964. North Korea is accused of stockpiling at least 60 pounds of unseparated plutonium in fuel rods at its nuclear facility at Yongbyon. Iran began work on nuclear power reactors at Bushehr on the Gulf coast during the 1970s. Although Iraq bombed the Iranian reactors during the 1980s, Iran has received Russian help in rebuilding them, raising suspicions in the United States and elsewhere that Iran still hopes to build a nuclear bomb.

The same suspicions could have been raised in the 1970s about Iraq. At the time, however, the international community did not view Iraq as a particularly aggressive nation, so the nuclear program raised few eyebrows at first. I myself believed the French reactor would be used as a research tool to prepare our scientists to produce energy. After all, Iraq had signed the 1968 Treaty on the Non-Proliferation of Nuclear Weapons, which provided for international oversight of its nuclear program.

In 1979 political upheavals inside and around Iraq shook the region in ways that would reverberate for years to come. In neighboring Iran, Shi'ite militants seized control of the government and imposed a radical version of sharia law, a code of conduct based on a strict interpretation of Islam. Iranian demonstrators angry at U.S. support for the deposed shah took dozens of people hostage in the American embassy in a standoff that lasted more than a year. The Iranian revolution alarmed Iraq's military regime. Despite this, Saddam Hussein, already the de facto ruler of Iraq even though he had not yet assumed the presidency, sent a formal letter of congratulations to Iran's new ruler, Ayatollah Ruhollah Khomeini. The conciliatory gesture went nowhere. Khomeini returned the letter with part of a verse from the Koran: "Peace be upon those who follow righteousness." He may as well have slapped Saddam in the face. The verse relates to Moses admonishing the pharaoh, implying that Saddam, like the pharaoh, was a dictator, a killer, and an unbeliever.

I remember telling my family, "War is inevitable, and it is coming soon."

A few months later Saddam seized the presidency in a manner that sent a chill down the spine of the nation. After the resignation of President Hasan al-Baqr, he called a meeting of leading government officials in a Baghdad conference hall on July 18, 1979. To make sure his message was unmistakable, he had the proceedings videotaped for public consumption. As soon as the several hundred most powerful men in Iraq had taken their seats, Saddam strode to a lectern with a lit cigar between his fingers and a look of concern on his face. In a melodramatic voice, he told the audience that he had uncovered a plot to undermine the government. He lowered his voice and scanned the room. Some of those gathered in this very room are traitors, he said. On this cue the secretary general of the Revolutionary Command Council, Muhyi Abd al-Hussein Mashadi, emerged from behind a curtain and stood beside Saddam. Secretary General Mashadi had been arrested a few days earlier. As if in a trance, he confessed that he was one of the plotters against the government. Then he began reading from a list of alleged coconspirators. As he pronounced each name, armed guards moved through the audience and dragged the accused from the hall. Many of the condemned men shouted pleas of innocence, and others wept as they anticipated the worst.

"*Itla!*" Saddam shouted at the sound of each name, punctuating the roll call of the doomed. "Get out!"

Secretary General Mashadi read sixty names. When he finished, he seemed surprised when guards grabbed him and ushered him out of the chamber, too. The surviving members of the assembly rose to their feet, trying to outdo each other with cheers to Saddam's health and long rule. In the following days, we learned that many of the sixty accused officials were executed by firing squad, along with hundreds of others Saddam had deemed untrustworthy.

I remember seeing a parade that Saddam organized shortly afterwards. Just behind the new president stood Taha Yassin Ramadan, who later became vice president and would remain loyal to Saddam until the end of the regime in 2003. I noticed the look in Taha Yassin's eyes. He appeared nervous and frightened. Some of his comrades had been shot during Saddam's purge of the government, and even though he was already one of Saddam's right-hand men, he obviously felt insecure about his safety. The bloody purges continued during the next few years, as Saddam had thousands of perceived enemies rounded up and killed. Purges were not new to Iraq, but the scope and public manner in which Saddam took the presidency sent the unmistakable message that opposition would not be tolerated.

By 1979 the IAEC had expanded to the point where I oversaw a staff of more than two hundred in the Materials Department of the Nuclear Research Center at Tuwaitha. Although I was only thirty-five years old, I shared a department directorship alongside other distinguished scientists such as Dr. Jaffar Dhia Jaffar, head of the Physics Department, and Hussain al-Shahrastani, head of the Chemistry Department. The head of the Nuclear Research Center, Dr. Humam Abdul al-Khalek Ghaffour, reported to the political head of the IAEC, a short, stocky man named Dr. Abdul Razzak al-Hashimi, and Saddam Hussein himself.

Construction was nearly complete on a facility for the 40-megawatt French reactor at Tuwaitha. Adjacent to a multistory office building for hundreds of IAEC staff, the main reactor hall stood ten stories high, with three cooling towers and a dome over the main cylinder. Inside the hall, giant pumps were installed to circulate water in a cavernous pool that would dissipate the heat of the reactor block. A 40-megawatt reactor generates a tremendous amount of heat, about twenty thousand times more than a typical 2-kilowatt home water heater. We called the reactor Tammuz, which is the Arabic word for the month of July, the hottest period of the year, when temperatures reach unbearable levels, and the month of the coup that brought the Baathists to power in 1968. The French called the entire project Osiraq, a blending of the name of the French reactor, Osiris, with the name of my country.

My colleagues had been intimately involved in closing the deal with the French Atomic Energy Commission. I had not yet met our French counterparts, so it came as a surprise when, in the autumn of 1979, I received a written order from IAEC director al-Hashimi to travel to France and represent the IAEC as director of the Experimental Group. This meant that I would be responsible for defining the experiments to be conducted in the new reactor: an unexpected honor.

I flew to Paris in December 1979 to discuss the configuration of the reactor at the Center for Nuclear Studies at Saclay. A prominent employee of the French Atomic Energy Commission picked me up at Charles de Gaulle Airport. He spoke fluent English and we exchanged formal pleasantries, but as I loaded my suitcase into his car, I felt a vague sense of mistrust on his part.

"I understand you will be defining the experiments for the reactor," he said. "I hope you will be successful."

As an Arab accustomed to the poetry of the unsaid, I am attentive to the subtleties of dialogue and hidden meanings behind a person's words. I immediately picked up on the irony of his remark. As we drove out of the airport in silence, I considered the implications of his attitude. On some level, at least, the French doubted Iraq's declared intentions for the reactor. This could complicate my task of defining experiments, because I would be operating under a cloud of suspicion. As we drove through Paris, I felt the need to break the ice as my French host politely but coolly pointed out several landmarks.

"This is the famous Seine River," he said as we crossed a bridge over the waterway that winds through Paris.

"The 'Sin' River?" I asked, trying to make a pun in English. "So tell me, how many sins have been committed on your famous 'Sin' River?"

At first he didn't understand my silly wordplay, so I repeated, "The Sin River!"

"Oh," he said, with a genuine laugh. "Many sins have been committed here, I assure you. Many!"

As we chuckled over this, the atmosphere between us lightened. When we reached the hotel, he shook my hand warmly and agreed to meet for coffee the next morning. The following day he took me to Saclay and introduced me to the scientists who ran experiments at the French Osiris reactor, which was the model for the reactor the IAEC had purchased. As soon as my new friend departed, however, the goodwill established the day before evaporated. I experienced a complete lack of cooperation from the Saclay scientists. After several frustrating days, I told the head of operations at Saclay that I intended to return to Iraq because I was unable to fulfill my obligations. This put my French colleagues in an uncomfortable spot, because they had committed to an expensive contract that was difficult to break. I imagine that a number of high-level telephone calls were made that evening. The next day I was told to expect a different reception at Saclay.

I suspect that the French scientists were relieved to put political considerations behind them and to be allowed to deal with me as a fellow engineer. The turnabout in attitude was so complete that I suddenly felt as if I owned the place. I quickly established six experiments to test materials in the reactor. Four of them would explore the effect of neutrons on structural materials, and two physics experiments would test the viability of enriched fuel in a reactor environment. The French scientists were impressed by my knowledge of nuclear reactor engineering, much of which I had learned from the Italians.

Before I returned to Iraq, Jacques Genton, the head of experiments at Saclay, invited me to dinner and an evening out in Paris. After a meal at a fine French restaurant, we were joined by three men introduced as high-ranking officials from the French Atomic Energy Commission. They escorted us to an establishment called the Crazy Horse. We entered the dark lounge, and I realized it was a strip club. Women wearing almost no clothing danced ballet-style on stage, illuminated by colored lights. The rhythmic music rose and fell like heavy breathing.

"Don't worry," one of the Frenchmen confided, taking my elbow, "this is a classy establishment."

It seemed odd that my first visit to a strip club should be with top scientists in the French nuclear establishment. They led me to a private table overlooking the show and seated me in the place of honor, directly facing the stage. The whole encounter seemed designed for my benefit, to create an atmosphere of intimacy.

"Tell me something, Mahdi," said one of my hosts. Fat, ebullient, and the most eloquent in English of the group, he leaned toward me in a conspiratorial way. "Iraq must have a lot of money. You have so much oil. I'd like to ask something. What does Iraq want with a nuclear reactor?"

The question seemed obvious, but it took me aback under the circumstances. I looked down at the stage and considered how to respond. I now suspected that some of the men might be French intelligence agents, and I put my guard up.

"As you know," I said, smiling, "Iraq is a nation trying to join the industrialized world and become a great nation like France."

"You appear to be a clever man," another of my hosts said. "Why haven't we met you before? We met Dr. Jaffar, Dr. Shahrastani, and Dr. Hashimi. Aren't these the most prominent people in the Iraqi Atomic Energy Commission?"

It was clear to me that my hosts wanted to learn more about the hierarchy of the IAEC as well as its intentions for the reactor. Here, too, I felt I should be careful.

"They keep me very busy," I said, answering in the same light-hearted spirit.

The Frenchmen seemed to have prepared an orchestrated line of inquiry. As in the game of volleyball, they took turns setting each other up to hit me with probing questions.

"Dr. Mahdi," one of the Frenchmen said, leaning across the table. "We know that Iraq is a very forward-thinking country to anticipate a future without oil. But there are those who would use a nuclear reactor to make a bomb."

All the cards were on the table now. These men thought I knew something that I didn't.

"Of course," I said. "Many of your people have expressed concern about this. But I believe that in a republic such as France, one is presumed innocent until he is proven guilty. Isn't this the case?"

I was relieved when the inquiry ended there. Well past midnight I returned to my hotel with a lingering sense of unease. It felt uncomfortable to be caught between fellow scientists from another country and murky forces at home. I had no way of knowing that I would find myself in this awkward position many times in the years to come. The next day I returned to Iraq with a head full of doubts.

Meanwhile, the Iraqi nuclear reactor project had become a dangerous game, both inside and outside Iraq. Soon after I returned from France, Saddam's men arrested Dr. Hussain al-Shahrastani on suspicion of having ties to an orthodox Islamic party seen as hostile to the Baathist government. The truth of the accusations—something nearly impossible to discern under Saddam—was never made clear to us. But if Dr. Hussain was mixed up in opposition politics, it was a suicidal move for a government-employed scientist. He spent most of the next decade in solitary confinement in prison. Dr. Jaffar was next on the target list. He fell under suspicion after visiting Dr. Hussain's distraught wife and children and, in early 1980, was confined to house arrest for the next twenty months.

Foreign plots against the Iraqi nuclear program turned the pressure up further. In April of 1979, saboteurs had entered the storage facility in Toulon, France, where the cores destined for the Tammuz reactor were kept, and detonated five explosive charges that severely damaged them. Many fingers pointed to the Israeli secret service, Mossad. Then, in 1980, the plotting turned lethal. Within months three scientists working on behalf of the Iraqi nuclear program were dead.

The first was Yehia al-Meshad, an Egyptian physicist hired by Iraq to oversee the integrity of the uranium fuel for the reactor. I had met him on a number of occasions in Baghdad and genuinely liked the man. In June of 1980, he was clubbed to death in his Paris hotel room in an attack blamed on a French woman, suspected of being a prostitute, who died soon afterward in a hit-and-run auto accident. The same year, an electrical engineer named Salman Rashid, who worked with Dr. Jaffar, came down with a mysterious illness and died suddenly while in Geneva looking into electromagnetic separators. Dr. Rashid had been a friend of mine, and I was horrified by his death. Six months later one of the chief IAEC engineers with whom I had worked closely, Abdul Rahman Abdul Rasool, was poisoned to death at a dinner party in France.

These killings shook me to the core, as I realized I was now involved in an endeavor that someone was determined to stop at any cost. I lived in fear that I would be next on the list. The fact that two of the three victims had been working on the actual reactor, while my concern was only with the experiments, did little to comfort me.

In this tense climate, the IAEC negotiated with the French to repair the damaged reactor cores, which delayed their delivery by more than six months. X-rays of the cores revealed fractures throughout the inner layers. Several of my colleagues and I called this to the attention of our superiors at the IAEC, but they shrugged off the concerns. They insisted that the reactor core could function safely for years before any real problems might develop. I couldn't understand their reckless attitude. Why would anyone take even a small risk with something as dangerous as a nuclear reactor?

By coincidence, around the same time I was scheduled to attend the International Congress on Structural Mechanics in Berlin, along with hundreds of other scientists from around the world. The assistant to the head of the American Nuclear Regulatory Commission gave a lecture on the cracking of stainless steel due to stress and corrosion in nuclear reactors. After his lecture, I took him aside for a cup of tea. Without mentioning the specifics of the dilemma I faced or that I believed our reactor core had been damaged by a deliberate explosion, I asked his opinion about a hypothetical, and less serious, problem.

"If stainless steel is exposed to stresses due to heating, but the metal appears strong otherwise, isn't it still possible to put fuel in it?" I asked.

"Never," he said. "I would never dream of using a material that I knew had been exposed to stresses beforehand."

I returned to Iraq and told my colleagues that under no circumstances should we place fuel in the reactor, because of the damage to the integrity of the core. Although the risk of a radioactive leak was limited, the consequences could be disastrous. We had several meetings in which very heated words were exchanged. In the end my objections were simply overridden.

Around this time an incident confirmed my sense that the IAEC had an ulterior motive in acquiring a reactor from France. The IAEC director, the short, stocky Dr. al-Hashimi, called me one day to inquire about the progress of my work. He asked me to come to a small conference room near his office. I was surprised when I arrived at the meeting to find a number of the heads of the IAEC, including Dr. Khalid Ibrahim Sa'id, the head of the Projects Department, Chief Manager Dhafer Selbi, and Dr. Humam. I immediately sensed a tense atmosphere, and when I seated myself, Dr. al-Hashimi went directly to the point.

"Dr. Mahdi, how are things progressing with the experiments?"

It was a vague question, so I answered in an equally vague fashion. "Fine," I said. "Very well."

"I mean," he said, "how are we in terms of strategies? Will the reactor be able to fulfill its strategic requirements?"

One of the members of the committee who was sitting beside me pinched my leg and said, "Mahdi, please put him at ease. The man is terrified."

I didn't know Dr. al-Hashimi very well, but it seemed obvious he was leaving something unsaid. It was not a great leap to imagine that the unstated question was whether the reactor could be used to develop bomb-grade material. Why else would he speak in such generalities? But I also knew better than to ask, "What strategic requirements?" I had to answer carefully.

"Sir," I said, "I am sure the experiments will fulfill whatever expectations are required of them."

Dr. al-Hashimi seemed only partly satisfied, but he refrained from asking anything further and turned to the other IAEC directors. "Look here," he said. "You can all rest assured that my head shall be the last one to be chopped off."

The significance of al-Hashimi's remarks was plain. The Tammuz reactor was to serve a purpose so important that the head of the IAEC feared that failure would cost him his life. Dr. al-Hashimi's question about "strategic requirements" indicated the government's wish to develop nuclear weapons. But desire is one thing, and having a coherent plan to achieve a particular goal is quite another. When I stepped back to look at the larger picture, I saw a mismatch between the idea and reality. By purchasing the French reactor, the IAEC was possibly taking the first few steps on the road toward a nuclear weapons program. The 40-megawatt reactor wouldn't contain enough uranium fuel to enrich for a weapon, however. And I was almost certain that the IAEC had no strategy for turning the fissile material into weapons even if the material could be produced.

The delusions within the IAEC did not concern me directly. My responsibility was the experiments in the reactor, nothing more. Scientists generally do not like to get mixed up in politics, and as a task-oriented professional, I kept my focus on my narrow assignment. Looking back, I suppose some of the burning idealism of my youth had already given way to the more practical considerations of a family man in his mid-thirties. My job was prestigious and scientifically intriguing, and Layla and I already had two young children to feed.

After months of low-level border skirmishes, Saddam launched a full-scale attack against Iran in the fall of 1980. Iraqi warplanes struck Iranian airfields and bombed the oil refineries, while Saddam's ground troops surrounded the Iranian border towns and invaded as much Iranian territory as possible. The Iranians retaliated by bombing Baghdad and other Iraqi cities, including a strike that destroyed a building at Tuwaitha but left the reactor facility unscathed.

Despite foreign peace initiatives, hostilities between Iraq and Iran escalated with each month. By 1981 the situation had reached a dreadful stalemate. Iraqi troops were mired in a standoff with tens of thousands of Iranian revolutionary soldiers in the marshes of southern Iraq. Like many Iraqis, I believed that this border dispute would be settled in the near future. No one expected it to grind on for eight bloody years and become the twentieth century's longest conventional war.

The final components for the French reactor arrived in Iraq in early 1981. As they were installed at the Tuwaitha facility, I noticed another problem. The aluminum piping leading to the reactor block was pitted, due to a fragment of metal that had fallen into the pool when it was filled. Although the damage presented no danger of a radioactive leak, I argued that the flaw would need repairing eventually and it seemed best to do so before the reactor went live with radioactive fuel. The French were reluctant to fix it, however, and said it would cost $25 million. I suspected that the French were getting cold feet about the Tammuz project, due to doubts about the true intentions of the IAEC.

As we made final preparations for the reactor in May 1981, Saddam presented twenty new automobiles as gifts to the top officials and scientists of the IAEC. It was a time of heady anticipation. I was excluded from the rewards, however, despite the fact that I was the head of the Materials Division and one of the top scientists at the IAEC. When I saw that cars were awarded to a number of employees beneath my rank, I was left with only one conclusion. My superiors had singled me out because I had cautioned against using the reactor block. I learned another enduring lesson that day: it was taboo for a scientist to raise issues that were inconvenient to Saddam's government.

In the end, the Tammuz reactor never went live. Just days before we planned to install the radioactive reactor core, on Sunday, June 7, eight Israeli F-16 fighter jets flew more than a thousand miles to reach Baghdad, weaving across the borders of Jordan and Saudi Arabia and flying at low altitude through western Iraq to avoid detection by radar. They roared over the capital just after 5:30 P.M. as the sun shone directly behind them in the west. Caught completely off guard, the Iraqi air defenses had trouble targeting the fighters in the blinding sunlight. The first F-16 dropped an unguided bomb directly onto the dome over the reactor, tearing a gaping hole in it. With incredible precision, six of the other seven jets dropped bombs straight through the hole and they exploded within the reactor hall. The entire attack lasted less than two minutes.

After delivering their payload, the Israeli pilots outmaneuvered Iraqi surface-to-air missiles and returned home unscathed.

I heard about the bombing at home that evening on the radio. Several colleagues called me during the night to express their disbelief, and we agreed to meet at Tuwaitha first thing in the morning. Daybreak revealed the extent of the damage. The cylindrical beam that had supported the dome tilted wildly to one side, and the dome had collapsed down onto the reactor core. Sunlight streamed in from above, and we could see that the bombing had completely destroyed the reactor block. It was irreparable, finished.

A large group of IAEC officials and employees had gathered at the site by now, somberly inspecting the debris. Years of work lay in ruins. All around the reactor hall, administrative and support buildings stood without a scratch. But without the reactor, these buildings seemed suddenly meaningless.

Despite myself I let out a chuckle of amazement.

"What is so funny, Dr. Mahdi?" Dr. Humam asked. "Is there something about this tragedy we should find humorous?"

"The boldness of it, in broad daylight," I said, shaking my head. "And the precision. Look how nothing was touched except the reactor."

Within two weeks of the bombing, the United Nations Security Council condemned Israel for violating international law in the unprovoked attack. Israel's Prime Minister Menachem Begin countered that once the Tammuz reactor was functioning, it could soon lead to a nuclear-armed Iraq that would threaten his country. Prefiguring by more than twenty years the rationale of the 2003 war on Iraq, Israel claimed it was acting in "anticipatory self-defense." It argued that as a belligerent state Iraq couldn't be allowed to develop the ultimate weapon of mass destruction, and that unilateral action had been needed to remove a perceived threat.

The bombing of the Tammuz reactor ignited an international debate about how close Iraq had come to developing nuclear weapons and what should be done about Saddam's appetite for an atomic bomb. Our French counterparts at Saclay argued on Iraq's behalf that the Tammuz reactor was unfit for the production of plutonium and that inspections by the International Atomic Energy Agency (IAEA) and French technicians would have prevented the misuse of the reactor.

At first, France declared its intention to help rebuild the reactor and continue assisting the Iraqi nuclear program, but under a stricter program of safeguards. They offered no timetable for doing so, however. Inspectors from the IAEA eventually toured the Tuwaitha facility, inventoried the enriched uranium, and set a schedule of future inspections of the material to ensure that Iraq could not secretly use it for other ends. Months passed, and the promised French cooperation never materialized. For those of us who had once envisioned an Iraqi nuclear program to produce power and undertake important research, the dream died on the vine.

After the bombing of the Tammuz reactor, the atmosphere at the Iraqi Atomic Energy Commission was filled with apathy. I went to my office at the Tuwaitha facility every day on schedule, but without much motivation to work. Others stayed away as much as possible. The Tammuz reactor had been our common focus for years, and suddenly it was gone. My heart felt as empty as the corridors of the administration building, which echoed with the slow footsteps of the few scientists who bothered to come to work.

CHAPTER 3

The Centrifuge

The loss of the Tammuz reactor caused the IAEC to fundamentally shift course. In early 1982 Saddam established the Directorate of Studies to explore methods of producing weapons-grade material without the knowledge of the international community. The government had released Dr. Jaffar from confinement in September 1981 and assigned him to lead the new office and its staff, including my Materials Department, which supported the emerging enrichment programs. I was very fond of Dr. Jaffar, a brilliant, soft-spoken physicist from an aristocratic family. Although we met frequently, I never dared to ask him about his experience in confinement. In Iraq this was a taboo subject that could lead to nothing but trouble, but I imagined that those horrible memories served as a daily motivation to fulfill his responsibilities.

Dr. Jaffar chose a uranium enrichment technology called electromagnetic isotope separation (EMIS), based in part on a familiarity with accelerators and magnets he had gained at CERN, the world's largest particle physics laboratory, in Switzerland during the 1970s. The EMIS method separates uranium isotopes using electromagnetic fields created in giant iron cores. Although it is a cumbersome process that consumes tremendous amounts of power, Dr. Jaffar apparently felt it was the method most within reach of Iraq's industrial abilities.

He also began research into an enrichment method known as gas diffusion, in which solid uranium oxide is turned into a gaseous compound called uranium hexafluoride and then forced through a barrier that filters out the uranium isotopes. A marvel of science, a diffusion barrier is thinner than a sheet of paper and contains ten thousand billion holes per square centimeter.

The development of these two methods did not directly concern me until 1984, when Dr. Jaffar asked me to prepare a report on making diffusion barriers. I was surprised, because he already had a team of seventy scientists working on the project. Dr. Jaffar explained that he wanted a fresh perspective from an outsider, but I suspected that the work on the barrier had fared poorly and that he was under heavy pressure to find another solution. I spent a week in the library and prepared a brief suggesting the use of anodized aluminum for the barrier, along with a thorough rationale for doing so based on my knowledge of materials. A few days later, Dr. Jaffar came into my office with an even more surprising request.

"Your report is most impressive, and I would be pleased if you could continue developing it in practical terms," he said. "I want you to work on producing an actual diffusion barrier."

I was skeptical about taking on a project that overlapped with two years of work already undertaken by another team, so I tried to dismiss the idea.

"Why should I work on the diffusion project when you have seventy people working along the same lines?" I asked. "Surely this doesn't make sense."

"Unfortunately," Dr. Jaffar said, "this is the decision of the IAEC, not mine alone. So there is little choice in the matter."

When Dr. Jaffar spoke of "little choice," I knew he spoke from frightening experience. I asked two of my engineers to collect all of the literature on the diffusion technique that we had not yet studied, and we began experimenting with anodized aluminum in the Materials Department. We were quickly caught up in the enthusiasm of having a new challenge. I followed a complex electrochemical method that was quite different from the process used by the other IAEC team. A barrier consists of an aluminum film so thin that it is translucent. In theory, the structure of the material is a network of hexagons, each with a tiny hole bored into its center, so that under a microscope it resembles a honeycomb. After weeks of experiment-ation I began to see progress, and on the fiftieth day we looked at a piece of aluminum we had created and realized we had succeeded. When I bent down to the microscope, I was stunned to see that the structure was hexagonally shaped. As my engineers and I celebrated, I suggested that we keep our achievement secret because we could present it as a surprise at an upcoming IAEC seminar on the diffusion technique.

The seminar took place a couple of weeks later in an auditorium at IAEC headquarters, and I was scheduled to be the last speaker. As my colleagues used projections to illustrate their research into the types of nickel the Americans and the British were using and the alumina that the French were working with, I sat in the audience eager to take the stage. Finally, my turn came. I stood at the lectern in the dimmed lights and announced that I would not need to use projections because we had turned theory into a tangible reality. I asked for the lights to be turned on and held up an anodized barrier tube for all to see. The audience buzzed with excitement, and a number of my IAEC associates jealously congratulated me when they saw the structure of the material.

For a scientist, such a moment is a pinnacle of achievement. I imagine it is on par with the rush a soccer player experiences after scoring a winning goal, or what a mountain climber feels after scaling Mount Everest. I basked in the praise from my colleagues, unaware of how this achievement would bring me to the attention of Saddam Hussein's powerful henchmen.

. . .

The war with Iran dragged on disastrously. Outnumbered two to one, Iraqi troops had retreated from much of its captured territory, and Iranian revolutionary soldiers crossed the Shatt al-Arab River and mounted repeated attacks on the defenses surrounding the million residents in the southern Iraqi city of Basra. Saddam desperately needed new armaments, but the support he received from the United States, Britain, and other countries was at best lukewarm and unreliable. In 1986 it became clear that the United States was supporting both sides when it admitted to providing arms to the Iranian government in a secret deal aimed at both securing the release of American hostages in the Middle East and covertly funding the antigovernment contras in faraway Nicaragua.

Pressure on the IAEC increased during the mid-1980s, as Saddam was obviously getting impatient for results. Although I had enjoyed the scientific challenge, I felt in my heart that the diffusion technique was not a practical method for Iraq. It requires thousands of stages, involving many different types of highly advanced compressors and other equipment to push the uranium hexafluoride through the barriers. Where would Iraq get so many compressors, which were restricted under antiproliferation export controls? Manufacturing them in Iraq was out of the question. The country simply lacked the infrastructure. I settled on a scaled-down project involving a prototype barrier with two compressors. I considered it a scientific exercise, not something that could lead to enriching uranium for a nuclear bomb.

At 10 P.M. on a sultry Friday night in July 1987, my home telephone rang. I was watching TV in the living room, and I heard Layla answer it in the adjoining room.

"Yes, . . . who is speaking please?" She came into the living room with her hand over the mouthpiece of the telephone and a startled look on her face.

"It's Hussein Kamel," she whispered. "He says it is important." The president's son-in-law. I took the receiver. The voice on the other end of the line said polite words, but the tone was abrupt.

"Forgive me for calling so late, but I must see you tonight. May I come to your house?"

It was late at night on the weekly Muslim day of prayer, a strange time to receive an urgent call from a powerful stranger. Almost too flustered to speak, I began giving directions to my street in the al-Ghazaliya quarter. Our neighborhood was a pleasant middle-class suburb west of the city center, built for educated Iraqis in the years before Saddam came to power. As I described the route, Hussein Kamel cut me off.

"That sounds difficult," he said. "Let us meet somewhere else."

He suggested the parking lot of al-Hilal Hospital in al-Mansour, which is one of the finest residential areas in Baghdad, and near Hussein Kamel's home. I said I would set out right away. As I made my way along the Abu Ghraib Expressway, a feeling of dread crept into my heart. Why would Hussein Kamel want to meet me, and why at such a late hour? We had met briefly only once a few weeks earlier at the IAEC, after Saddam appointed him to oversee MIC.

I pulled my Toyota sedan into the dim parking lot of al-Hilal Hospital and saw Hussein Kamel standing under a lone service light next to his Mercedes limousine. As I stepped out of my car, he strode toward me through the long shadows. He was shorter than I am, but he walked with an air of authority, pushing his chest forward in the same way that some animals inflate themselves to warn off predators. We shook hands and exchanged the typical greeting, "Salaam aleikum." In the lamplight I could make out his hawklike nose and his small and fierce eyes as they studied my face for a few moments. My gut told me to be careful of this man. He motioned for me to join him in his car.

He drove us along al-Zaytoun Street, between the sand-colored homes of the Kadisiya quarter and the al-Zawra gardens, and skirted the Tigris River to a main drive lined with the silhouettes of majestic eucalyptus trees that led to the Republican Palace. I remembered the last time I had been to this area in 1968, when I still worked for the Ministry of Oil, to pick up a colleague from Baghdad's al-Daura refinery. It was a wealthy residential neighborhood at the time, but since then Saddam had evicted families from their homes and converted the entire area into palace grounds and official residences. Now most Baghdadis were too frightened of the area to venture anywhere near it.

Hussein Kamel remained unnervingly silent as he drove. I considered what I knew about the man. A cousin of Saddam's from Tikrit, he had served as Saddam's personal driver and bodyguard during the 1970s and then commanded the elite Republican Guard. In 1986 he married Saddam's fifteen-year-old daughter Raghad, who was supposedly the president's favorite. In a culture where the concept of *asabiya*, the loyalty to one's tribe and family, dominated social and political life, there was almost no one closer to, or more trusted by, Saddam.

As we drove into the main palace compound, he rolled down his window, and after recognizing him, a security guard waved us through. Hussein Kamel proceeded down a service road to the right of the main drive, and we parked behind a large trailer truck. The back of the truck was open, and Hussein Kamel motioned for me to follow him. My heart leapt with fear. I wondered if there were security men inside the trailer. Was I going to prison? I hesitated but followed him as he climbed up into the darkness.

Hussein Kamel turned on a flashlight, and I breathed a sigh of relief as he directed its beam to a large machine in the back of the trailer. It was an exact replica of a very specialized compressor I had recently told the IAEC we needed for the diffusion barrier prototype. I was impressed that Hussein Kamel had been able to acquire it in such a short time.

"I believe this is the device you requested to be manufactured by reverse engineering," Hussein Kamel said, as I nodded with approval. "I hope you will accept this as a sign of support for your work. But this is not the only reason I asked you to meet me tonight."

When I said nothing, he continued.

"As of tomorrow you will join the Special Security apparatus under my command, along with the two-hundred engineers and technicians you now oversee at the IAEC. You and your group will lead a uranium enrichment program separate from the work at Tuwaitha. The project will be completely secret. Do you understand?"

There are moments in our lives when time seems to stop, when conflicting emotions battle one another for supremacy. I felt a surge of patriotism and pride that the government had recognized my work. It was a tremendous vote of confidence. Hussein Kamel's instruction meant my staff of two hundred and I would compete directly with the programs of Dr. Jaffar, the IAEC, and its more than seven thousand employees. But anxiety took hold as I contemplated the heavy responsibility being placed on my shoulders and the penalty for failure. The president's son-in-law would directly oversee our work, and I would be held accountable for meeting the government's nuclear goals. I felt as though I were on the edge of an awful abyss that could easily swallow me up into its darkness. Yet I suspected that walking away from it was not an option.

In the shadows of the trailer, Hussein Kamel must have noticed the look of indecision on my face.

"Dr. Mahdi," he said in an almost apologetic tone, "please try to understand that this is not only my decision. This is a direct order of Saddam Hussein, president of Iraq."

Hussein Kamel led me out of the trailer to an office in a recently constructed building on the palace grounds. He poured me a glass of orange juice, which soothed my throat and calmed me as I began to consider my new situation. Another man entered the room. Hussein Kamel introduced him as Abu Rugaiba, a chemist from the MIC's al-Qaaqaa establishment who would be assigned to assist me, and then began asking questions.

"I have heard about your work developing a diffusion barrier, which is the heart of a diffusion program, is it not?" Hussein Kamel asked. "Tell me more about it. How is it produced?"

We had a short technical conversation, and I noticed that Hussein Kamel was listening attentively. I explained that the barrier is not easy to manufacture and that each square centimeter contains ten thousand billion holes. There were many technical problems to solve. Hoping to throw cold water on his expectations, I told him that in the 1940s the Americans and the British devoted years of research in hundreds of laboratories to developing a diffusion barrier, and that during the 1980s the Americans invested more than a billion dollars to improve a barrier for their nuclear power program.

"How is it produced?" Hussein Kamel asked.

"The Americans make it out of nickel powder," I said. "It is a very special and fine powder, and it is extremely difficult to acquire."

"We can make the nickel powder," Abu Rugaiba suggested. I couldn't help rolling my eyes, because producing this powder was well beyond Iraqi technical expertise at the time.

"I understand you are making your own barrier," Hussein Kamel said, ignoring Abu Rugaiba's suggestion. "Is it the same type as the Americans have made?"

I explained that our barrier was different because it was made from anodized aluminum, which was a substance that had never before been used successfully. But if we were successful, our barrier might have better characteristics than any barrier yet developed by any country. Hussein Kamel nodded and then dismissed Abu Rugaiba.

"I have also heard that you have other reservations about the diffusion technique," he said once we were alone again. "Tell me what they are."

I described the practical problem of acquiring thousands of compressors and diffusers of such varying specifications. I believed that a production-scale diffusion plant would be impossible in Iraq. Also, I said, even if we could purchase and manufacture the massive amount of equipment needed, it would be nearly impossible to keep such a large-scale project secret from the eyes of the international community. Hussein Kamel appeared to understand this drawback immediately. Although he was technically not a well-educated man, he seemed to possess the kind of raw intelligence that one finds among the Bedouin tribes. Unlike many at the IAEC, he quickly grasped the basic hopelessness of the diffusion method, given Iraq's poor infrastructure and the political position it held in the world. A look of profound worry spread over his face.

"Dr. Mahdi," he said, "is there no other method for enriching uranium that Iraq has not yet explored?"

I was taken aback by such a simple and elemental question. The same question had occupied my mind in an abstract way throughout my work on the diffusion barrier. I hadn't expected this cousin of Saddam's to ask such a thing.

"There is another method," I said.

"Well, what is it?" Hussein Kamel asked impatiently.

"It is called a centrifuge."

"I have heard of it. What is it?"

I explained that the gas centrifuge cylinder rotates at high speeds on a vertical axis to create great centrifugal force, which separates a gaseous mixture of the uranium isotopes. The heavier isotope, uranium-238, falls from the lighter uranium-235 in much the same way that water is drawn out of laundry in the spin cycle of a washing machine. In fact, the idea for a centrifuge was based on the same principle as a dairy cream separator. Once the heavier isotopes have been drawn out, the highly enriched uranium in the center may be siphoned from the cylinder. The centrifuge was more practical than the diffusion technique because of its efficiency. A centrifuge requires only dozens of stages instead of the thousands needed to enrich uranium through diffusion.

Although it sounded simple as I described it to Hussein Kamel, the difficulty lay in engineering a six-inch-wide cylinder that could spin more than fifty thousand revolutions per minute, at least twenty times faster than the most advanced motor Iraq had ever seen. A successful centrifuge, I told Hussein Kamel, is a near miracle of engineering that is one of the most closely guarded secrets by the few countries that have developed them. Technologically, it was an idea well out on the edge of the imagination. The IAEC had decided that developing a centrifuge program was as far-fetched in Iraq as attempting to build a space shuttle.

"Who is using this technique?" Hussein Kamel asked.

"It was developed in America a few decades ago, but now it is used mainly by the Europeans," I said. "The Brazilians have experimented with it, unsuccessfully so far. And the Pakistanis are also said to be working on a centrifuge program."

"The Pakistanis!" Hussein Kamel practically gasped. "Surely, if the Pakistanis can develop such a thing, then so can we. Iraq is at least as advanced as Pakistan!"

Though by now it was about 2 A.M., he leaped at the idea with the eagerness of a child let loose in a candy shop. The idea that another Muslim nation was developing a centrifuge program seemed to inspire him. He leaned forward in his chair, suddenly animated.

"Let us discuss the time frame," he said. "How long would it take to pursue this centrifuge method?"

Because I had considered the idea only as a hypothetical brain-teaser, I had no time frame in mind. I figured it would take at least two years to build a basic prototype, assuming we could acquire the know-how and the technology required. But I sensed that two years would not be acceptable to Hussein Kamel, who was obviously under a great deal of pressure.

"We might be able to have a prototype ready in a year, sir," I said. "Of course, there is no guarantee that it will work."

"Too much time," Hussein Kamel said, almost to himself.

Then he hit me with a barrage of commands. Within three days, he said, I should select a facility for the program, which would be called the Engineering Design Directorate. I must outfit the facility to continue the diffusion program, as well as for a new centrifuge program to begin immediately. Both programs should proceed simultaneously. By Monday, Hussein Kamel said, I was to provide him with a list of materials and other requirements, and he would take care of our requests personally. Secrecy would surround the entire project, he said; even the IAEC would not know of its details.

As Hussein Kamel took me back to al-Hilal Hospital, my mind reeled as I considered the enormity of the task ahead. It was nearly dawn when I arrived home. I entered the front door quietly, hoping not to awaken my family, but Layla was waiting up for me. She was pregnant with our youngest daughter, Ayat, at the time, and I gently told her she should have gone to sleep without me. But she had been as worried about my summons from Saddam's son-in-law as I had been. I told her about the meeting at the Republican Palace and emphasized that from now on my work would have to remain a strict secret between us.

"The good news is that I received a promotion," I said. "The bad news is that I can never tell anyone about it."

The next day I got a first taste of the frenzied schedule that would dominate my life for the next few years. A security agent called early in the morning with a list of facilities available for the new Engineering Design Directorate. After looking at about a half dozen sites, I finally chose an irrigation research center in Rashdiya, north of Baghdad, that was operated by the Department of Agriculture. A walled enclosure of several acres of land and buildings, it had plenty of space for the research and design facilities I envisioned. In addition to a central office building, it contained laboratories, an auditorium, a small theater, and a library. The irrigation center was also perfect in terms of security requirements. At the edge of a semirural suburb north of Baghdad, its western edge abutted an embankment that separated empty fields from a marsh of reeds adjacent to the Tigris River. To the south, the main entrance to the compound opened onto groves of date palm trees and a road dotted with a few small farmhouses. It was secluded and yet near enough to the city to be convenient and discreet. In fact, my security escort informed me, the area was known as a "love nest" spot where unmarried couples would occasionally come to enjoy late-night trysts in their parked cars.

The following day, the security services cleared the entire facility of its Department of Agriculture employees and their personal equipment. I don't know what explanation the surprised researchers were given for the urgent evacuation, but they undoubtedly knew better than to question the word of Saddam's Special Security Organization. My staff of two hundred and I moved onto the premises Monday morning to find signs of a hurried departure, among them all the Department of Agriculture library books still on their shelves. I divided my team into five departments and assigned each a section of the main four-story building in roughly ascending order corresponding to the steps of the program. The ground floor would house the Materials Department, to deal with the building blocks of our program. The Mechanical Department and Physical Process Department, which would oversee the separation of enriched uranium, occupied the second floor. I assigned the third floor to the Chemical Process Department, which was in charge of producing uranium hexafluoride, and the fourth floor to offices for administration and support. My office on a corner of the second floor had a grand view of the river and a date palm plantation. Next to it, rooms full of drafting tables received natural light from westward-facing windows.

As my staff hurried about installing furniture brought from the IAEC, the head of the Special Security Organization arrived to discuss the security arrangements with me. He said the Engineering Design Directorate would be assigned twenty security men who would drive nongovernmental cars so they would not bring undue attention to the facility. No outsiders were ever to visit our premises, and any meetings my staff needed to conduct had to be held outside of Rashdiya. Finally, he said, Hussein Kamel had ordered that I be accompanied by a bodyguard at all times. He said it was believed that if foreign intelligence ever discovered our work, I could become a target for assassination. I strongly objected to this idea. In Iraq, "protection" was often another word for surveillance, and I felt that having a twenty-four-hour bodyguard would not only be inconvenient, it would also jeopardize the privacy of my family.

"If someone wants to kill me it is very easy, even with a bodyguard," I argued. "A killer could assassinate me in a market or while I am sitting in my garden at home."

The security chief said the decision was not his, but I protested so vigorously that he agreed to review the issue further, and the idea was eventually dropped.

Just after lunchtime, Hussein Kamel called and asked about our progress and whether we needed anything. For some reason, I mentioned the poor condition of the midday meal, which had been provided by army chefs and delivered by the security services. A number of my employees had complained that the meat was poorly cooked and the rice seemed dirty. Hussein Kamel must have taken my comment to heart. Within an hour a courier arrived with a sack containing 50,000 Iraqi dinars in cash, an amount roughly equivalent to $150,000 at the time, to hire a private caterer. Such largesse had never been a feature of the IAEC, and I marveled at the funds suddenly available to Hussein Kamel. He seemed to be able to open a floodgate of cash for the nuclear program that had been severely restricted before he took over responsibility in early 1987. It occurred to me that Hussein Kamel may have been behind the renewed quest for the bomb. In fact, it wasn't until Hussein Kamel took over that the IAEC formed a separate group to investigate an explosive device for the nuclear material. At first, he gave responsibility for the weaponization effort to Dr. Khidir Hamza, but after several months he let him go and shifted responsibility for it to Dr. Khalid Ibrahim Sa'id.

Later that afternoon, Hussein Kamel himself arrived to check on our situation, and I gave him a preliminary list of equipment needed for the laboratories. He came again the next morning unannounced, as my staff was still settling in. I hastily organized a meeting with my department heads in a conference room still decorated with Department of Agriculture pictures on the walls.

"Tell me, Dr. Mahdi, what is your schedule for the centrifuge?" Hussein Kamel asked, once we were all seated.

I hesitated for a moment. At the IAEC, my department heads and I were accustomed to a rigorous scientific schedule of about two years for most experiments. Yet I had already halved that timetable to Hussein Kamel.

"Sir, you may remember that I said we could possibly have a prototype of the centrifuge ready in one year's time," I said. "If we work extra hours, I believe this is an optimistic, yet still feasible, timeline."

Hussein Kamel put his fists on the table and directed his piercing gaze toward me and my department heads.

"That is not acceptable," he said. "You have a month and a half. Nothing more. I will provide whatever materials you need, but you must have a working centrifuge within forty-five days. It is an order." Then he stood up and walked out.

Left sitting around the conference table, my department heads and I were stunned. It was inconceivable that a centrifuge, never seen by any of us, could be designed, manufactured, assembled, and run in a month and a half. Getting to the moon would be easier. However, we all realized that the orders from Saddam's son-in-law were deadly serious, and it was pointless to despair or think of quitting.

I drew up a hypothetical schedule for the next six weeks: one week for design of a centrifuge, three weeks for manufacturing, one week for assembly, and the final week for testing and operation. We would work from eight o'clock in the morning until ten at night, with everyone getting a full night's rest each day to keep our minds fresh. Even then such a schedule seemed like a hopeless dream. As I looked at the worried faces of my department heads, one thing at least gave me a ray of confidence. Seated around me was, in my opinion, one of the best scientific teams Iraq had ever assembled. These men had worked for me for years at the IAEC, and I felt that if anyone could achieve the impossible it was our group.

Dr. Farid Bashir, head of the Mechanics Department, was one of the most brilliant men I have ever met. He was born in Basra but had the thin face and fine features typical of the Assyrian Christian people of northern Iraq. A quiet and reserved man, his eyes revealed a formidable intelligence that had been refined in the best schools of England since he was a young man. As my right hand, Dr. Farid would be in charge of the mechanics of the centrifuge. Seated next to him, Dr. Adil Ridha would be the head of the Materials Division. Round-faced and round-bellied from his healthy appetite, he had a thick mane of hair that would turn prematurely white during the difficult years ahead. Besides his skill as a scientist, the round-faced, British-educated Dr. Adil possessed a warm sense of humor and a diplomatic way of communicating that would prove very helpful in keeping my staff's spirits up. Dr. Abdul Fattah, the head of the Chemical Process Department, would produce the uranium hexafluoride gas for both the diffusion and the centrifuge programs. The Physical Process Department head, Dr. Mikdam, had been trained in nuclear engineering in the United States. Of the six of us at the table, he looked the most frightened by the idea of working under Hussein Kamel, and although he was extremely competent, I began to worry that he might collapse under the pressure. Finally, Dr. Faris Abdul Aziz ran the Engineering Support Department and oversaw the largest number of staff. Although Dr. Faris lacked the visionary intelligence of Dr. Farid, he made up for it with his energy and enthusiasm. In later years I always teased him that he was the greatest workhorse on our Orwellian animal farm. He was earnest and kindly, and my children liked him very much and often asked when "Uncle" Faris would visit.

"Well, it seems we have our work cut out for us," said Dr. Adil, making an understatement. "Where should we begin?"

I asked a member of my staff to check the IAEC library for any materials that could be of use, and was astonished when he returned hours later with American designs for a basic centrifuge. The designs were from the 1940s. They described the earliest working centrifuge developed by University of Virginia professor Jesse Beams as part of the Manhattan Project during World War II. In the end, the Americans dropped the centrifuge technique in favor of diffusion for practical reasons: the embryonic Beams centrifuge consumed too much power and was unreasonably expensive in comparison with the diffusion method. The gas centrifuge had become a realistic option only after new developments in its design during the 1960s. But the Beams model had worked. He used these very designs for a centrifuge that successfully enriched uranium in the labs of the University of Virginia, and the fact that Iraq possessed copies of them seemed a stroke of incredible good fortune.

I never discovered how the IAEC got their hands on the Beams reports, but I suspected they had been provided during the 1950s, during the early phases of Iraq's nuclear program when international restrictions were looser.

From that afternoon, we worked frantically to turn the Beams documents into designs workable for production by Iraq's best industrial firms. Hussein Kamel came almost daily to breathe down our necks, but he also supplied the connections for manufacturing the components we needed. The cylindrical section that spins, called the rotor, was outsourced to the Nasser & Saddam Company, which manufactured cannons and other armaments for MIC. An establishment at Kadisiya, which made machine guns, manufactured other fine parts. The IAEC supplied the special oil for the lower bearing; technicians at the Daura oil refinery balanced the rotor on its vertical axis.

Because none of us could predict what would happen if the system broke at high speeds, I took the precaution of building a bunker where the centrifuge could be operated via remote control. We were all exhilarated when a test run achieved the speed of five thousand rotations per minute. Although this was less than one-tenth the speed necessary for the enrichment of uranium, it was nearly two thousand rpm faster than anything ever before produced in Iraq. Hussein Kamel was traveling with Saddam to an Arab summit in Amman, Jordan, at the time, and when he returned to Baghdad and heard the news, he ordered the slaughter of ten head of sheep for a celebratory meal at the Rashdiya facility. Even though it was now November and his six-week schedule had turned into several months, Hussein Kamel temporarily forgave us because we were showing progress. His spirit of benevolence lasted only a few hours, however. Before he left with his security men, he ordered us to bring the centrifuge to fifty thousand rpm by the end of the year.

By now construction was nearly complete on a larger building to further test the prototype. Inside, a special room for the centrifuge stood twenty feet tall with reinforced walls three feet thick. From a control platform we could observe the centrifuge, which was suspended among a jumble of piping, through a thick Plexiglas window.

On a chilly morning in early January, I felt ready to increase its speed in stages. My five department heads and I stood on the observation deck as I gave the orders to raise the rpm levels. A monitor in front of us read ten thousand. Then fifteen thousand. As the counter neared the eighteen thousand mark, we heard a muffled whistling noise that rose in tone and became almost deafening. Dr. Farid and I exchanged an alarmed look. Before I could order a reduction in speed, we heard a sharp bang like the crack of a gunshot. I shouted to a technician to cut the motor. After it finally wound down to a standstill, we hurried into the centrifuge chamber. When we removed the rotor, I saw a discolored patch in its metal. It was ruined.

An examination of the aluminum rotor afterwards confirmed fears that had plagued me throughout the process. We had not properly understood the stresses on the materials that occur at such stratospheric speeds. The centrifugal force produced pressures that may be understood only through an advanced knowledge of vibration and harmonics. We had tried to shortcut the difficult science of rotor dynamics, and our centrifuge simply cracked under pressure.

I called Hussein Kamel with apprehension.

"Sir," I said, "there is a problem with the centrifuge."

"What?" Hussein Kamel asked in a low voice.

"The rotor is broken."

Hussein Kamel arrived minutes later. He could see that my entire staff was heartbroken, but he did not say a word. He walked over to the table where my technicians were dissecting the rotor, picked it up, and held it for a few moments. His lips began to tremble and I could see tears of rage in his eyes. Then he put the rotor back on the table and turned toward his waiting car. I followed him, and as he was getting in, I apologized, using an Arabic expression: "Sir, we have tried to beat time, but time has beaten us instead."

Hussein Kamel paused for a moment, and I thought he would say something, but he only stared at me with a look of such menace that I instinctively took a step backward. Then he shut the door in my face and drove out the gates.

We were all terrified by Hussein Kamel's behavior. His reputation for cruelty was spreading throughout Iraq, as he solidified his position as Saddam's right hand. He had become a little Saddam. My staff began speculating about the horrible punishments he might inflict on them for the failure of the centrifuge. I decided to try to shield them from Hussein Kamel's presence as much as possible in the future. The ordeal shattered the nerves of Dr. Mikdam, who took me aside and said he was scared for his life and begged me to relieve him of his responsibility. He looked so nervous that I grew afraid for his mental health and his ability to perform. I truly pitied the man. A few days later I informed Hussein Kamel that Dr. Mikdam suffered from an eye disease and that I needed a replacement, and Dr. Mikdam was transferred safely to the University of Baghdad.

This was obviously not an option for the rest of my employees. It was clear that we would have to rethink our strategy and try again, and that the failure of the centrifuge was not the end of our work, but the beginning.

CHAPTER 4

Saddam's Grip

The centrifuge rotor lay dissected on a table in our laboratory like a corpse after an autopsy. My technicians and I walked around it wordlessly as we cleaned up the mess around the stand where it had stood, and disassembled much of the apparatus. Oil had leaked onto other parts of the machinery, and our hands became slick with the stuff. I wiped my hands on a towel in disgust. The difference between the neat conceptual drawings and lofty goals we had at the outset and the messy reality of the broken rotor offended my engineer's desire for a perfect outcome.

My fear of repercussions from Hussein Kamel mixed with the disheartening feeling that comes with failure. But I knew I couldn't quit. Saddam's government would not let us off the hook so easily. I had to find another solution. I remembered the image of my father setting off into our orchard with a shovel over one shoulder and his other arm in a sling, and resolved to persevere in my task.

I considered the lessons I had learned from our experiment with the Beams oil centrifuge. The first was that possession of designs alone would not lead us to a functioning centrifuge, just as having the pattern for a dress does not make one a clothing designer. Understanding the basis for the designs, the tolerances of the materials, the environment in which they would be used, and issues related to balance was equally important. Of course, I reasoned, that is why the Americans had allowed the Beams oil centrifuge designs out into open literature in the 1950s. The designs themselves were very basic and failed to provide a strong enough foundation for a centrifuge program.

I became convinced that the Beams centrifuge was unworkable for our purposes. For a covert operation like ours, it carried risks of exposure. It consumed many kilowatts of energy, and at high speeds it emitted a high-pitched whine that could be heard a half mile away. Hundreds of Beams centrifuges operating at the same time would have been difficult to conceal.

I turned my focus to the state-of-the-art magnetic centrifuge. Conceived in Russia in the late 1940s and later refined in the United States and Europe, the use of electromagnets to support the rotor had revolutionized centrifuge technology. A magnetic centrifuge balances in a vacuum on virtually zero-friction bearings. A ghostly machine, it spins in silence, touching almost nothing. The gracefulness of its motion seems an almost supernatural phenomenon. It consumes energy measured in watts rather than kilowatts. It is so efficient that a facility for a small, yet dangerous, nuclear weapons program could be hidden inside a single warehouse. For Iraq and other countries that had to conceal their nuclear ambitions, a magnetic centrifuge program was the ideal solution.

The IAEC had long ago rejected the idea of building a magnetic centrifuge as an impossible fantasy, the stuff of science fiction. They felt that Iraq could never accomplish a feat that had taken years of development in the world's most technologically sophisticated nations. But I thought it was time to reevaluate their conclusions. Despite our failure with the Beams centrifuge, I reflected on the accomplishments of my team with pride. The engineers and physicists on my staff were among Iraq's greatest minds, as astute as the best Western scientists. During the past months, they had proved themselves to be quick learners with an innate ability to adapt.

The obstacles we foresaw were indeed formidable. The fundamental problem was that we had neither the designs for a magnetic centrifuge nor the expertise to interpret such designs if we had them. Also, I guessed that Iraq lacked the infrastructure to manufacture the components. As our failure with the Beams centrifuge showed, the job was far too complex for an Iraqi artillery factory. If we were to undertake a magnetic centrifuge program, we would need assistance every step of the way from foreigners who might become suspicious of our motives. This was the soft spot.

Several days after the destruction of the oil centrifuge, Hussein Kamel reappeared at Rashdiya. I nervously ushered him into my office in an attempt to protect my employees from his wrath. Brooding and distracted, he was obviously still smoldering over our failure and in a dangerous mood. He demanded to know what we intended to do next, and I was relieved to have at least a conceptual plan. I explained the beauty of the magnetic centrifuge, along with the practical drawbacks to building one.

"I don't want to hear about difficulties," he practically shouted at me. "I only want to see progress, do you understand me?"

I understood perfectly that Hussein Kamel was under great pressure to show results to Saddam, but I also knew that in order to save our necks I needed some leeway in the time frame. We could not produce a magnetic centrifuge based on a whim.

"I will need to travel to the United States," I said. "And I would like to take Dr. Farid with me."

I explained that according to our research, some of the first comprehensive experiments on the magnetic centrifuge were done by an Austrian physicist named Gernot Zippe in the late 1950s. He had worked at the University of Virginia, and some of his reports were supposedly still in the open literature there. These reports could provide a valuable basis on which to build a more modern centrifuge program. Also, I said, an American company in upstate New York, called Mechanical Technology Inc. (MTI), had developed the world's most sophisticated computer programs related to the cadence of rotational devices. The programs went to the very heart of our failure with the Beams centrifuge. If we could manage to slip under the radar of the Americans and acquire these things, I told Hussein Kamel, we would have in our hands the seeds necessary to grow a true nuclear program.

Hussein Kamel ran a hand across his brow and seemed to consider the implications of what I was saying: that a magnetic centrifuge program would take years rather than months. I almost pitied him at that moment. Just as I was squeezed between his demands and the reality of science, he was crushed between me and Saddam's blind quest for a bomb.

"Go ahead to America," he said, shooting me a look full of mistrust. "But it is better if you go alone."

Hussein Kamel must have known that Dr. Farid had a brother living in the United States, and I could read on his face a momentary suspicion that Dr. Farid, or both of us, might try to defect. It was an unthinkable idea. We were both married with children who would remain behind in Baghdad, and we would never abandon them. Also, I had traveled abroad frequently during the past twenty-five years without deserting the country.

"Sir, you have placed a great responsibility on us," I said. "I must be allowed to depend on my staff. If you lack confidence in one of my colleagues then remove him from my department. Otherwise, I beg you to let them follow my orders."

Hussein Kamel shrugged. "It is on your head," he said. "And I expect to see results."

His suspicious look deepened my worry that he would place our families under surveillance. I began to look over my shoulder for undercover agents following me and listening to my private conversations. I could never be sure, of course. This is part of the effectiveness of a police state. Fear shadowed us just as effectively as any agent and made us alter our behavior. The climate of general surveillance made the entire populace wary and secretive. And my position in the sights of Iraq's second most powerful man put me and my department heads directly in the line of fire.

When Dr. Farid and I boarded a flight to the United States via Germany in April 1988, I considered telling him of Hussein Kamel's stern warning but decided against it. Dr. Farid was a man who understood things without having to be told. During our travels, it would become an unspoken rule that we should hide the true nature of our work. Even with each other, Dr. Farid and I discussed obtaining "the report" rather than "the Zippe report" or mentioning the word "centrifuge." We wore our secrecy as though it were our own skin.

It was my first trip to the United States in twenty years. On a bumpy afternoon flight from New York's John F. Kennedy Airport to the little airfield in Charlottesville, Virginia, I caught glimpses of the green fields of Pennsylvania and Maryland through the clouds, and my mind drifted back to my college days at the Colorado School of Mines. I remembered long talks about the future with my hiking companion David Johnson, my friend Bill Hunzeker, the captain of our swim team, and my Iraqi friend Hamid al-Hakeem. We all had plans to make the world a better place. Those days of freedom seemed distant now. I could not imagine what they would say if they knew I was directing Saddam Hussein's centrifuge enrichment program. We lost touch after graduation, and I wondered what paths their lives had taken.

The next morning Dr. Farid and I visited the University of Virginia, where Jesse Beams and Gernot Zippe had pioneered two generations of centrifuge techniques. According to the IAEC, the Zippe report was one of the last unclassified documents on magnetic centrifuges, and few copies of it existed. Although it lacked actual designs, it contained crucial knowledge. Zippe had prepared the report at the bidding of the U.S. Atomic Energy Commission, after a career that had been shaped by the international events of his era.

I felt a sort of distant kinship with Zippe. He too had been pressed into the service of a nuclear weapons program in a totalitarian state. At the end of World War II, Soviet agents seized him and put him to work on the USSR's nuclear centrifuge program. The Soviets finally allowed him to return home in 1956, but American agents quickly convinced him to re-create some of the work he had done in Russia. What Zippe produced at the University of Virginia was supposedly so comprehensive that it formed the basis for the development of magnetic centrifuges in the West.

Our first stop was at the Department of Mechanical Engineering, not far from the Department of Physics, where Zippe and Beams had worked. We were eager to see this legendary place with our own eyes. We entered the reception area of the Department of Mechanical Engineering, and just as the receptionist asked if she could help us, I spotted the name of the department head on his office door.

"May we see Dr. Townsend, please?" I asked.

"Do you have an appointment?"

"I'm awfully sorry, we do not," I said, glancing at Dr. Farid. "We are professors from the University of Baghdad in Iraq. It was rather hard to phone ahead from there, but we hoped Dr. Townsend could spare us a few minutes."

The receptionist seemed to understand, and a short telephone call later the department chairman emerged from his office. Dr. Miles A. Townsend was an elegant-looking gray-haired man of medium build. He shook our hands and graciously invited us into his office. I told him that rotating machinery was a new line of research at the University of Baghdad, and he immediately called two of his junior assistants to show us around the department.

The University of Virginia no longer had a centrifuge research program. But I could see its fingerprints. The Department of Mechanical Engineering still focused heavily on high-speed rotors for various applications, such as turbines for helicopters and power generators.

Dr. Farid and I peppered the technicians with questions, and they seemed surprised by our grasp of the subject matter. We discussed rotor dynamics on a very complex level. I felt honored that these accomplished American engineers quickly recognized us as their scientific equals. I was also relieved that they appeared to have bought into our story completely, never questioning how the University of Baghdad had such accomplished faculty in the field in which they specialized.

My interest perked up when they led us to a computer terminal to show us a program they had developed to simulate rotational forces. By entering different variables, one could use it to understand the basic dynamics of anything that rotates, from a truck axle to a centrifuge. I immediately saw how valuable this tool could be in our hands. When I returned to Dr. Townsend's office to ask about purchasing the program, however, the receptionist told me he was busy. I suggested we could return later in the afternoon, and asked her for directions to the library, where I hoped we would find the Zippe report.

I had no trouble locating the catalogue number, and Dr. Farid and I entered the library stacks with a great deal of excitement. But in the space where the Zippe report should have been we found only a slip of paper with instructions to make a special request at the rare collections library.

I approached a wiry, bespectacled librarian with the catalogue number, and he disappeared into a closed-off area of the library. When he returned several minutes later, he handed me a lengthy form and a ballpoint pen.

"You have to fill this out first," he said. "For security purposes. And I will need some identification."

This put me in an uncomfortable position, because filling in such forms would leave a dangerous paper trail. American intelligence agents would surely be very interested to learn that two Iraqi men had asked to see a centrifuge report at the University of Virginia. We couldn't afford to leave such a revealing piece of evidence, particularly at the very outset of our secret program.

"Would it be possible to ensure that the report is indeed here," I asked, "before I fill out all these forms for it?"

The librarian gave me an annoyed look, then returned to the back section of the library. We waited at his desk for what seemed like hours. Next to me, Dr. Farid fidgeted and began to sweat.

"Do you think he will call the authorities?" Dr. Farid whispered.

"Don't worry," I said. "We are in a university, making an everyday request. He is probably having trouble finding the report."

But I shared his nervousness. The word "security" triggered a subconscious reaction of fear in both of us. In Iraq, it usually meant just the opposite. Dr. Farid's seemingly irrational notion suddenly took hold of me. What if a request for the Zippe report triggered an automatic security alert? If the librarian made a phone call and we were questioned, our cover story that we were from the University of Baghdad would hardly hold up. I thought of the awful consequences if Hussein Kamel learned we had exposed ourselves through such a foolish blunder.

To my relief, the librarian finally returned with a thick sheaf of papers in one hand.

"Here it is," he said, holding it back from us. "Now please fill out these forms."

"Could I see it for a moment to be sure it is the right document?" I asked.

He handed me the report and watched closely as I took it to a nearby table and flipped through its pages. As I had hoped, it was a key piece of literature. It did not contain blueprints or dimensions of centrifuge pieces but offered a broad view of the engineering principles behind the magnetic centrifuge. It was exactly the primer our team needed. But there was no way of reading it without filling out the release forms, and almost certainly no way of copying it. I noticed the librarian glowering at me several feet away. I intently scanned the chapter headings of the report while trying to appear as though I were only riffling through the pages.

"Is that what you are looking for?" the librarian asked impatiently.

"I'm still not sure," I said.

I knew I had only a few more seconds to look at the report. Then I came to an appendix that listed the recipients of the report when it was first issued in 1960: the holders of the precious few copies. Scanning down the list, I recognized the name of a Milan-based professor associated with the Italian nuclear program. That was the piece of information I needed.

"No, I'm afraid this is not the document we were looking for at all," I said, handing the report back to the librarian. "But thank you for your time."

As we left the library, I confided my discovery to Dr. Farid.

"It looks as though I will need to make another trip to our friends in Italy," I said. "It has been a long time. I hope they remember me kindly."

We returned to the Department of Mechanical Engineering late that afternoon and found Dr. Townsend in a receptive mood. His assistants must have spoken highly of the knowledgeable professors from the University of Baghdad, because he greeted us as peers and said he was at our service. It occurred to me that some of my technicians could gain valuable experience in Dr. Townsend's labs.

"We are interested in sending a few postdoctoral students here to conduct their research," I said. "Of course, we would not expect a grant. Our university would cover all the associated costs."

The idea pleased Dr. Townsend. He asked about our facilities in Baghdad.

"Oh," I said, "they are nothing like your department here. They really do not compare."

Our cover story had undoubtedly convinced Dr. Townsend by the time I offered to purchase a copy of the rotor dynamics program. He agreed without blinking, and we settled on a price of $90,000.

As useful as it was, the program would not help us solve all of the complicated problems associated with rotor dynamics. As anyone who has listened to a washing machine wobble during its spin cycle knows, a rotating cylinder is easily thrown off balance. A centrifuge of nearly six inches in diameter spinning at 60,000 rpm or higher—roughly 1,000 rotations per second—requires a science imaginatively called hairy mathematics. As the centrifuge walls spin at more than the speed of sound, issues of cadence and harmonic vibrations wreak havoc with the structure of the materials, posing riddles solved only through sophisticated calculus.

MTI in Latham, New York, was one of the few companies in the world that had unraveled these mathematical secrets in a computer program. Most large-scale centrifuge producers such as Westinghouse in the United States or Urenco in Europe develop these programs in-house and guard them as company secrets. But MTI was different. As a contractor it dealt not only with highly classified engine and rotor projects for the U.S. military and NASA, but also with private companies, according to my research. Getting our hands on this program could subtract years from the time required to develop an Iraqi centrifuge.

We called ahead for an appointment with the technology manager, introducing ourselves as engineers from the Iraqi Ministry of Oil. As we drove our rental car north from New York City, however, Dr. Farid and I were unsure of what level of security we would find or how open MTI administrators might be to two scientists from Baghdad. We arrived late in the afternoon and checked into a motel in Latham, where we rehearsed our cover story for the following day.

The modern buildings of the MTI complex looked like a typical technology company from the outside, but as soon as Dr. Farid and I entered the reception area, we were confronted by a choice of two lanes: one for visitors on classified business and the other for nonclassified business. I had never seen such a thing before; it was like passing through customs at an international airport. Without hesitating, I led Dr. Farid through the lane for nonclassified business.

After we checked in at the low-security desk, a man named Bob arrived and led us to a meeting room. He was a tall, good-humored fellow with a rugged face. We exchanged pleasantries and then got to the point. Using my intimate knowledge of the oil business in Iraq, I gave Bob a credible explanation of the Oil Ministry's need for the MTI cadence program for our rotating machines such as pumps, blowers, and compressors.

"Whenever the rotating parts break, we have to send them abroad for analysis and repairs," I said. "Then we have problems maintaining our production of oil, which, as you know, is the driver of the Iraqi economy. We want to be able to make firsthand appraisals instead of calling on foreign experts. It could save us millions of dollars."

Bob saw the logic of this argument. After asking me a number of technical questions, he picked up a telephone and dialed an extension.

"David, do you have a moment?" he asked. "I want you to meet these people."

When David arrived, we explained our story again in greater detail. A thin, quiet man, David offered us coffee, and I couldn't help smiling with appreciation when he went to a vending machine and bought cups for us with coins from his own pocket. In Iraq, managers of David's caliber felt they were too important to serve coffee, for which they had secretaries or servants.

After a tour of some of the MTI laboratories, Bob and David invited us to lunch at a beautiful restaurant in the middle of a nearby golf course. Spring leaves fluttered on the trees, and the bright grass where golfers strolled in the distance shone in the mid-day sun. In this quiet setting full of greenery and birdsong, our conversation drifted away from business and onto more general topics of science and our professional lives. Bob and David asked many questions about Iraq's oil industry, and I described it in vivid detail. They laughed when I asked them if they played golf, and both admitted to being addicted to the sport. I marveled at their carefree lives in America, with time to golf and relax, never fearing that the government would unexpectedly throw them or their families in prison. I had nearly forgotten that such freedom could exist. It occurred to me that this was part of what made them so gullible. Their culture of straightforwardness and trust between people was at least partly the result of a lack of fear. It had helped Americans develop a great nation. But the openness of people such as David, Bob, and Dr. Townsend also made my job easier. I approached them with confidence and a viable story that held up to their questions, and they gave me the benefit of the doubt.

When we returned from lunch to arrange for our purchase of the cadence program, David informed me that the application required the signatures of twenty-two people, including officials from the U.S. government, due to the sensitivity of the material.

"As you can imagine, this program could have applications that are highly classified," he said. "We have to be very careful with it."

Twenty-two signatures. I felt my nerves tighten again. Surely someone would investigate further before twenty-two people signed off on the deal. I calmed myself with the thought that unlike the centrifuge reports at the University of Virginia, the MTI program had various legitimate uses, and we would put all of the paperwork through the Iraqi Ministry of Oil. Still, the need for so many signatures seemed to invite scrutiny.

"Will it take long to be approved?" I asked, trying to disguise my anxiety.

"I don't think so," David said. "I will see it through."

David's misplaced confidence in us must have carried a lot of weight, because the American authorities granted permission to sell it to us two days after our meeting. At a price of about $200,000 this classified program was not cheap, but it proved invaluable to our efforts.

After our success in Latham, I had decided to take a trip to my alma mater and, for two days at least, try to mentally escape the clutches of Hussein Kamel and the Iraqi centrifuge program. As the flight descended into Denver International Airport, the snow-capped Rocky Mountains appeared just as I remembered them, rugged and eternal. As Dr. Farid and I stepped out of the terminal, the crisp mountain breeze brought forth a rush of memories. I drove us to the Colorado School of Mines campus in nearby Golden. So much had changed. The town had grown into a little city in my absence. At the administration office, I learned that most of my old professors had retired. I briefly stopped in on Dr. Stermole, a junior professor at the time I was a student, and I was saddened to learn that Dr. Dickson, the head of the Chemical Engineering Department who supervised my master's work, had died. I showed Dr. Farid the classrooms and laboratories where I had taken my first steps as an engineering student and the hills where I studied compass mapping and surveying.

The next evening we dined at a steak restaurant with my college sweetheart Phyllis Mulhausen and her mother. They had been like a second family to me and the only "relatives" who had been able to attend my graduation ceremony in 1967. They stood up smiling as we entered the restaurant and rushed over to embrace me. They made quite a fuss over Dr. Farid when I introduced him, and the warm camaraderie of our past instantly flooded back. Phyllis showed me pictures of her husband, whom she married two years after I graduated. I told her about my wife, Layla, and my own four children. Soon we were reminiscing about college days and our mutual friends. The conversation flowed so easily we nearly forgot to eat our meals.

"But Mahdi," Phyllis's mother said. "You haven't told us what you are doing with yourself? Where are you working?"

For a moment I stumbled. I hadn't thought to prepare an alibi for my old friends.

"The Ministry of Oil sent me to Wales for my Ph.D.," I said, holding on to the truth as long as possible. "So I am Dr. Mahdi now."

"And are you still with the Ministry of Oil, *Doctor* Mahdi?" Phyllis's mother teased.

I clearly couldn't tell Phyllis and her mother that I was leading a top-secret program to enrich uranium.

"Yes," I lied. "Dr. Farid and I are engineers with the Ministry of Oil."

"And do you like it there, Dr. Farid?" Phyllis asked.

"Oh yes," Dr. Farid said without looking at me. "It is a fine place to work."

I felt a pang of shame. Fabricating a cover story at MTI and the University of Virginia had been a necessary part of my assignment from Hussein Kamel. But it was another thing to have to deceive these people who had been so dear to me in freer days, a cruel by-product of my position at the heart of Saddam's secretive regime. As I continued smiling and chatting with Phyllis and her mother, a sense of melancholy slid over me. Truth is the firm earth on which every good scientist hopes to tread. I had tried to live on the principles of honesty. But now I saw truth slipping away from me like a receding continent, as the need for deception swept me helplessly out into deeper waters. The small group of people I could confide in was reduced to my family and a few colleagues. And even within that small group in Iraq, I had to hold back details. I could not risk telling my young children or family friends the true nature of my work. They knew only that I was involved in engineering research, about which I could not be specific. And I could not discuss my conflicting feelings about the nuclear program with my colleagues. The only person with whom I could share such confidences was Layla. Suddenly, seven thousand miles away from her, I felt very alone.

We parted ways graciously after dinner, and the next day Dr. Farid and I flew to New York with a ten-hour layover before the flight back to Germany. Dr. Farid invited me for a short visit to his brother's home in New Jersey, but I wanted to shop for some gifts for my family in Manhattan. We agreed to meet at Kennedy Airport.

Waiting for him at the gate that evening, I grew increasingly nervous as our departure time approached. The flight crew called the first group of passengers to begin boarding, then the second. I looked around frantically for Dr. Farid, but he was nowhere to be seen. I boarded with the final group, and as I took my seat the unthinkable idea that he might have defected began to sink in. The consequences of returning home alone would be severe. Hussein Kamel had put the responsibility for Dr. Farid on my head. Then I thought of Dr. Farid's wife and children. It seemed inconceivable that he would leave them behind, because Saddam's security men would surely put them in prison. Did Dr. Farid have a secret plan? Maybe he had arranged for his family to flee the country during our trip to the United States. But he had invited me to his brother's home during the layover. It didn't make sense. Was that part of a ruse? I looked at the empty seat next to me and began to panic as I imagined the punishments Hussein Kamel would inflict on me.

A few stragglers boarded the plane, searching for empty spaces in the overhead compartments. When I saw the anxious face of Dr. Farid behind them, I sighed with relief.

"I am terribly sorry," he said as he slid into the seat next to me. "The traffic was worse than I expected."

"You had me fearing the worst," I said. Dr. Farid caught my meaning.

"You mustn't worry about that," he said. "We are in the same boat."

After our stopover in Germany, I flew directly to Milan in search of a copy of the Zippe reports. Desperate to get my hands on this essential document, I checked into a hotel near La Scala Opera House and phoned an old acquaintance.

Dr. Giorgio Morandi had been my closest Italian colleague during the work on the nuclear reactor complex in the 1970s. He spent several months in Baghdad as the Italian project manager for a $50 million contract to build facilities for materials testing, fuel fabrication, and processing. My admiration for his talent was such that, when he was drawing designs for the inner workings of the Russian reactor, I used to call him the Leonardo da Vinci of the nuclear field. We always relished our time together as we spoke the common language of engineering, and I considered him a friend.

"Giorgio? It's Mahdi," I said when he answered. "I am in Milan."

"Mahdi! After all these years, what are you doing in my city?"

"Oh, just a bit of sightseeing," I demurred. "I am eager to see you."

"I can't believe you are only sightseeing," Giorgio laughed. "Do you have plans for dinner tonight?"

We met at a wonderful Milanese restaurant and caught up on nearly a decade of our personal lives. After the waiter had cleared our plates and served coffee, Dr. Morandi lit his pipe and asked the question that hovered in the air.

"I know you have not come to see an opera. What really brings you to Milan, Mahdi?"

Unsure of how to broach the subject, I explained in general terms that I was working on a new project, and that I had sought compressors in France and would need other forms of help from abroad. Dr. Morandi smiled indulgently.

"You are dancing around the subject, Mahdi," he said. "Spell it out."

"I am after the Zippe report on magnetic centrifuges," I said, coming directly to the point. "I understand that an original was issued to one of your colleagues."

I mentioned the colleague by name, and Dr. Morandi sat back and puffed on his pipe pensively. Although the report itself was not classified, he seemed taken aback by the implications of my request. But he quickly regained his composure.

"There are two problems at hand," he said. "The first is that I no longer work directly with the gentleman you mentioned. The second is that he is reluctant by nature."

"I don't mean to sound desperate, Giorgio," I said, "but I really need that report."

Dr. Morandi shook his head in mild exasperation.

"Mahdi, you are breaking my balls," he said. "But how can I refuse an old friend?"

I flew back to Baghdad the next day, and within two weeks the Zippe report was in our hands. It was like a torch's light in the darkness. It detailed all the early experiments conducted with the magnetic centrifuge and indicated the difficulties we would need to overcome. The experiments revealed the brilliance of Zippe as a scientist. I devoured this material as though I were reading an exciting novel.

The report gave us only a grip on theory, however. We could see the nature of the lock, but we lacked the key to open it. To actually build a magnetic centrifuge, we would have to acquire classified drawings and blueprints. I knew that the assistance from Dr. Morandi was the last time I would be able to call on a favor from an old friend, and I didn't want to risk drawing the attention of the United States to our efforts by returning there for designs that would surely be locked under tight security. I needed new foreign contacts. Although much early laboratory work on centrifuges took place in the United States, the Americans had largely shelved centrifuge enrichment in favor of the diffusion technique and other methods. It was the Europeans who developed and perfected the technology for commercial purposes. Blueprints had to exist in the European private sector, I reasoned. During the next few months I made several attempts to penetrate companies that produced centrifuges to enrich uranium for power reactors.

The mother of the commercial centrifuge was a Dutch-British-German consortium called Urenco in the Netherlands, which had first solved the mathematical riddle of how to run magnetic centrifuges on a large scale in the 1970s. It also had a history of divulging its secrets. The Pakistani scientist Abdul Qadeer Khan infiltrated Urenco for two years at the height of its development program and, in 1975, returned to his native land with a complete set of copied designs, calculations, and contacts for component manufacturers that formed the basis of the Pakistani nuclear weapons program. Educated in Europe, Dr. Khan had slipped past security measures partly because he spoke Dutch and was married to a Dutch-speaking South African woman, and was viewed almost as a citizen of that country. Although I lacked these connections, I was nonetheless eager to find out what sort of reception I might receive in the Netherlands.

I arranged a visit to a large Dutch company, Almelo, which among other things built cascades for centrifuges and was closely associated with Urenco. I flew to Amsterdam with Dr. Farid, Dr. Adil, and Mr. Ali Mutalib Ali, who had been the cultural attaché at the Iraqi embassy in Germany for the past ten years and played a crucial role in our procurement network. He became our calling card throughout Europe. Fair-skinned with a medium build and the graceful demeanor of a diplomat, Mr. Ali always wore fine suits and enjoyed dining at the best restaurants. He spoke elegant German and beautifully handled any logistical challenge we sent his way, whether it was opening lines of credit at foreign banks, negotiating with German companies, or making arrangements at restaurants and rental car agencies.

The officials at Almelo received us politely, but I could see right away that they were wary about in dealing with us. We professed an interest in chlorine for Iraqi water treatment plants, which was another area of their business, but I could tell they sensed we were of a higher caliber than scientists who would normally approach them for such a project. They gave us a brief tour of their premises but declined to show us the more sensitive areas, including the centrifuge operation. It seemed the espionage of Dr. Khan, which set off a storm of negative publicity in the Netherlands, had made officials there extremely guarded. I left convinced this was a dead-end street. Before leaving Amsterdam I visited an indoor nursery and bought a small lime tree for my garden, which was all I had to show for my trip to the Netherlands.

A German centrifuge manufacturer, the giant M.A.N. New Technology in Munich, proved equally unhelpful. A producer of everything from trailer trucks to rocket launchers, M.A.N. had also developed centrifuges to produce fuel for nuclear power reactors after Dr. Zippe returned to Germany and spent the final years of his career at the company in the 1960s. Hoping to open up a preliminary business relationship, we arranged to purchase from M.A.N. ten truck trailers to be used for artillery rocket launchers. After this sweetener, I arranged for Dr. Adil to visit the company in Munich to see, among other things, the Materials Department where the centrifuge parts were manufactured. At first he was given permission, but when he arrived, the M.A.N. staff denied him access to all sensitive departments, citing ongoing classified work on the European space rocket program, Ariane. I never learned whether this was a legitimate security concern or simply a false pretext to deny us access to the centrifuge facility because they doubted our stated intentions.

I still could show no great progress on the magnetic version of the centrifuge. We had rebuilt the Beams oil centrifuge with a new rotor, which over time proved useful for studying basic concepts. But this, along with the fact that we were gaining important knowledge from the Zippe reports, was not enough to please Hussein Kamel, who wanted tangible results. By July of 1988, he had put the Engineering Design Directorate under his authority at MIC and renamed it the Engineering Design Center. He visited Rashdiya less frequently, and each time he arrived, his demeanor was more aggressive and his questions more sarcastic. Something had to be done quickly or we would feel the tip of Hussein Kamel's knife at our necks. I finally asked him to contact Dr. Safa Habobi, the director general of the Nasser Establishment, one of many front companies that were used to buy armaments for the Iraqi government. Dr. Safa used these companies to form business relationships with firms in other countries, in order to disguise the purchases of weapons parts that violated export restrictions. The network between Iraqi front companies and foreign suppliers was the key to our illicit procurements. I learned that Dr. Safa had a secret partnership in a German company, H&H Metalform, which had business dealings with M.A.N.

Hussein Kamel called him from my office, and his abruptness showed that his patience was reaching an end.

"Dr. Safa," he said, "I am sending Dr. Mahdi to see you. You are to devote all your efforts to helping him. Do not let me down, or you will be ousted."

Then he turned and looked me directly in the eye.

"This is a last chance for you," he said. "You understand what it means if you fail. I have had enough failures."

I drove directly to Dr. Safa's office, where I explained to him the basics of our covert centrifuge program. Dr. Safa didn't need to be told to keep this information secret. He was the picture of discretion. We compared notes on H&H Metalform and M.A.N. The prospects for cooperation from the German company seemed good. Not only had Dr. Safa given lucrative contracts to the company to build tubes for Iraqi artillery rockets, he had also organized a cash loan for its two owners a year earlier in exchange for a silent 50 percent partnership in H&H. It would be difficult for them to refuse a request for a favor from a partner. Dr. Safa and I discussed the ways in which the company could assist me.

The German co-owners, Dietrich Hinze and Peter Huetten, were experts in a process called flow forming, which stretches metal under intense pressure in order to manufacture rotationally symmetrical tubes, including the casings for rockets and missiles. At the most precise level of machining, it is also the process used to make centrifuge rotors from high-quality steel. I told Dr. Safa I would like to discuss flow-forming machines with Hinze. Because my direst need was still to acquire detailed designs for a magnetic centrifuge, I also asked if Hinze could put me in contact with any engineers who had connections at M.A.N.

Soon afterward we flew to Munich, where Hinze met us. A clean-shaven, businesslike man in his late forties, he wore a well-tailored suit and drove a blue Mercedes-Benz and was married to a beautiful blonde woman. The Hinzes were obviously prospering from their Iraqi business deals. Hinze introduced me to two former M.A.N. employees, Walter Busse and Bruno Stemmler, both of whom had been instrumental in the German company's centrifuge program. Busse was an expert in working with a lightweight metal called maraging steel that allows rotors to spin faster. Stemmler had built and directed the first M.A.N. uranium separation laboratory, which housed about twenty magnetic centrifuges. Hinze had done well; these were perfect contacts.

At first we discussed business in general, and I spoke of the desire in the Iraqi scientific community to learn from the achievements of German science. Stemmler and Busse listened very attentively, nodding their heads, and I could tell they smelled money behind my words. I gambled and went straight to the point.

"We would be very grateful for designs that would assist us in developing a centrifuge prototype," I said. "There are a number of technical issues we have been unable to resolve."

None of them blinked, which I took as a good sign. I continued with an esoteric description of the difficulties Iraq faced in terms of centrifuge theory, in order to deflect their attention from the fact that I had just asked them to provide classified information to a foreign country. I referred to several intriguing issues involving hairy mathematics. Scientists are natural problem solvers, and I appealed directly to their pride as specialists. Reading their body language, I noticed that Hinze sat back and tried to disengage slightly from the conversation. Busse was more receptive. But it was

Stemmler who leaned forward in his chair and took the greatest interest. I figured he was our man. About fifty years old and slightly dumpy, Stemmler chain-smoked cigarettes throughout the meeting. He wore thick-rimmed glasses and had the air of an absent-minded professor. Dr. Safa had said he was bitter against his former employer, who he felt didn't compensate him well enough for his contributions to centrifuge technology. I later heard that he had serious financial problems and was desperate for money for personal reasons. Whether motivated by scientific interest or the need for cash, he cooperated wholeheartedly with our every request.

Dr. Safa and I invited the threesome to Baghdad, and they arrived a few weeks later, in August of 1998. As soon as Dr. Adil, Dr. Farid, and I sat down with them, I realized that Stemmler had brought us gold. From his briefcase he pulled out a set of blueprints of assembly drawings for the magnetic centrifuge developed at M.A.N. in the 1970s. I didn't ask how they came into his hands. As I eagerly thumbed through page after page, I felt my pulse quicken as the significance of these documents dawned on me. They were a virtual instruction manual for the M.A.N. centrifuge. But that wasn't all Stemmler brought. He proudly reached back into his briefcase and pulled out prototypes of centrifuge components, including the motor and the bearings for both the top and bottom of the rotor. We tried to contain our excitement. For scientists who knew what they were looking at, it was as though Stemmler had pulled the moon out of the sky.

Stemmler and I settled on a price of two million deutsche marks, or just over a million dollars, for everything he provided, including ongoing technical assistance. I felt the price was more than fair, and I wondered why Stemmler would risk everything for such an amount.

I brought some of my best technical engineers in to interview Stemmler about the finer points of centrifuge design. For several days we questioned him in an empty office at MIC headquarters. His mind seemed hazy at times, and he often wandered off topic, but he possessed a deep hands-on knowledge. I wanted Stemmler to look into problems with our Beams centrifuge and risked exposing our Rashdiya facility in bringing him there. Instead of driving north from central Baghdad, we took him southward and made a number of circuitous detours on the way to Rashdiya to confuse his sense of direction. The risk was worth it. After studying our Beams centrifuge, Stemmler suggested a few key adjustments that improved its performance. He seemed slightly amused that we had tried to build a nuclear program based on an oil centrifuge, but he agreed that it would serve as a useful research tool as we prepared to build a magnetic version.

The dialogue with Stemmler opened my eyes even further to the need for technical assistance from experienced foreigners. As we frantically worked to turn Stemmler's assembly drawings into detailed designs for the manufacture of individual parts, I also realized that Iraq's industrial capabilities were not up to the task. Our indigenous facilities simply lacked the level of precision required for many of the materials. Certain parts required manufacturing on a microscopic scale. After the Germans left Baghdad, I began to put together a strategy for acquiring parts, materials, and know-how on the international black market.

As I researched the centrifuge technique, I also followed Hussein Kamel's order to continue developing a diffusion enrichment program. I had set up special groups of scientists to investigate how to progress from the barrier we developed early on to a version that would handle the flow of uranium hexafluoride. The barrier laboratory was housed in a separate building at the Engineering Design Center. Even though we were making headway, I considered the project more of a hobby than a job. As I bent over the electron microscope to observe the pores of the barrier, I found myself delightfully transported into a micro universe. I saw the molecular flow through the barrier as though it were a traffic jam of cars passing through a tunnel. My greatest concern was that the tunnel walls would crack under the flow of those uranium hexafluoride molecules. At other times, the process seemed like bees filling the holes of their delicate honeycomb, and I told my engineers that we must be careful to ensure its strength to safeguard the honey. We made endless micromechanical tests of the material and refined it each step of the way. Years later, when I described our diffusion experiments to weapons inspectors from the United States, Europe, and Japan, they conceded that our efforts had been ingenious.

When we finally experimented with the barrier using uranium hexafluoride over the course of six months, the results were beautiful. By the end of 1988, we had proved the theoretical efficacy of our barrier. I called Hussein Kamel, and when he arrived and saw the prototype, his face lit up with enthusiasm. It was the first time I had seen him pleased in many months, and I hoped this would buy us some time on the centrifuge program.

Three hours after Hussein Kamel left, he called my office and dropped a bomb on me.

"President Saddam has asked to see you in person," he said. "You should be prepared for a meeting tomorrow morning. Bring the prototype of the diffusion barrier you have made and the top technicians on the project. I will send a car for you."

I felt flattered but extremely nervous. Saddam very rarely asked for meetings with scientists. The son of peasants with only a minimal level of education, he preferred to receive reports from trusted intermediaries who digested information for him. He surrounded himself with military men and members of his tribe in Tikrit, who told him what he wanted to hear. I always suspected that Saddam suffered an inferiority complex in the company of academics or scientists.

At 9 A.M., a black minibus came to the Rashdiya facility to collect me and four of my junior assistants. As we climbed inside the minivan, we could see nothing, because the windows were blacked out from the inside to prevent us from seeing where we were going. In my lap I held the prototype barrier in a leather box our department had specially made the night before for presentation to the dictator.

All of us were edgy. Meetings with Saddam were notoriously unpredictable experiences that could end with a promotion, a gift, or imprisonment. I remembered with a chill how Saddam had consolidated his power nine years earlier at the meeting in which he ordered the execution of many government officials.

After about half an hour of driving, the minivan came to a halt, and we were let out into a parking area lined with fine olive trees. As my eyes adjusted to the sunlight, my first impression was that I had never seen so many olives on a tree. Hussein Kamel greeted us and led us to a small compound where uniformed guards frisked us. We were then ushered through a courtyard full of flowers into another building. Its interior was decorated simply, with high ceilings and floors and banisters of fine Italian marble. Finally, we entered a salon filled with tea tables placed in front of ornate, colorfully cushioned chairs.

Saddam Hussein walked forward to greet us. I was surprised at his appearance. He had dressed theatrically in an Arabic *abiaa* robe of yellow silk with a matching *igal* wrapped around his head. I was accustomed to seeing him on TV wearing his olive green military uniform, and my first thought was that this was a bit on the silly side. Why would the president dress in the garb of an Arabic noble-man for a formal meeting with scientists?

As he approached, however, these thoughts vanished. I felt my throat tighten with nervousness. I didn't dare look back at my four assistants, but I could sense them behind me standing as straight as boards. I offered my hand as calmly as I could as he came within reach.

"This is the man who will deliver the enriched uranium," Hussein Kamel said to Saddam, nodding at me. "He has already made great strides."

Saddam took my hand in a noncommittal grip, without saying a word. I had done my homework, and I knew it was impolite to shake his hands with too much force, so I regulated the pressure of my handshake to be slightly softer than his to show deference. I'd heard about Saddam's unnerving habit of probing people's personalities by looking them in the eye for long periods of time. So I held his gaze as we shook hands. His eyes were brown and sturdy, but the whites were cracked with veins and slightly yellowed. I wondered if he had been drinking the night before. His pupils locked on mine as though they were trying to bore a hole in me. He did not let my hand go and began shaking it gently as though trying to rock me into a hypnotic state like a snake charmer, while pulling me in with his eyes. I felt rather ridiculous and extremely uncomfortable. But I knew I mustn't look away.

The room became quiet around us. I wondered how long this could go on. I silently counted the seconds until they added up to nearly two minutes, and still the dictator held me in his juvenile staring contest. I softened my gaze and took in the features of the president's face. A web of broken capillaries spread over his broad, pear-shaped nose, and his mustache and eyebrows sprang from his face like thick shrubs. He squinted slightly as he searched my eyes, and I was petrified that he might somehow be able to read my mind. I thought of the thousands of Iraqis this man had executed or imprisoned. Those who displeased Saddam and lived were said to be rotting away in airless cells, fed once a day through slots in their doors. There is an Arabic expression for sympathy that translates, "When we see a cat's blood, we feel itchy." I imagined the pain of so many fathers and wives and children who never knew if their loved ones were dead or locked in Saddam's dungeons. I imagined my own family members in this situation, if Saddam were to imprison one of them to "encourage" me to enrich uranium more quickly.

The president must have sensed my unease.

"Come now, Dr. Mahdi, drink a cup of tea with me," he said, finally releasing my hand and gesturing for me to take a chair next to his. We sat, and he placed a cup of tea and a bowl of sugar in front of me. "I am pleased to hear of your progress. Tell me more about it."

I tried to explain the main aspects of the barrier and the diffusion technique in nontechnical terms. As with smoke, which diffuses through the air with the lightest particles leading the way and the heaviest remaining behind, uranium hexafluoride can be enriched by forcing it to diffuse through a series of barriers, I said. I held up the prototype and explained that the process involved thousands of such barriers and the creation of large-scale processing plants. I could tell Saddam was beginning to lose interest, so I finished quickly.

"To build a house, you must first design a brick," I said. "This is the brick."

Saddam paused and then launched into a general speech about the technological progress of Iraq and the Arab nation.

"Soon we will be on par with countries like Switzerland in technological terms," he said. "Hussein Kamel, how long will it take Iraq to reach the level of Switzerland?"

"Not long, for sure," Hussein Kamel said dutifully.

This was a preposterous notion. Few people understood the state of Iraq's technological infrastructure better than I did, and I knew that although Iraq had advanced further than most of its neighbors in the Middle East, the comparison with Switzerland bordered on lunacy. The grandiose words from a man who had never visited Switzerland showed just how disconnected he was from reality. Then the president turned to me.

"You say the gas is called uranium hexafluoride?" He took a pen and notepad from the tea table and wrote "UF6" on it. "Is that the chemical compound?"

I felt he was making a show of being interested in the technical aspects of the program. It was obvious he cared little about the process. He wanted only to see the end product.

"Yes," I said, "that is it."

Saddam removed the piece of paper from the notepad, and we all watched as he slowly tore it into tiny pieces, which he put in an ashtray. The double message of this was subtle but clear: the program was top secret, and the president had finished listening to the technical side of things.

"Dr. Mahdi, when will we see results from this diffusion program?" he asked bluntly. "You say you have the brick; when will we be able to live in the house?"

The metaphor to "live in the house" needed no explaining, but I didn't know how to answer. I groped for words. I am a scientist, not a flatterer. The path ahead for the diffusion program was very long and perhaps impossible. The program would need to pass from the prototype stage to a pilot stage with dozens of diffusers of different types, and finally to an industrial stage with thousands of highly complex machines we were unlikely to produce even within the next few years. But it wasn't hard to guess that Saddam wouldn't be satisfied with an answer in terms of years. I glanced at Hussein Kamel and Saddam's advisor, Lieutenant General Amir al-Saadi. They nodded to me to answer the question.

"It is very difficult to put it into a precise time frame," I said carefully. "There are many challenges facing the diffusion program. What we have here is only the cornerstone, and many other materials are needed to build the house. On the other hand, we have begun exploring the potential of the centrifuge with more confidence."

Hussein Kamel gave me a sharp look to cut me off. It was instantly clear that he had not briefed Saddam on the centrifuge program, which was still at the theoretical level, because he needed to show progress and not a new beginning. Even though he was married to the dictator's daughter, Hussein Kamel was so afraid of Saddam that he feared bringing anything but good news.

"Dr. Mahdi is a very humble man who hates to boast," Hussein Kamel interjected. "He believes that results will be shown within the next few months."

My heart sank. This was an absolutely impossible time frame in which to show tangible progress with either the diffusion or the centrifuge program. Saddam stood up from his chair, indicating that our meeting had come to an end. Hussein Kamel and General al-Saadi ushered me out into the palace courtyard and then dressed me down in front of my assistants.

"Why didn't you tell the president what he wanted to hear?" General al-Saadi screamed at me. "Did you fear for your neck? You should be more afraid to disappoint him now than to disappoint him later!"

General al-Saadi's attitude was revealing. Saddam's entire era was characterized by lies from subordinates and false commands from bosses. Everyone deceived each other in order to survive. And as the scientist leading Iraq's great hope for enriching uranium, I was at the hinge point between deception and reality.

CHAPTER 5

Shopping in Europe

I walked into the lobby of a grand hotel in Paris in late 1988 with only a vague description of the men Dr. Farid, Dr. Adil, Mr. Ali, and I were going to meet. In search of maraging steel to begin producing materials based on our centrifuge blueprints, we had approached a French businessman who went by the alias Jacques Rough and who had supplied other types of steel for the Iraqi cannon industry. He promised to find a supplier, knowing this would be a clandestine deal. Maraging steel was difficult to come by on the open market. Its potential use in sophisticated weapons and centrifuges made it one of the materials closely monitored by international intelligence agencies. We scanned the lobby as nonchalantly as possible until two men approached.

"My Iraqi colleagues, I presume?" the Frenchman asked. "I am Jacques."

I offered my hand, and Jacques Rough introduced us to the man accompanying him, an Englishman of Pakistani origin whom he called Malik. Well dressed, with a thin mustache, Malik suggested that the hotel was not the best place for a meeting, and invited us to ride with him to another location. His demeanor suggested he was experienced with transactions on the black market. The six of us piled into two waiting cars and for about a half hour drove west through Paris into the suburbs. When we finally pulled into the driveway of a quiet estate, I was surprised to find that it was a rest home for the elderly. Malik's connection to the place was unclear, but it was a perfect spot for a confidential discussion away from the prying eyes of the city.

Inside the reception area, Jacques greeted an attendant in French. The two men obviously knew each other, and we were cheerfully waved through to the large grounds in back of the estate. We walked through well-tended rose gardens and wide, crisply trimmed lawns as we began discussing the purchase of maraging steel. The only witnesses to our conversation were the colorful, spotted koi fish swimming lazily in a pond. In the distance, well out of earshot, a few elderly people strolled along paths with a serenity befitting their age.

Malik raised an eyebrow when I specified that I was interested in maraging steel of the highest quality available, called maraging 350.

"What do you intend to use it for?" he asked.

"Rockets," I said, "for our artillery program."

It is true that maraging steel is sometimes used to manufacture artillery rockets, but the highest quality they require is an inferior grade, maraging 250. Malik let the matter go for the time being, and we continued discussing specifications in a very cordial and professional manner as we walked through the gardens. I emphasized our need to have a sample tested, and Malik assured me he could deliver one the following day. He nodded without commenting when I said we required about one hundred tons, a large and costly amount.

My staff had hotly debated whether to develop the prototype before collecting materials for large-scale manufacturing. The natural process for a conventional project would have been to avoid large purchases of raw material until a prototype had proven its viability. I had weighed the pros and cons. Saddam and Hussein Kamel might punish us if we wasted money on premature purchases. But surely it would be worse for us if foreign governments discovered and compromised our procurement program before we had all the materials. I had finally decided we should get our hands on every piece of equipment we could as soon as possible.

That night Malik invited us for an evening out on the town, and I was surprised by his choice of venue: a cabaret on the Champs Elysées. We entered a dimly lit auditorium with flashing lights and semi-naked women dancing on a giant stage, and I was reminded of my experience nearly a decade earlier with the men from the French Atomic Energy Commission. We took our places in a long row of seats facing the stage. As Dr. Farid, Dr. Adil and Mr. Ali became engrossed in the performance, Malik began a more focused line of questioning with me, leaning over to speak directly into my ear. He mentioned the end of the war with Iran and sympathized with Iraq's need to replenish its stocks of artillery rockets.

"The material you asked for is of a much higher standard than is normally used for artillery," he said. "Are you sure you wouldn't prefer a more economical grade?"

"No, maraging 350 is what we need," I said, practically shouting over the music.

"But the specifications you mentioned are more appropriate for higher levels of stress on the material," he said, "for example, as at high rotational speeds."

His insinuation went straight to the heart of the matter. Evidently, this Malik had some acquaintance with the subject of centrifuges, although he refrained from mentioning them by name. I wondered whether he was involved in the centrifuge programs of Pakistan or Brazil. There was no way of telling in this murky underworld. He could have been an intelligence agent, for all I knew. As I glanced at a row of dancing girls onstage, I was suddenly struck with the odd notion that Parisian strip clubs doubled as interrogation chambers for foreign nuclear scientists.

My only option was to pretend I didn't understand the meaning behind his remark.

"When it comes to rocketry," I said, "we are determined not to cut corners."

Malik shrugged, and I felt relieved when his line of inquiry seemed to end there.

The next day, I asked the Iraqi ambassador to France to send by diplomatic pouch a sample of the maraging steel to the German firm Interatom for testing. The ambassador seemed startled to see me. In a strange shuffle by Saddam's government, it was none other than Dr. al-Hashimi, the head of the IAEC in the 1970s, who had quizzed me years earlier about experiments for the Tammuz reactor. But one look from him showed me he understood the gravity of my request. Without a comment on our past connection, he assured me a driver was waiting outside. Two days later, I received the results. The maraging steel was of the highest quality and met our specifications exactly.

I flew to meet Malik in London. He seemed to prefer to spread his dealings around geographically. After Paris, where I hardly understood the language, arriving at Heathrow Airport was like coming home. It was a rare sunny winter day in London, and through the window of the black taxicab the silhouettes of the old brick buildings against the setting sun seemed like a postcard of the city.

Malik and I met at a nearly empty tea house in Wimbledon the following morning. As the waitress brought biscuits and poured tea, we settled on a price of $7 million for one hundred tons of maraging 350 steel. I casually asked after the name of the manufacturer, but it was evident Malik didn't want to divulge the source. However, he assured me that the full shipment would meet our specifications and suggested sending it through either Lloyd's of London or Bureau Veritas for quality control. We agreed on Bureau Veritas. Malik refrained from asking further questions about our intended use of the material, and as we lapsed into pleasant small talk, my confidence in him increased.

Looking back on that episode, it seems strange that I was able to enjoy that quiet morning in Wimbledon as we were laying the foundation for an arsenal that could play havoc with the destiny of the world. One hundred tons of maraging steel was conceivably enough to produce ten thousand centrifuges, which in turn could yield 150 kilograms of highly enriched uranium per year. That would be enough uranium for Iraq to annually produce ten bombs with the destructive power of the bomb dropped on Hiroshima in 1945, or nearly one a month. The idea of dozens of nuclear bombs in Saddam's hands is horrifying in retrospect. When I think of leaders like Saddam in the world today and those who will no doubt emerge in the future, we are bound to see a proliferation of the world's most destructive weapon. The specter arises of dozens of countries with nuclear arsenals at their disposal, with all their potential quarrels and conflicts, raising the likelihood of devastating nuclear encounters.

Out of necessity, I put these concerns out of my mind as I focused on assembling the components and resources for the centrifuge program. Every success led us closer to the urgent goal of pleasing Saddam and keeping me and my staff out of his dungeons. But it required a careful strategy. We needed both the materials and the technical skills to build a prototype and, later, the large-scale manufacturing facilities. I developed a two-pronged approach: purchasing the tools and raw materials to manufacture as many of the components as possible inside Iraq and outsourcing the manufacture of other parts. We followed both tracks for many of the most sensitive parts. Secrecy was essential. I scattered our efforts throughout many countries in an effort to avoid detection. I broke the centrifuge designs into subcomponents that, individually, would be hard to recognize. I focused on soft targets in the private sector: companies that could produce fine parts and machines without suspecting their final use.

We had learned many lessons since the outset of our program, one of which was how much expertise we still lacked. A centrifuge is like a delicate soufflé that will fall apart if anything is done incorrectly, and our chefs were woefully unprepared. I put top priority on training my technicians abroad. Several of our engineers honed their skills in hydrodynamics at Imperial College London. Others went to

Munich to study the complex motors needed to generate the magnetic fields to turn the centrifuge rotor. Twenty-two of my staff underwent intensive training at the German company Interatom, where they learned how to build and work inside a "clean room" environment. Another team went to Interatom posing as Oil Ministry engineers to learn the secrets of cryogenics, the study of extremely low temperatures, which were necessary for the production of uranium hexafluoride gas. To maintain the illusion that they were oil engineers, they also spent several weeks in the study of furnaces, since both disciplines are needed in oil refineries.

As we grew more familiar with the cadence program from the American company MTI, it became painfully clear that our new knowledge of rotor dynamics had merely scratched the surface. Our experience with the Beams oil centrifuge showed that a little knowledge is dangerous indeed and could imperil our project and possibly our lives. I contacted Dave at MTI, who agreed on a contract for one of our engineers to study the application of the cadence program with an elderly professor there. I sent a bright young engineer named Dr. Makee Rashid, with specific instructions. We worked out experiments to perform at MTI that could apply to slower-spinning rotors used in the oil industry, but also included a model specific to a centrifuge rotor at more than 50,000 rpm. It wasn't until Dr. Makee returned to Iraq months later that I learned we had nearly been exposed.

As I debriefed him, I grew increasingly apprehensive. For several weeks, Dr. Makee said, his studies progressed beautifully, until a young Ph.D. overseeing his training with the professor became inquisitive.

"He noticed that the rotor model I was working on was beyond the requirements of the oil industry," Dr. Makee said. "He kept asking what I was designing."

"What did you tell him?" I asked.

"As we discussed, I told him it was only a hypothetical model."

That was a potentially disastrous development. Driven by our fear of not producing fast enough for Saddam, we were taking risks by pursuing our program right under the nose of a major American defense contractor. Perhaps we had gone too far. Because of the close ties between MTI and the U.S. government and intelligence services, the suspicions of one young engineer could endanger our entire program. I worried that we would soon hear an accusation coming from the U.S. government, but one never materialized.

With our growing network of contacts supplied by Hinze and others, we began putting together the other pieces. Malik was true to his promise, and several weeks after our meeting in Wimbledon, the maraging steel arrived in Dubai and was trucked across the Saudi Arabian desert in three shipments to Baghdad. We purchased vacuum valves and pipes from the German company Leybold, in Cologne. From Leybold's U.S. subsidiary, we bought electron beam welders to attach the ball to the shaft of the lower bearing. Although specially manufactured to the exact measurements for our centrifuge, the company did not question the end use. The German firm Reutlinger sold us machines to balance the rotors. We sought other parts in Yugoslavia, England, and Switzerland.

Our efforts to procure materials led us to many dead-end streets, some spectacular successes, and a few hair-raising close calls. One of the most difficult pieces to obtain was the small high-powered magnet that sits atop the centrifuge. A marvelous piece of engineering, the upper magnetic bearing holds the rotor in place, without ever touching it, as it spins in a vacuum. No ordinary magnet, its specifications identify it as a key piece of a centrifuge. No matter whom we asked, suspicions were bound to be aroused.

When we asked an Iraqi front company for procurements in Britain, called the Technology Development Group (TDG), about acquiring such a magnet, they recommended an Englishman and a Chinese-born American, who had approached TDG in an attempt to sell Chinese technology on the black market. At first it seemed a promising lead, and I flew to Bonn, Germany, with Dr. Farid, Dr. Adil, and Mr. Ali for a prearranged meeting at a hotel there.

I stood on the balcony of my third-floor room at the luxurious little four-star hotel, overlooking a large garden, awaiting the arrival of the Englishman for our two o'clock meeting. A few minutes before the hour, as I was admiring the flower beds below, I spotted a bald man approaching the entrance. He wore a business suit and carried a briefcase. I had a strange feeling as I watched him disappear under the hotel's awning. A sixth sense, which my mother always trusted, told me this was our man but that he wasn't to be dealt with. I decided not to meet him. Instead, I sent Dr. Adil and Dr. Farid downstairs to speak to the gentleman. Two hours later, they returned from the lobby and confirmed that the bald man had been the contact. They said they had agreed for a sample magnet to be shipped from China.

Back in Baghdad two weeks later, we received a sample of the Chinese magnet and an offer to build a production facility for 4.7 million British pounds. But the sample looked disgusting. Its surfaces were shabby and pitted, and to a trained eye the piece was not at all proper. I sent a message through TDG vehemently refusing to continue with the offer. My intuition about the bald-headed Englishman had been correct. A few days afterward, an article appeared in a newsletter called *Middle East Markets* published by London's *Financial Times*, accusing Iraq of trying to obtain highly sophisticated Chinese-made magnets for an effort to build centrifuges. It stated that the attempt to purchase magnets was an essential part of Iraq's quest for a nuclear bomb. We had been exposed in a setup.

I learned about the article only after a phone call from Hussein Kamel summoning me to his office. When I arrived, I saw a copy of the newsletter spread out on his desk. He stood over me as I read it.

"How did this happen?" he asked, his voice uncharacteristically calm.

"Sir," I said, "the man we were supplied with must have been a British intelligence agent. I don't have any information about him. I didn't meet him."

"Do you realize what this means if it becomes a bigger story in the media?" he asked. "Do you?"

"Yes," I said. "It could jeopardize our program."

"You must be more careful," he said, dismissing me in his usual brusque manner. "Be sure that it doesn't happen again."

I anxiously waited to hear whether more foreign news media had picked up on the story, and tried to gauge the potential fallout. Public awareness of Iraq's centrifuge program in Europe or the United States would lead to tighter scrutiny on exports to Iraq, and this would hurt not only our chances of success but also those of Iraq's armaments programs overall. Saddam and Hussein Kamel would hang the blame on someone, and the noose most likely would tighten around our necks. Weeks passed, however, and to my relief nothing new appeared about the matter in the foreign media. Newspaper editors must have found the details of the case too sketchy and the evidence too weak. All they had to go on was a single aborted attempt to purchase a magnet, with no paper trail to prove it. I never learned whether anyone at TDG in London suffered consequences for the slipup.

We made an appointment at the prominent German magnet producer MagnetoBonn. To disguise our true interest, we sent a list of dozens of types of magnets and suggested that we might purchase a large range of MagnetoBonn products, hoping this would draw attention away from the centrifuge magnet. When I arrived at the company, however, the technology manager met me in the reception area and said that, regrettably, the company could not allow me onto its premises. Evidently someone had carefully studied our list of requirements and sounded an alarm bell when they saw the specifications for the centrifuge magnet.

"But sir, you have invited me to come all the way from Baghdad for this visit," I said, fearing that I would once again return to Iraq with nothing to show for my trip. "That is a long way to travel for a last-minute cancellation."

"Please accept my apologies for the mistake," the technology manager said. "Our plant is simply off-limits at the moment."

I felt I simply couldn't go back empty-handed once again. But there seemed no other way to press my case. I quickly racked my brains for something I could ask of this man that would not unduly raise his suspicions but still be useful.

"Well, in order not to have wasted my time completely, could I at least ask you a few technical questions?"

"By all means," he said, looking at his watch. "But I'm afraid I still can't invite you inside."

I asked about the pressing and treatment of the metal for the magnets, and the methods used for shaping the particles inside of them. Although the topics were theoretical, these were highly specialized questions, the answers to which touched on classified applications.

The technology manager let my questions hang in the air for a few seconds. He looked around the reception area at fellow employees coming and going through the front door. Perhaps he was assuring himself that it was safe to speak to me in this environment. Then I was seized by a moment of panic. Maybe my line of questioning had spooked him, and he was about to call security. Or he might file a report on an inquisitive Iraqi who had asked dangerous questions. I looked around the reception hall at passersby who seemed to pay us no notice, worried that I had gone too far over the line.

Then, either because he felt guilty for canceling my appointment at the last minute or due to a scientist's natural love of explaining things, he began answering in a general way. I eagerly fished a notebook and pen out of my pocket and offered them to help illustrate his points. He hesitated for a moment, looking at my notebook skeptically, but then he took it. He refused my pen, preferring to use one from his own shirt pocket. He sketched a few notes and diagrams, and I asked pointed follow-up questions about the length of the pressing time needed to make magnets, the temperature, the surface finish, and other technical issues. For a short while he seemed caught up in the enthusiasm of describing the essence of his work, like a schoolteacher pleased to find an attentive student. I memorized his every word. After about twenty minutes, perhaps he realized that he had given me a lot more than he had intended to, because he abruptly stopped his impromptu lecture.

"I think I have said enough," he said. "Are you satisfied now?"

"You have done more than enough, and I thank you very much for your kindness," I said, and hurriedly left.

In those twenty minutes I had learned enough to conceptualize these high-end magnets from the ground up. Understanding the technology behind them gave me the credibility needed to negotiate with manufacturers.

I set our sights on the Austrian high-tech firm Treibacher, one of the world's preeminent magnet makers.

On a chilly morning in the autumn of 1988, we set off on a long drive from Germany toward Vienna. Mr. Ali navigated our rented Opel up icy roads into the snowcapped Alps, which treated us to breathtaking views. As we entered Austria, a heavy rain began lashing our windshield, reducing visibility to zero. Mr. Ali slowed us to a crawl, but as we descended a hill, the tires lost their grip on a long patch of ice. The car careened sideways and then spun out of control. Mr. Ali tried in vain to correct the steering as we hydroplaned across the wet ice, picking up speed. I gripped the dashboard. Suddenly I felt a bump and we skidded several feet and crashed into a small snow bank. I opened my door and saw to my horror that we had come to a stop only a few feet from a steep precipice. Only the little snow bank had stopped us from falling to our deaths. The Iraqi centrifuge program had nearly been dealt a decapitating blow.

The skies cleared as we safely descended into the flat meadows around Vienna, where we stopped for a traditional Austrian lunch and, still feeling the adrenaline, relived our narrow escape. Because our meeting at Treibacher was not until the next morning, we had made a date with an engineer from H&H Metalform. We spent the afternoon driving through the outskirts of Vienna, marveling at the greenery and the majestic mountains. The German engineer showed us the former home of Ludwig van Beethoven and several castles with exquisite lawns and gardens. As we were leaving one of them, he turned to me and made a remark that made painfully clear the lack of understanding foreigners had for the reality we lived under in Iraq.

"All of these luxurious castles are like the palaces Saddam is building in your country," he said. "Isn't that right?"

I nodded politely. But his comment brought a dark cloud over the pleasant afternoon. I would never dare to mention Saddam's castles in public, even in a foreign country. In Iraq, you could disappear into the clutches of the security forces for saying such a thing aloud. Saddam, his palaces, and his personal life were taboo subjects. Outside of Saddam's entourage, no one knew how many he had built for himself. They were feared places, the mere mention of which put ordinary citizens on edge. The Austrian castles may have witnessed atrocities in the distant past, but unlike Saddam's palaces, they were now open to the public as tourist attractions.

In the morning we drove to the Treibacher headquarters nestled in an Alpine valley in the southern Austrian town of Villach. We entered a well-furnished waiting room with a window onto a section of the plant itself. The facilities were immaculate, as though one could eat a meal off the shiny surfaces of the machines. The manager of Treibacher introduced himself to us in flawless English and invited us into his office. After we exchanged pleasantries, he asked about the nature of our business. Armed with the knowledge I had gained in Germany, I told him we hoped to purchase sophisticated magnets that few manufacturers could provide. I described the specifications of the magnet we wanted to use for our centrifuge, but with important differences in terms of its performance.

"For what application do you intend to use this magnet?" he asked.

"We are experimenting with more advanced pumps for the oil industry," I said, "and we want to find a better way of generating a magnetic seal."

The Treibacher manager looked at me quizzically, and then begged our pardon as he left us alone in his office. He was gone for minutes that seemed to stretch on endlessly. I began to fear that he had already guessed the true purpose of our visit and would alert some authority to it. I wondered who he could call. The Austrian intelligence agency? Interpol? I tried to calm myself with rational thoughts. We had given a plausible reason for our visit, and these people were in the business of selling magnets. Yet I could not shake the fear that comes with such a high-stakes negotiation. I never knew what these counterparts knew or suspected. I knew only the consequences of getting caught.

He returned a few minutes later with a diagram showing the properties of a sophisticated magnet.

"Is this what you are looking for?" he asked.

My heart leapt. It was a graph of the exact specifications for a centrifuge magnet. I instinctively wanted to take the diagram and study it further. But it was not what I had asked for. I had indicated specifications appropriate for oil industry pumps. Although the magnet itself was the same, his graph showed a performance level well beyond our stated requirements. It was as though I had asked to purchase a sports car able to reach speeds of two hundred miles per hour, but claimed I would use it only on city streets and obey legal speed limits. He was showing me a graph of how the car would perform on a race track at full throttle. I sensed a trap, so I feigned ignorance.

"I'm afraid that isn't it," I said. "I am unfamiliar with this design."

The Treibacher manager seemed pleased with this answer as he rolled up the diagram. He called two of his assistants into the office and instructed them to show us around the premises and cater to our requirements. We had struck a gold mine. After an impressive tour of the Treibacher establishment and lengthy negotiations, we settled on a deal to provide thousands of magnets for the Iraqi oil industry.

The fact that the Austrians were willing to sell us these magnets shows the difficulty of keeping technology that has a range of uses out of the hands of those who might apply it to a secret weapons program. It also speaks to the complicated nature of Iraq's relations with the West during the late 1980s. Many countries had secretly aided Saddam in the eight-year war against Iran, and he was not yet perceived as a threat to Western security. On the other hand, no country could have publicly supported an Iraqi nuclear weapons program.

Our relationships with foreign companies always carried some element of risk. We could never tell how closely foreign intelligence agencies were watching exports, but at least some members of Western governments seemed to turn a blind eye to our procurements. In retrospect, it is hard to imagine that our program would have progressed so quickly if the Europeans and Americans had been more vigilant.

I sent one of our highly skilled physicists, Dr. Widad Hattam, to a company in the United Kingdom, where she refined our ability to work with the Treibacher magnets. The British scientists she worked with might easily have guessed the true nature of her research. One of them, she later told me, even cautioned her against taking a magnet in her carry-on luggage on a flight back to Baghdad, because it might arouse suspicions at the airport security check. The inability of airport security to check all items of every passenger allowed small but dangerous materials to be smuggled between the Middle East and Europe. One of my staff members managed to bring a sample of uranium hexafluoride from Baghdad through Heathrow Airport to the University of Dundee in Scotland, where several resident Iraqi scientists helped him test the material. He sneaked it through customs by strapping it to his shin under the cuff of his pants. The fact that my colleague was able to bring radioactive material on an international flight is very scary indeed.

As much as our procurement successes depended on lax security and our well-planned cover stories, we would have made little progress were it not for the network of Iraqi front companies and international business relationships. A machine tools company in Coventry called Matrix Churchill built many components for our centrifuge program. A formerly struggling, British-owned company, Matrix Churchill was another well-timed acquisition by Dr. Safa al-Habobi. In 1987, after purchasing a majority of shares, he was named chairman of its board. As was the case with H&H Metalform, it would have been difficult for Matrix Churchill to turn down Iraqi business. Iraq claimed that items Matrix Churchill produced were for civilian use, and the British government approved their export. During the 1990s, however, a scandal broke out when evidence showed that British intelligence had known about the true end uses of many components, and that the government tacitly approved exports to arm Saddam before the 1991 Gulf War.

The real keys, however, were the Germans connected to H&H Metalform, which by now turned handsome profits from Iraqi commissions. Dietrich Hinze provided dozens of connections to high-tech firms who cooperated because of their long relationship with him and the ample funds we could provide. Walter Busse, the expert in machining centrifuge parts, taught us many of the finer points of working with maraging steel, and both made repeated trips to Iraq to help guide our program. Using the assembly drawings provided by Stemmler, we designed the ball bearing on which the centrifuge sat. We found several Swiss companies that specialized in the pins and balls used in high-rpm dental drills, which could be adapted for a centrifuge bearing.

At the bottom of the centrifuge rotor, the bearing spins in a bath of special oil in a customized cup. To reduce friction to nearly zero, the ball must be etched with grooves that maintain a thin layer of oil between the bearing and the surface of the cup. The complicated design and techniques for etching these grooves are highly classified secrets. But after we offered enough financial incentive, Stemmler provided a photograph of the microscopic groove pattern used in M.A.N. bearings, and we overcame this hurdle, too.

When we needed to purchase machine tools for high-precision parts, the Germans directed me to a Swiss company, Schaublin S.A., which makes some of the world's most accurate lathes and other machines. In 1988 Dr. Farid and I called on Ulrich Spiess, the

Schaublin sales director, at the company's head office in the small town of Bevilard. Spiess was a thin man with a temperamental character, and we spent hours discussing the purchase of milling and turning machines. Although these machines have many applications, including the manufacture of rotor caps and other centrifuge parts, he finally agreed to supply fifteen machines without asking about our intended use for them. But when he mentioned a price, I said it seemed unreasonably high and suggested at least a 10 percent reduction. Sitting in front of his desk, Dr. Farid and I negotiated back and forth with him until Mr. Spiess's patience snapped and he became suddenly furious.

"This is impossible," he said. "It seems you are nothing but horse traders!"

I felt Dr. Farid stiffen with rage at this cheap and racist remark. Mr. Spiess seemed to regard us as nothing more than peasants from an underdeveloped country who were somehow beneath his level. He may as well have called us camel herders. My own cheeks flushed with indignation, too.

"Mr. Spiess," I said. "Evidently this is not the time or place to come to an agreement. Why don't you visit us in Baghdad and we will discuss things further?"

"I'm sorry, but I cannot," he said emphatically. "I simply don't have the time."

We shook hands coolly, and Dr. Farid and I returned to Baghdad.

I temporarily swallowed my pride, because emotions have no place at a negotiating table. I knew that Schaublin could be a valuable partner, and I resolved to court Spiess on a more intimate level and to try to develop a more productive relationship, rather than simply caving in to the price he had offered. I decided I would get the better of Spiess by showing him the beauty and mystery of the land he had just insulted. I would offer him the most memorable vacation of his life and in the process get exactly what we needed for our centrifuge program.

It was true that Swiss technology was light-years ahead of what we had developed in Iraq, as even Saddam could acknowledge. This inequity had brought us to Europe to shop for parts and expertise in the first place. But no one likes to be labeled inferior, and Mr. Spiess's comment stirred my pride. My country was full of people with highly educated minds and skilled hands, who managed to preserve a sense of integrity despite Saddam's tyranny. It is a testament to the spirit of the Iraqi people that an educated class endured the dictatorship of brutes.

Several days later, after tempers had cooled, I called Mr. Spiess and followed up on my gambit, assuring him that we would pay all of his expenses for a first-class trip to Iraq on a weekend of his choice. Combined with the prospect of an ongoing business relationship, the carrot proved too inviting to refuse.

I picked up Mr. Spiess at Saddam International Airport, wondering how his Swiss eyes saw the spacious, spotlessly clean arrivals hall whose walls were covered with beautiful designs and murals. Very different from the Zurich Airport, Saddam International was not the sort of place that would be built by "horse traders." A waiting Mercedes limousine ferried us out of the airport, along a smooth highway lined with date palm and eucalyptus trees. I pointed out the sights as we took the Qadisiya Expressway into central Baghdad, watching Spiess carefully to see what impressed him and what raised his eyebrows. He seemed surprised at how modern the supposed backwater of Baghdad was. I had chosen a route that would show this aspect of my home to best effect.

The Qadisiya Expressway threaded us through several green parks to the left and the Tigris River to our right, past the festival and parade grounds and the new, modernistic dome of the Monument to the Unknown Soldier, to the Al Rashid Hotel, where we had arranged a suite for him.

The next morning, Dr. Adil, Dr. Farid, and I met with Mr. Spiess for a general discussion of technology. I dropped the hint that the machine tools we had discussed earlier were only the tip of the iceberg of potential contracts. He seemed receptive, even eager to hear more, but I cut this dialogue short.

"Let's not ruin your vacation with too much business, Mr. Spiess," I said. "I have arranged as a special treat for you a private tour of the ruins of Babylon."

After lunch I escorted the Swiss manager to Babylon, about fifty miles south of Baghdad near the banks of the Euphrates River. I showed him the spot where in the sixth century B.C. in his calendar, the Babylonian King Nebuchadnezzar II built for his wife the Hanging Gardens, one of the ancient Seven Wonders of the World, and the foundation of the ziggurat believed to be the legendary Tower of Babel. Mr. Spiess seemed to take interest when I told him about the Babylonian architect Gudea of Lagash, whose temple plans carved in stone nearly five thousand years ago are the earliest engineering graphics in the world.

"I knew that algebra was invented here," he said, as we strolled among the ruins.

"The quadratic equation they developed is still used in every child's textbook around the world," I said. "Did you know that the Babylonians also invented the concept of 'zero'?"

Mr. Spiess supposed that he had learned that once. I described a Babylonian temple in the ancient city of Nippur that more than four thousand years ago was filled with clay tablets, making it the first known library. The Babylonians, I told him, sketched man's first maps on clay tiles, including the earliest map of the world that shows waters surrounding a circle of land with Babylon at its center.

Mr. Spiess seemed truly moved by our field trip, and on the drive back to Baghdad we had an animated conversation about the history of the world and the great scientists and thinkers who had defined human progress. I felt the barriers between us melting away.

On the last day of his trip, I brought some of our more talented engineers to MIC to discuss the specifications of the Schaublin machines with Mr. Spiess. Without mentioning prices, I asked him if it would be possible to send some of our engineers to Bevilard for hands-on training. He seemed surprised by my request.

"What do you need training for?" he said. "It seems to me you already have some of the finest engineers in the world."

I smiled at this. Mr. Spiess didn't know that he had met only my finest scientists. It was like the old habit in Iraqi market stalls of putting the healthy tomatoes on top of the bucket while hiding the bad ones underneath. But I appreciated his sentiment. Without his saying so, I felt it was a full retraction of his remark about "horse traders." More important, I felt we had reached a level of mutual respect on which to build a working relationship.

"We may have some talented engineers," I said, returning his compliment, "but no one knows how to operate fine machinery like your fellow Swiss."

My aim for training our engineers at Schaublin was twofold. I wanted them to become familiar with the machines under expert guidance and, even more crucially, to produce the centrifuge rotor caps and other parts to the correct specifications. Maraging steel is very hard to machine, and the precision of the caps was just as important as that of the rotor itself. Because Schaublin made machines and did not deal in parts, I felt that it would be easier to manufacture centrifuge components there with less risk of discovery. Mr. Spiess and I settled on an increased price for the milling and turning machines that included on-site training on parts we wanted to manufacture. What had begun as a strained relationship became a cooperation that benefited us both.

Mr. Spiess was curious about the strange-looking components my engineers intended to produce on his machines, of course. I attended several of the early training sessions at Schaublin to make sure everything went smoothly, with a prepared excuse that the centrifuge caps were intended for a highly specialized machine called a laser chopper, which is used in experiments with lasers. It was a gamble, because my familiarity with laser choppers was superficial at best. I knew only they were spinning devices that stop laser beams and refocus them. It was a technology well beyond our reach. But I guessed that as a manager and not a technician, Mr. Spiess knew as little about them as I did. One afternoon, as one of our young engineers named Jamal looked over one of our sensitive designs, I noticed Mr. Spiess within earshot.

"Look, Jamal," I said in English for Spiess's benefit, "when you rotate this part, the beam gets intercepted."

Jamal looked at me in confusion, but he knew better than to say anything. Mr. Spiess obviously picked up the hint, because the next day he approached one of my engineers with an air of confidentiality.

"I know what you're doing," he said. "You are working on laser choppers. I didn't know that Iraq was working with such technology."

Our increasingly good relations with Mr. Spiess had other advantages, as well. He opened up many contacts for our engineers at other Swiss companies. A few times, he even sent his own engineers to accompany mine to neighboring high-tech firms, to vouch for them. Soon Switzerland became an Iraqi workshop.

CHAPTER 6

The Crash Program

When I stepped back to look at everything we had achieved during the past eighteen months, I saw tremendous progress. We possessed the designs, raw materials, and many of the tools for an indigenous centrifuge effort. Dozens of my engineers and researchers were training undercover in the world's best institutes and high-tech companies. Technicians throughout Europe worked on sensitive subcomponents, unaware that they were helping to piece together an Iraqi centrifuge. It was very likely the most efficient covert enrichment program in history.

In any other circumstances, the boss of such a complex engineering task might have praised us and showered us with bonuses. But Hussein Kamel focused on our shortcomings. I was forced to acknowledge that, just as many of the elements of our centrifuge program seemed to be coming together, we had encountered a couple of serious problems. Our calculations showed that the permanent magnet would burst at the high speeds of the centrifuge, due to extreme rotational forces. Even more troubling, we were finding it difficult to use the flow-forming machines provided by H&H Metalform to manufacture rotors precise enough to withstand the rotational speeds of the centrifuge. They were fine for producing artillery rocket casings, but they lacked the precision to consistently create perfectly uniform tubes of maraging steel, and even the slightest imperfection rendered the tubes useless to us.

After the debilitating war with Iran, Saddam's government was militarily vulnerable and engaged in a spending spree to rebuild his defenses, including discussions of a billion-dollar conventional arms contract with Brazil. And to judge by Hussein Kamel's frantic pressure on us, Saddam was more eager than ever for enriched uranium. Internationally, the government embarked on a charm offensive to rebuild its standing, especially in the eyes of the West, in order to encourage the relief of debts run up during the war. Saddam held elections on April 1, 1989, in which many women and non-Baathists took seats in the National Assembly, and he announced intentions to create a constitution that would guarantee democratic rule. It was little more than a publicity stunt, however.

Saddam's security men stationed at Rashdiya began asking technical questions well beyond their understanding. Some of my engineers told me they seemed to be probing for flaws in our program that they could report to their superiors.

When I brought our technical challenges to the attention of Stemmler, he suggested a more sophisticated method for producing rotors using a material called carbon fiber, which is even stronger than maraging steel. I was eager to explore this other technology. Any successful project must be able to adapt to changing realities. Stemmler said he had a friend and former colleague from the centrifuge program at M.A.N. who specialized in carbon fiber. His name was Karl Heinz Schaab, and though I didn't know it at the time, he would provide the last keys necessary to the development of the Iraqi centrifuge.

Schaab had quit M.A.N. in the early 1980s and set up a private business, making him more approachable than an employee of a large company under strict controls. His company, RoSch, a composite of the first letters of his surname and that of his wife, Brigitte

Ronniger, produced carbon fiber plating for automobile and computer companies, as well as bulletproofing for the Egyptian Air Force. With his background in centrifuge technology, he fit our needs perfectly.

In April 1989 Stemmler and I visited Mr. Schaab at his company in the Bavarian town of Kaufbeuren. I brought Dr. Farid and Dr. Adil along, as well as Mr. Ali. We were careful not to mention our centrifuge project when we set up the meeting.

I liked Schaab from the moment we met. At fifty-five, he was ten years older than I, with graying hair combed back over a wide forehead. His light blue eyes seemed like tiny pools of water that gravity had sunk into his broad face, and when his mouth rested, its corners turned downward in a sad and thoughtful frown. He moved in a lumbering way, as though he carried an invisible weight on his back. But his hands were magical. They seemed to think independently of his brain they were so graceful. As he trudged around his workshop explaining his operation in German, his hands danced over the machines as though in a private conversation with them that even Schaab himself couldn't hear. He demonstrated a rotor winding machine used to form tubes out of carbon fiber, along with ballistic armored shields and other items he produced. Then he showed us a centrifuge rotor, which surprised me because it was a highly classified object. Roughly the same dimensions as our maraging steel rotors, its smooth, dark gray surface reflected no light. Schaab held it gently in his fingers, caressing it as though he had pulled it out of the earth and sculpted it into form with his own hands rather than winding it on a machine.

When I casually mentioned our interest in centrifuge rotors, I was pleased to see that Schaab did not recoil from the idea. We spoke of many issues still facing our program, including machines to set the balance of the rotors once they were produced and the elaborate process of testing them. When I finally asked Schaab if he could provide us with rotors of carbon fiber like the one we had seen at his workshop, he seemed amenable. He also agreed to help us purchase a winding machine, so that we could make the rotors ourselves in Iraq. I found his level of cooperation remarkable.

It soon became clear that Schaab's wife, Brigitte, wielded a heavy influence over his decision making. During our collaboration, I invited Schaab to Iraq several times, and on one occasion she accompanied him. We footed the entire bill, including the most luxurious accommodations Iraq had to offer, and I could see that this pleased Brigitte immensely. She was a stern woman with a stout frame and an air of determination. Unlike Schaab, who shuffled laboriously from place to place, his wife moved quickly, and I remember him always struggling to catch up to her as they walked. One evening I took them to dinner at one of Baghdad's finest Western-style restaurants, the Hinaydi in the Jadriya district, along with Mr. Ali, Dr. Farid, and Dr. Adil. The restaurant owner gave us a corner table away from the other patrons. As we dined on steaks and potatoes, I began proposing other ways in which RoSch could assist us.

We discussed the details of a contract to manufacture the centrifuge rotors, as well as the process for gluing the end caps onto them. Schaab also agreed to work on the ball bearing. His willingness to help us seemed boundless, and I let the requests pour forth until Schaab shook his head, appearing suddenly hesitant.

"He says you are asking too much," Mr. Ali translated.

Schaab's wife intervened, however, speaking to him rapidly in German. Out of good manners, Mr. Ali stopped his translation during their private conversation, but her tone was unmistakably sharp and commanding. When she stopped speaking, Schaab reversed himself.

"He will see what he can do," Mr. Ali said.

Schaab was true to every commitment he made, and his work on the ball bearing, magnet rings, and other parts pushed our program forward by many months, if not years. In the summer of 1989, I received a sample rotor tube Schaab had custom-produced to our specifications. We tested it on the cadence programs from MTI in New York and sent back a request for specific changes in its texture.

Schaab complied immediately, and a few weeks later, I sent two Iraqi engineers to Munich to collect a shipment of twenty rotor tubes, to be delivered via diplomatic pouch. When they arrived at our Rashdiya facility, the rotors tested perfectly on the MTI program. Schaab's expert hands had worked wonders.

Schaab said he could provide us with even more advanced blueprints for what is known as a super-critical centrifuge. Five times the height of the centrifuge on which we were working, the super-critical centrifuge consisted of rotors stacked end to end and held together by a band of maraging steel called a bellows. It produced many times the amount of enriched uranium generated by the centrifuge in Stemmler's designs, which dated from the 1970s. These blueprints were state-of-the-art, representing a decade of research and development in Europe. We settled on a price of 100,000 German marks: an incredible bargain, and a sign that these German scientists were unaware of the true value of the assistance they provided. Someone desperate for these classified blueprints might have paid millions for them. The real prize was the bellows with its microscopic crimp. I had heard that even the Japanese, with their superior technology, had so far failed to unlock the secrets of the centrifuge bellows.

In the winter of 1989, Schaab spent more than a week in Baghdad helping us solve problems related to the rotors. He provided machines to both balance the tubes and analyze them at slow rotational speeds, and he showed us how to use them. He also agreed to build the cup in which the ball bearing sits, which must be machined to a precision of two-thousandths of a millimeter.

In the spring of 1990, with components arriving by secret shipment from manufacturers in England, Germany, Switzerland, and elsewhere in Europe, we were ready to begin assembling our prototype at Rashdiya. Schaab made his final trip to Iraq in April. For three days we brought him to Rashdiya, driving him in circuitous routes to confuse his sense of direction, as we had done with Stemmler. With Schaab's oversight, we assembled a test stand for the prototype and pressed the permanent magnet into his carbon-fiber rings. As technicians, we shared a sense of excitement at watching our creation finally come together, and we worked with a giddy enthusiasm late into the night. We glued the upper and lower end caps onto one of Schaab's carbon-fiber rotors along with other parts and set them to harden overnight. The next evening, we connected the magnet to the upper end of the rotor and attached the needle and ball bearing to its lower end. Before Schaab left, we started the balancing machine to test the equilibrium of the rotor. To my dismay, it wobbled faintly on its bearing. When I pointed this out to Schaab, he shrugged and bent over the bearing for a closer look. He slid his index finger under the tiny ball, nearly touching it. I couldn't imagine what he meant to do. I watched with fascination as Schaab's hand hovered under the centrifuge, his fingers spread wide like a bird suspended in a pocket of air. With an almost imperceptible flick, he stroked the bearing with the tip of his forefinger at what must have been the dead center of the ball, because suddenly the centrifuge balanced. I shook my head in wonder. That soft touch of Shaab was better than a hundred machines, and I realized that all the theory in the world can never replace an experienced hand.

We moved the apparatus into the large vacuum tube, and before Schaab left for Germany, he witnessed the prototype spinning perfectly at low speeds. The moment of truth had arrived, and my entire staff felt a sense of anticipation. Hussein Kamel made frequent visits to Rashdiya as we incrementally increased the speeds. The memory of the failed Beams oil centrifuge haunted us.

Armed with his knowledge of rotor dynamics from MTI, Dr. Makee accelerated the motor. As my other senior staff looked on nervously, Mr. Sinan, the motor designer, attended to the power supply. The centrifuge reached 20,000 rotations per minute, and we congratulated ourselves on reaching a new high mark. When the speed arrived at 32,000 rpm, however, we heard a bang. My heart dropped to the floor as I thought of the price of another failure. We cut the motor and the centrifuge began to slowly wind down. It was nearly three in the morning, and as I looked around the laboratory

I saw the faces of my staff etched with fear. They knew we could not afford to disappoint Hussein Kamel again. Despair would get us nowhere, though, and I rallied my spirits knowing that we had learned a great deal during the past two and a half years. This time, I told my staff, I felt we had enough expertise to understand and fix the problem.

"Dr. Makee," I asked rhetorically, "where is all this power going?"

"To accelerate the motor, of course," he said, looking at me with a strange smile, as though I shouldn't ask such an obvious question.

"But does all of the power go to acceleration?" I asked.

"Of course it all goes to acceleration; where else would it go?" he said. He was unable to heed my suggestion, but I could tell that Dr. Farid picked up on it.

"Okay, let us leave everything until the morning because we are all tired," I said. "But I believe that my question may contain the answer to our problem."

When I arrived the next morning I found Dr. Farid and Dr. Makee opening the centrifuge. We noticed a dark coloration on the lower side of the rotor, and Dr. Farid and I agreed that the coloration was due to excessive heat leaking out of the magnetic motor. As Mr. Sinan worked to fix the motor's frequency converter, I assigned Dr. Farid and my best engineers to attach components to a new rotor for a second trial run. Hussein Kamel turned up shortly afterwards, and I took him aside and said that although we had suffered a minor setback, we were confident of success.

Despite my assurances to my staff and Hussein Kamel, the apprehension I felt was taking a toll on my health. As we reconstructed the centrifuge, I felt lightheaded and dizzy at times, and I worried about a dark spot that had appeared on the skin of my upper left chest. The fist-sized purple stain perplexed me. It was as though the discoloration of the centrifuge rotor had somehow transferred itself to my own body. Not wanting to alarm my staff, I hid my symptoms as best I could. It was a different matter at home, however. Layla took one look at me and asked me to see a doctor. I am not a man who gives in easily to weakness, but I agreed. The doctor said the discoloration on my chest was due to high levels of stress, and he warned me that if I didn't take several days of rest, I might not survive. I reluctantly tried to relax at home by pruning fruit trees and hedging the lawn. After a few hours, however, I could think of nothing other than my engineers working on the new centrifuge prototype, and I hurried back to Rashdiya.

We were able to balance the new rotor without Schaab's magic touch. Nervously, we watched the speed of the new centrifuge climb beyond the 30,000 rpm mark. By late evening, we had increased it to 63,000 rpm, and everybody was hugging each other in triumph.

The next morning Hussein Kamel came to see the centrifuge working. When he entered the laboratory, he seemed surprised, evidently anticipating the high whistling sound that had come from the Beams oil version. The magnetic centrifuge spun silently in its vacuum.

"Is it working?" he asked.

"Yes, sir," I said, showing him the digital counter that read 63,000 rpm.

He laughed and said, "You bear responsibility for my guilt if it's not true," using an Iraqi expression of guarded appreciation.

Naturally, the next step was to attempt to enrich uranium. The success of the prototype in reaching critical speeds gave us confidence that our centrifuge would pass its ultimate test. It was like having manufactured an automobile and checked its motor in the factory. We were now ready to put the key in the ignition and test-drive it for the first time.

The trial run with radioactive material would be fraught with risks. We built a new centrifuge and installed the auxiliary equipment for feeding and extracting the uranium hexafluoride gas. After several weeks, in late June, a complex network of piping, valves, and controls surrounded the new centrifuge in a clean room walled off by a Plexiglas partition. I stood in the control room with my department heads, Dr. Adil, Dr. Farid, Dr. Abdul Fattah, and Dr. Faris, peering in at the floodlit system. Dr. Abdullah, who led the Physical Process

Department, scurried around in his white lab coat making last-minute checks of the feeding system. He seemed jittery, shouting commands to his assistants in a loud voice uncharacteristic of his normally subdued nature.

As I gave the order to start the centrifuge, the chatter among the technicians turned to whispers and you could have heard a pin drop as silence fell over the control room. The centrifuge ran as smoothly as the original prototype next door, and before long the counter registered the 60,000 rpm mark. Contained in a vacuum close to one billionth of an atmosphere, it whirred silently, like a good baby awaiting the feed of uranium hexafluoride.

My department heads kept looking at me as though I could alleviate some of their fears and I did my best to hold my composure, smiling at them to indicate that success was all but assured. But my heart pounded frantically against my ribs. My mind leapt to the oil refinery fires I had witnessed and the industrial accidents I had studied. They were nothing compared to the horror of a possible nuclear accident. The feeding system contained about two kilograms of uranium hexafluoride, and if the system burst or sprang a major leak, the corrosive gas could kill all of us in the room. The possibility was remote, but we were playing with the most destructive fire man has ever created. Our faces were as tight as death masks as we watched the brightly lit system. I looked around at my assembled technicians, all of them good men with families, suddenly feeling the weight of responsibility for their safety.

I nodded to Dr. Abdullah. He led the cryogenic end of the feed into the centrifuge, and the pressure instantly rose with a jerk, registering vibration on the recorder. Our hearts jerked with it, and I could feel the sweat pouring from my skin. But the pressure reached only a fraction of an atmosphere and then safely stabilized. As the uranium gas fed into the system, I felt every molecule moving through the veins of the complex piping as though it were my own circulatory system.

The streams of gas were under strict control, but any deviation would scrap all our efforts and possibly lead to disaster. I thought of the hairy mathematics my colleagues learned at the Imperial College of London and the knowledge we had gained from the hydrodynamics reports obtained abroad, and I felt comforted that we had mastered the required techniques. Sometimes the scientist must let intuition guide him into the unknown, and as the uranium hexafluoride circulated through the centrifuge, my intuition told me that our efforts would pass this test.

After several tense hours, Dr. Abdullah announced that all of the radioactive gas had successfully passed through the centrifuge into the extraction chamber. I ordered the centrifuge shut down, and a cheer went up among my staff. We were struck with such exhilaration that my department heads and I spontaneously embraced each other in the control room. Pumped up with adrenaline, we couldn't stop grinning, as though we had just reached a treacherous mountain summit.

We sent the enriched uranium hexafluoride to the IAEC for analysis, and when the results came in two days later, they confirmed our success. We had produced enriched uranium, a green light to proceeding with an industrial-scale plant.

When Hussein Kamel came to Rashdiya to congratulate us, his normally harsh face was softened with a gleeful smile that I had seen three times before: when I first described the possibilities of the centrifuge at the Republican Palace, at the premature success of the Beams oil centrifuge a few months later, and when we had produced a diffusion barrier.

"Slaughter ten head of sheep!" he commanded, as he had years earlier. He spent several minutes commending me and my department heads, and then, as was his habit, he quickly left the premises. Government chefs arrived and lit several large barbecues for an outdoor banquet of *tishrib* and other Iraqi delicacies for my entire staff. Ten sheep were brought into the courtyard of the Engineering Design Center. Following the traditional method, the chefs slit their throats with long knives and let the blood flow onto the ground. Some of my junior engineers wet their hands in the pools of blood and made red handprints on the walls of the centrifuge laboratory as a blessing.

We had good reason to feel proud. In less than three years, our staff of only two hundred talented men and women had progressed from almost total ignorance of centrifuge technology to the successful enrichment of uranium and to the verge of large-scale production. One key to our success was adaptability. We shifted our strategy when we found holes in our domestic infrastructure and pursued a parallel track of outsourcing the most delicate components. But we also had an extremely talented team of scientists and engineers who worked under the greatest motivating force known to man: fear for their lives and their families.

At Hussein Kamel's bidding, I ordered construction sped up at the al-Furat facility in Yusufiya, about thirty kilometers southwest of Baghdad, to complete the industrial framework needed to build a hundred centrifuges in a network called a cascade. A cascade links centrifuges together so that uranium hexafluoride passed through them in a series, becoming more highly enriched at each stage until it reaches the grade needed for a nuclear weapon.

The al-Furat facility was designed to incorporate three huge structures, with 33,000 square meters of space, along with smaller support buildings. One building was already complete, built by a German firm as a training center and workshop, in which we had installed the Schaublin machines to manufacture parts. Another building under construction would contain the H&H flow-forming machines to manufacture rotors. The third was designed by the German company Interatom with clean room facilities to house the piping workshop, an assembly room, and the centrifuge cascade hall. After I received the designs for the super-critical centrifuge from Schaab, I ordered changes in the cascade hall design to accommodate the more powerful three-meter centrifuge versions.

The idea of arming Saddam Hussein with nuclear weapons still seemed remote as my staff and I basked in the rare goodwill of Hussein Kamel. Although Saddam's government used the stick of intimidation to motivate its scientists, it also dangled carrots. About a week and a half after our successful test run with the prototype,

Hussein Kamel called with the news that Saddam had given us official commendations. Eight of my top engineers and I were awarded new cars, and the rest of my staff received various amounts of money. I went to a government lot and picked out a four-door Japanese sedan large enough to squeeze in my entire family. When I drove it home and parked it in our driveway, Layla and the children ran out of the house and made quite a fuss over it. On the spot I promised to take them on a vacation to the mountains of northern Iraq to escape Baghdad's punishing summer heat. I longed for a chance to get away and relax after three years of constant secrecy and worry, and especially to spend some precious days alone with my family. Hussein Kamel's demands had kept me from them for too long, and I resolved to spend more time at home in the future.

This was not to be, however.

A few weeks later, on the morning of August 3, 1990, I was eating breakfast with Layla in our kitchen when I turned on the TV and heard the shocking news from an Iraqi state broadcaster. Tens of thousands of Saddam's troops had swept into Kuwait during the night and overwhelmed local resistance, and they were already occupying Kuwait City, the capital of the tiny emirate. Iraqi fighter bombers attacked the airport and other targets, and many Kuwaitis were reportedly fleeing to neighboring Saudi Arabia. The invasion took the entire world by surprise.

Layla and I looked at each other in disbelief. For weeks Saddam had been accusing Kuwait of overproducing oil and driving down prices on the international market, as well as illegally drilling sideways across the border into the southern Iraqi oil field of Rumayla. But the possibility of a full-scale invasion, only two years after the war with Iran ended, had never crossed our minds. Perhaps because I had spent so much time abroad, I immediately sensed that Saddam's rash military strike would have serious repercussions, although it was too early to tell exactly what they would be.

The United Nations approved a series of resolutions condemning the invasion, and Security Council members threatened the use of military force if Saddam did not unconditionally withdraw from Kuwait by January 15, 1991. Suddenly the United States, the Soviet Union, and most European and Asian nations saw Iraq as a dangerous enemy, as did most of Iraq's neighbors. It was not hard to foresee the gathering battle.

Several days after the invasion, I received an unexpected visitor to my office in Rashdiya. I had seen little of Dr. Jaffar Dhia Jaffar since Hussein Kamel pulled me out of the IAEC in 1987. He had never set eyes on our facilities, and I knew only that Dr. Jaffar had overseen an electromagnetic enrichment program during the same years. I had only a vague notion of how his efforts had fared because Hussein Kamel kept us completely isolated from each other, perhaps to encourage a sense of competition between the two programs. It was indeed a surprise to see Dr. Jaffar walk through my door. I greeted him warmly, not only out of politeness, but also because I have always deeply respected him as a brilliant scientist. He asked about the progress of our centrifuge program. I suspected he already knew of our success, and that Hussein Kamel had sent him to open up an avenue of cooperation. We exchanged the gracious small talk that is customary to the beginning of any good Iraqi conversation, inquiring after each other's families and drinking a cup of tea together. Then he came to the point.

"We would like to use your centrifuges to enrich a limited amount of uranium from seventy to ninety-three percent," he said in his soft-spoken way.

I nodded as though this were a natural request between two scientists, even as I tried to gauge its implications. Apparently, the IAEC had not developed the ability to enrich uranium by any other method.

"Where would we get the seventy percent enriched uranium?" I asked, although I already guessed the answer.

"There are stores from the reactor," Dr. Jaffar said.

The reactor fuel had been lying dormant for years at Tuwaitha. But it fell under international monitoring as spelled out by the

Non-Proliferation Treaty, which Iraq had signed in 1968. Removing it for further enrichment would violate the treaty and would certainly be noticed by inspectors who, by international law, were to check on it once every four months. Such a step could mean only one thing: that Saddam was desperate for a nuclear weapon as soon as possible.

Dr. Jaffar did not mention the word "bomb," but his meaning was clear. To merit such a risk, the amount of highly enriched uranium must have been enough to build a single crude nuclear device. I had known Dr. Jaffar for nearly a quarter of a century. I knew his fine upbringing as the son of a minister in the former kingdom of Iraq and as a doctor of physics in Birmingham, England. And what I saw in his face was a disturbingly perplexed look. His intelligent eyes revealed his misgivings. I felt a deep sense of empathy with him at that moment. He had the appearance of a besieged man unable to pry Saddam's fingers from around his neck. I thought about how he had been put in confinement in the late 1970s. Although implied threats hung over all of Saddam's nuclear scientists, Dr. Jaffar had lived through the terrifying reality.

We exchanged a look that communicated the gravity of the request, as well as a shared sense of helplessness. Here were two scientists, powerful enough to give Saddam Hussein a nuclear weapon, sharing a moment of doubt. Yet we could not dare to act on our doubts, or even to speak up and give them a name.

"I would need to build at least fifty centrifuges," I said.

"Do whatever you need to do," Dr. Jaffar said. "I'm certain that Hussein Kamel will provide any extra funds you need, and I will assist you however I can."

The benevolence Hussein Kamel had shown after our successful test instantly evaporated under the strain of the crash program to build a bomb. He began frequent visits to Rashdiya again, demanding instantaneous results. He ordered me and my staff to stop further testing of prototypes and direct all our efforts toward a scaled-down uranium production facility. We would focus on the concepts and designs for a fifty-centrifuge cascade within our compound at Rashdiya.

I made an inventory of our parts and equipment, most of which had been manufactured abroad. Because I had planned to refine the centrifuge in prototypes before moving into the industrial phase at al-Furat, we already had fifty of many crucial pieces in hand. We probably had enough magnets from Treibacher, I figured, as long as no malfunctions damaged them. However, the invasion of Kuwait put an end to cooperation from companies in Germany, Switzerland, Great Britain, and elsewhere, which meant we had to manufacture missing parts ourselves. We possessed only about twenty carbon-fiber rotor tubes from Schaab, and the carbon-winding machine with which we could try to manufacture more had not yet arrived. I dispatched Mr. Ali and Dr. Ridha Fatlawi to Singapore to get a new letter of credit for the machine from a bank still doing business with Iraq.

They arranged for a rush shipment through Jordan, but in the meantime, our only other option was to try manufacturing tubes out of maraging steel and then use a combination of steel- and carbon-fiber rotors. I had sent Dr. Adil on a two-week training course with flow-forming machines at H&H Metalform, and now he was faced with the task of trying to manufacture rotor tubes. It was a formidable job that required precision down to the level of one micron, or twenty-five times smaller than the smallest particle visible to the naked eye. As for the carbon-winding machine, it would not arrive in Jordan until after the war had ended and our program was shelved. The machine sat in a Jordanian warehouse until weapons inspectors found it.

For now, we had incomplete numbers of other critical components, such as the molecular pump to create a vacuum in the system, the outer centrifuge jacket, and the motor casing. If we had ten brass connecting pieces, we needed forty more. The cup for the ball bearing alone consists of ten separate pieces; we had more than fifty of some and too few of others. Hussein Kamel outsourced the manufacture of missing parts to some of Dr. Jaffar's engineers, allowing me and my staff to dedicate ourselves to the cascade design and coordination of the whole crash centrifuge project. I sent a team of our engineers to discuss with Dr. Jaffar's group the use of the Schaublin milling and turning machines. But it was difficult. We had relied on foreign expertise and manufactured many of the sensitive parts in European workshops. Now we were on our own, trying to transfer recently acquired machining skills to engineers unfamiliar with our program. Many of the parts required precision down to two microns, and as with Dr. Adil's attempts to flow-form tubes, engineering enters a different world at this level. Conditions must remain tightly controlled in an environment where the body heat of a single person entering the room can raise the temperature enough to alter the machining. In October I sent Dr. Farid to visit our counterparts in Dr. Jaffar's group, and he returned with the opinion that it would take them many months to master the technology and properly manufacture the most difficult components.

At Rashdiya, Hussein Kamel's security men made their intimidating presence felt as we put up a new structure and built a cascade hall. We designed a meter-thick cement wall, about chest height, down the center of the room, with twenty-five evenly spaced alcoves on each side to hold mounted centrifuges. The structure, designed to completely eliminate vibration, was sometimes referred to as a pissoir, because it was reminiscent of a double-sided wall of urinals. As we had with the prototype centrifuge, we sealed the cascade block in a clean room. An adjacent control deck would give us a view over both the cascade hall and the feeding and extraction apparatus through thick windows.

Our main task was designing the flow of the cascade, which is quite a different science from the creation of a single centrifuge. For weeks we calculated how many kilograms of uranium hexafluoride should enter the cascade, and at what rate, given the amount in each centrifuge at any given time. The complex mathematical formulae led to the conclusion that the fifty-centrifuge cascade, if ever completed, could turn 70 percent enriched uranium into the 93 percent needed for a weapon in a few months.

On November 8, 1990, the United States announced preparations for an offensive against Iraq called Operation Desert Storm, which would be triggered if Saddam failed to meet the January 15 deadline. Hundreds of thousands of troops from more than thirty-five nations began landing in Saudi Arabia, where they took up attack positions along the borders with Kuwait and Iraq. Although I was forced to spend many long stretches at Rashdiya, I returned home at night as often as I could to be with my worried family. As Arab neighbors lined up against Iraq and the threats of an American-led invasion increased, Layla and I had many agonizing late-night conversations about the possibility of war.

What, I asked myself, was Saddam's endgame? The crash program showed his desperation for a single atomic weapon, a crude bomb. But in the face of the overwhelming force of nearly the entire world, what could he be thinking? In the absence of any obvious answer, I tried basic scientific reasoning. There are only two uses for any weapon: offensive or defensive. If the intended use was offensive, Saddam might want to use a nuclear weapon directly against one of the nations threatening to invade. But this would require the long-range means to deliver the payload, which he lacked. His only other offensive option was to launch a nuclear strike against a nearby country. The obvious target would be Israel, perhaps in an attempt to rally Arab nations behind him. But with a vast nuclear arsenal of its own, Israel would surely retaliate with an annihilating counterattack.

The defensive strategy made more sense, if Saddam wanted a nuclear weapon as a deterrent to an invasion. But if he truly felt that a nuclear weapon would serve as a deterrent, the only logical course of action would be to delay a confrontation until he had one. His refusal to budge showed that Iraq was in the grip of a delusional leader who lacked any long-term strategic thinking.

In any case, what was one bomb against the might of the rest of the world? A small fraction of the nuclear weapons possessed by the United States could turn Baghdad, or for that matter the whole of Iraq, into a wasteland in seconds. The very idea of using a crude bomb in the face of such devastating capability was insane. Horrific images came to mind of my fellow countrymen being incinerated in their homes in a nuclear counterstrike.

Thankfully, the world will never know what Saddam might have done with a nuclear bomb. By December of 1990, as the crisis over Kuwait was coming to a head, I knew that we were still many months away from producing enough material for a weapon. I gathered that Dr. Khalid Ibrahim Sa'id had made advances in building an actual explosive device but was far from ready to turn highly enriched uranium into a bomb. Another obstacle was the production of uranium hexafluoride. Although this was a far easier task than building a centrifuge, we had turned the job over to a team from the IAEC, and they were having trouble converting the reactor fuel into the dangerous and highly radioactive gas. This fact was later a source of puzzlement to UN weapons inspectors. During the 1990s they repeatedly asked whether we had produced large amounts of uranium hexafluoride. They felt that our success in building a centrifuge would indicate that we had the ability to produce any amount of raw fuel we desired, since it was an easier task. They couldn't understand that our resources were limited, and that for years I had put the vast majority of them into overcoming the more challenging problem of the centrifuge itself.

By late December, we had nearly completed the construction of our cascade hall. What we still lacked were key components to assemble fifty centrifuges. After many failures, Dr. Adil had succeeded in flow-forming a single perfect rotor tube from maraging steel, and perhaps could have produced more if time had allowed. Although Dr. Jaffar's team still had not produced the missing parts, the cascade was within reach. But it was doomed by the impossible time limit.

In the days before the January 15 deadline to withdraw from Kuwait, it seemed ludicrous that Saddam would violate international demands in the face of invasion. He shrugged off the ultimatum, however, and sealed the fate of everyone in Iraq for many years to come. On January 15 Baghdad was like a ghost town as everyone waited for the storm to hit. It began the following morning at around 2 A.M. with a bombing blitz that shook Baghdad awake.

My initial orders from Hussein Kamel were to stay at the

Engineering Design Center with my top staff twenty-four hours a day during the bombing. The order seemed cruel, and nothing more than a forced show of solidarity with Saddam's regime. During the next few weeks, foreign bombers attacked government facilities, including the nuclear sites of Tuwaitha; Dr. Jaffar's EMIS facilities at Tarmiya and Baiji, and Dr. Sa'id's facility at al-Atheer. We had gone to great lengths to keep our compound secret, but there was no way to know how much foreign intelligence agencies might have learned about our program at Rashdiya. We cleared out a row of shacks on the western end of the facility that had been used by maintenance and security crews. We slept on cots, dormitory style, terrified that Rashdiya would be hit and that the last thing we would hear in this life would be the whistle of an incoming bomb.

On the third day of the attack, Hussein Kamel came with orders to temporarily dismantle the entire centrifuge facility. During the following days, my staff and I carefully disassembled the rotors from their components and took apart the key pieces of the uranium hexafluoride system and turned them over to the Special Security Organization, which rushed around stashing them in suburban buildings and rural farmhouses. Besides the equipment installed in the cascade hall and the prototype laboratories, we emptied a six-thousand-square-meter warehouse with hundreds of tons of stockpiled equipment. I watched the skies, sure that the movement would be spotted by Western satellites or spy planes. About 150 trucks came and went from Rashdiya, carting off boxes of components and raw materials to hiding places. The security services took the heavy ingots of maraging steel and buried them in the farming area of Taji north of Baghdad. They evacuated the European machines and tools from al-Furat and other workshops. They collected about one hundred boxes of documents to be squirreled away for later use.

On one of my final sweeps through the administration building, I stopped in my office to collect my copy of the centrifuge designs, which I had decided to take home for safekeeping. I also collected prototypes of four components sitting on a shelf in my office: the ball bearing, the motor, the magnetic upper bearing, and the bellows for the super-critical centrifuge. I packed these valuable items in cardboard boxes along with more than two hundred reports that explained in detail how to build every piece of the centrifuge. The reports included design notes translated into Arabic as well as the technical specifications for making them. At the time I thought little of my decision to take these things home. It seemed natural to want to avoid their loss or destruction. They represented years of hard work and learning, and I regarded them with the same pride that a novelist must feel about an original manuscript. Had I known then the trouble they would cause me, I might have thought differently. Instead, I put the boxes in the trunk of my car, drove them home, and stored them in my garage for the time being.

The coalition of foreign armies launched its land offensive the night of February 23, with a three-pronged invasion of Kuwait and southwestern Iraq that quickly encircled Iraqi troops in and around the occupied kingdom. The crushing assault killed tens of thousands of Iraqi soldiers. Thousands more surrendered and many deserted. Within two days, Saddam announced a withdrawal from Kuwait. In a senseless campaign of vandalism, many of his troops followed orders to sabotage Kuwaiti infrastructure and industry as they retreated. They set dozens of oil wells on fire, creating massive oil spills and poisoning the air with thick black smoke. The cloud reached all the way to Baghdad, and the acrid fumes filled my nostrils.

Unwilling to risk alienating Arab members of the coalition, the United States and its allies backed off from threats to fully invade Iraq and depose Saddam. One hundred hours after the invasion began, a cease-fire was declared.

Perhaps emboldened by the vague terms of the cease-fire, Saddam ordered an immediate resumption of the centrifuge program. Hussein Kamel became as furious as I've ever seen him, urging us to redouble our efforts to produce enough enriched uranium for a nuclear weapon as soon as possible. My staff and I worked around the clock, as the Special Security Organization (SSO) brought equipment back from their hiding places. We took the first steps toward rebuilding the clean rooms and reassembling everything as it had been weeks earlier. Within several weeks, however, I could see the writing on the wall. The United Nations was setting out terms for a permanent truce that included disarming Iraq of its weapons of mass destruction. On April 2, 1991, the Security Council made strict demands: Iraq would have to accept liability for damages and pay reparations to Kuwait, destroy its chemical and biological weapons and ballistic missiles, and discontinue all nuclear weapons programs. Under threat of renewed military action, four days later, Saddam agreed to allow international weapons inspectors into Iraq.

Hussein Kamel ordered us to once again dismantle everything at Rashdiya, and then to disguise the entire facility. We removed the clean room and piping, plastered over the walls of the centrifuge laboratory, and modified a number of the structures. We poured a new concrete floor to disguise the pits designed for centrifuge stands. We cleared our offices of all incriminating documents, and set up drafting tables and materials that would suggest engineering work on water treatment projects.

I later heard that the SSO in charge of hiding materials had been given a strange order: to gather enough material for one hundred centrifuges and stash them separately. What was bizarre about this order was that my staff and I were not involved in selecting the material. It was a hopeless task for the largely uneducated security men. As it was we didn't have enough materials for even fifty complete centrifuges. It seemed a quixotic idea, ill-conceived in the midst of chaos.

Hussein Kamel ordered us to turn over to the security services all remaining designs, documents, spare parts, and prototypes we had in our possession. Many of my engineers had blueprints for the parts for which they were responsible, and they spent hours dumping their work into containers, like convicts handing over their personal belongings at the prison gates. I told Hussein Kamel I needed to drive home to collect my complete set and the components.

"A complete set?" he asked. "You have one at your home?"

"Yes," I said. "I took them there during the bombing, along with several prototype pieces."

He paused for a moment, mulling over some private thought.

"No," he said. "Keep them for now, until I tell you otherwise."

I couldn't tell what he had in mind, but it left me feeling uneasy. Whereas my junior engineers and staff left Rashdiya that day with nothing more than the knowledge in their heads, I possessed physical evidence that might someday become an issue with weapons inspectors and could bind me more closely to Hussein Kamel and Saddam. My misgivings were not fully formed at that moment, but I began to wish I had never brought the designs and components home.

CHAPTER 7

Nuclear Hide-and-Seek

"Tomorrow, you will be presented to inspectors from the International Atomic Energy Agency," said Dr. Humam Abdul al-Khalek Ghaffour. "So tell me, how have you enjoyed your years working at the Ministry of Industry?"

Dr. Humam smiled ironically from the other side of his director general's desk at the IAEC, as he coached me on my official cover story. It was the fall of 1991, nearly six months after the UN sent its first team of weapons inspectors to Iraq. Saddam's strategy to thwart them had locked me into a key role in the concealment effort. The centrifuge was considered the jewel in the crown of the WMD programs, to be hidden above all else. The officials directing Iraq's WMD concealment must have believed it would be easier to restart the centrifuge program if I were not compromised. I was its creator and the only person who knew intimately its every detail. So they treated me as an asset, a thing to be buried out of sight along with the materials, facilities, and designs.

Dr. Humam had concocted a story that I resigned from the IAEC in 1987 after a quarrel with Dr. Jaffar, and afterwards was moved to the Ministry of Industry. For several hours he cross-examined me on this tale, pacing back and forth behind his desk in the style of a courtroom attorney. Then he asked me to make up a list of questions I imagined inspectors might ask me.

The next morning a government chauffeur drove me to the IAEC headquarters. I dreaded the thought of meeting inspectors. They must have had an idea about who I was from their intelligence sources, because they had repeatedly asked to speak to me by name. I feared they would easily see through my story.

Two inspectors rose from their chairs when I walked into a small meeting room: an American whose name I do not recall and a Greek inspector, Dimitri Perricos, who was one of the IAEA Action Team leaders. I shook hands with the inspectors and nervously took a seat at the conference table. Three of my Iraqi colleagues from the IAEC sat opposite them. I gathered they had been interviewed before me.

The American asked most of the questions. He seemed quiet and understanding, while Perricos looked at me cynically throughout the interview. The American asked general questions about the period leading to the year 1987, and I was able to describe my work in the early stages of the diffusion program in a way that fit the truth perfectly. Then Perricos intervened to ask about the centrifuge program. I denied any relation to it.

"Oh, come off it, Dr. Mahdi," Perricos said. "We know better than that. What did you do after 1987?"

"I left for the Ministry of Industry," I said.

"Really, an important person like you?" he asked, baiting me. "How could the IAEC let you go?"

I fumbled for an answer. Perricos obviously knew something. For a few embarrassing moments I drew a blank on the words Dr. Humam had coached me on the day before. Dr. Abdul Halim al-Hajjaj, whom Dr. Humam had appointed as nuclear liaison to the inspector, came to my rescue.

"Dr. Mahdi came to a stalemate with Dr. Jaffar," he said. "Dr. Mahdi didn't think Iraq possessed the infrastructure for an extensive diffusion program, and the only way to resolve the differ-ences of opinion was to transfer him. So he went to the Ministry of Industry."

There was at least a small element of truth in this, but the cover story did not go over well with Perricos.

"Ha!" he scoffed. "This is simply not credible!"

He turned from Dr. Abdul Halim and looked me in the eye.

"Do you expect me to believe this story?"

I felt the urge to confront Perricos for lashing at me with his cynicism. I am a scientist, I wanted to tell him, and I respected the truth as much as he did. Didn't he know that I was speaking words forced out by the hands around my neck? Would he have the courage to speak the truth if he were in my position, and risk the lives of his family? Couldn't he understand the dilemma I was in? Of course, I held my tongue and finished the interview, fulfilling my duty to Saddam's committee. When the inspectors finally dismissed me, I felt tired and deeply humiliated.

I arrived home after that interview and collapsed on the sofa. Drained of all my energy, I gloomily pondered the meaning of my being hidden away. Where did that leave me, a man who had begun his career hoping only to take part in building a great nation? Would I spend the rest of my life as a mere tool in the hands of those who placed no value on human individuality? I thought of the fates of Dr. al-Shahrastani, who was imprisoned during the reactor program, and Dr. Jaffar, who was confined during the same period. How could a nation ever hope to achieve greatness by suppressing its top-caliber people?

Layla brought me a glass of tea, and I told her about my interrogation.

"You look terrible," she said.

"I've been lying all day about who I am," I said, trying to make a joke of the matter. "So I don't quite feel like myself."

After the 1991 war, Saddam dispersed most of the top scientists from Iraq's nuclear program into positions in state-run industries. I was made director general of a company called General Establishment of Engineering Technologies (GEET), based out of our converted offices at Rashdiya, which carried out industrial projects for the MIC. The government kept scientists away from inspectors as much as possible. To deal with the UN teams, Saddam had set up an Oversight Committee soon after accepting the terms of the truce. Deputy Prime Minister Tariq Aziz chaired this committee, which included Saddam's son Qusay as well as the head of the presidential Diwan, and others on an as-needed basis. The committee made the IAEC Director, Dr. Humam, the front man for questions regarding the nuclear program, with the assistance of Dr. Jaffar. In the early rounds of inspections during the spring of 1991, Dr. Humam revealed only that Iraq had tried to enrich uranium using Dr. Jaffar's electromagnetic isotope separation (EMIS) technique. He claimed that Iraq was researching how to enrich fuel for a possible nuclear power program in the future. For years Iraq would deny that the purpose of the nuclear program was to produce weapons. The inspectors were extremely skeptical, however, and they demanded more answers.

By the summer of 1991, several months before my interview with Perricos, the IAEA Action Team had gotten wind of the Iraqi centrifuge and diffusion programs, possibly through intelligence provided by UN member states. Dr. Humam conceded the existence of these programs. But he said that the centrifuge and diffusion techniques had reached only the investigative stages. When the inspectors asked who had led the centrifuge program, the Oversight Committee put forward Dr. Faris, the former head of our Engineering Support Department.

I remember the first time the committee ordered Dr. Faris to give a lecture about the Iraqi centrifuge to half a dozen inspectors. The presentation began at 4 P.M. in a hotel in downtown Baghdad. I slipped unnoticed into the auditorium just after it began and sat in the back row to listen. The inspectors took notes diligently as Dr. Faris presented an impressive slide show offering an overview of the program, in which there was not a shred of falsehood. But there were plenty of omissions. He neglected to mention the crash program to build fifty centrifuges in the months before the war, and the fact that we had design drawings for a much larger, three-meter centrifuge that would have dramatically increased our output of enriched uranium. He completely avoided the subject of procurement, and the assistance we had received from abroad. At one point, Dr. Faris peered into the back of the auditorium and I thought he might have recognized me in the semidarkness, because he quickly looked down at his notes again. I made an early exit before the lights came up.

The fourth round of inspections in the summer of 1991 marked the arrival of Dr. David Kay and a difficult period for Saddam's concealment effort. A native Texan, Dr. Kay had a brash, confrontational style. He rode around Iraq, acting like a cowboy on a big horse, and over time all the scientists became afraid he would expose their former work and land them in trouble.

The night before his plane touched down in Baghdad on one of his first missions, I attended a strategy meeting for Iraq's top nuclear scientists at the IAEC administrative building next to Firdos Square. Dr. Khalid Ibrahim Sa'id, who had led the bomb-making effort, called the meeting to order. He stressed, among other things, the need to hide our documents and procurement receipts. I assured him that all the paperwork from the centrifuge program had been collected by the security services. The irony is that some of Dr. Sa'id's own paperwork was still in that very building and had not been properly hidden. When Dr. Kay arrived the following morning, one of the first things he did was show up there. He barged in on members of Dr. Sa'id's staff packing up the last documents, snatched a couple of boxes, and attempted to leave with them. Alarmed, Dr. Sa'id's employees called security, which blocked Dr. Kay's exit from the premises and kept him penned up in the parking lot. A remarkable standoff ensued.

For three days, Dr. Kay refused to hand over the documents, and for three days the Iraqi security forces refused to allow him to leave the IAEC building with them. Dr. Kay made the most of the dramatic situation, giving interviews to journalists from the parking lot. As the impasse grabbed headlines around the world, pressure from the

UN and foreign governments mounted on Saddam's regime until Iraqi officials finally negotiated a compromise to let Dr. Kay leave with many of the documents. They included bundles of pay stubs that gave weapons inspectors a broad overview of the IAEC structure and names of employees. Saddam punished Dr. Sa'id lightly with only a demotion, but threw several of his underlings into prison for the foul-up. The centrifuge program avoided exposure because we had been separated financially and otherwise from the IAEC since 1987.

The inspectors made other high-profile inroads during those early months. They discovered Dr. Jaffar's electromagnetic isotope separation facility, which forced the disclosure of almost the whole EMIS program. They also demanded to see the equipment for the diffusion and centrifuge techniques. The Oversight Committee handed over much of it, including the carbon-fiber rotors. The inspectors laid them out on the ground and smashed them into pieces with their feet.

In a preemptive move, Saddam sent out a much-publicized memo to unilaterally destroy all materials related to weapons of mass destruction programs. The Special Security Organization (SSO) brought tons of equipment from all the programs and documented their destruction or handed them over to inspectors. They dug nearly one hundred tons of maraging steel out of the ground at Taji, melted it down, and mixed it with inferior metals to make it unusable for weapons purposes. They gave inspectors hundreds of tons of other centrifuge equipment, such as vacuum pumps, aluminum valves, and magnets.

Faced with evidence presented by inspectors, the Oversight Committee divulged the planned centrifuge plant at al-Furat, which exposed the ambitions of the program. Work on the buildings there had progressed nicely until the outbreak of the war, including a cavernous hall with centrifuge pits for large-scale production. Although little equipment had been installed yet, the facility was an awesome sight. I later heard that David Kay told the U.S. Congress that, in terms of nuclear facilities, he had never seen anything finer outside the Western Hemisphere. I admit that hearing this stirred my sense of pride, even as the inspectors went about nullifying our years of work.

The Oversight Committee stuck to the story that design and testing of the centrifuge program had taken place at Tuwaitha. The strategy was to keep the Engineering Design Center at Rashdiya a secret, in order to conceal the extent of our progress. The line fed to inspectors was that the grand plans for al-Furat had been a pipe dream. But they obviously suspected otherwise.

Four white Nissan sport utility vehicles pulled into the driveway of the Rashdiya facility without warning early one afternoon in December 1991. I was in my office working on a project to renovate a brass factory, which had been put on hold before the war. Through my office window I saw about a dozen very non-Iraqi-looking men and women step out of their vehicles wearing khaki pants and short-sleeved shirts and carrying clipboards and knapsacks.

I instinctively cast my mind around the entire facility, making a mental check. We had completely transformed it. The network of piping had been removed along with the clean room, the observation deck, and all of the equipment related to the centrifuge program. I had ordered the plastering over of holes, repainting, and the installation of a new floor. Drafting tables and a few machines for the brass factory project belied the former nature of the place. We had cleared our offices of every incriminating document. I reassured myself that a team of inspectors had made a brief visit to the facility the past summer and found nothing. But their decision to return for a surprise visit nearly six months later was troubling.

A knock on the front door downstairs jolted me into a realization. The one telltale sign of the previous use of the facility was the presence of me and Dr. Farid. I raced out of my office and shouted down the hall in the direction of his door.

"The inspectors are here! Come quickly or we will be discovered!"

We flew down the stairs and found two of my engineers near the entrance, unsure of what to do. They looked at me expectantly as the knocking continued.

"Don't let them in," I whispered. "Stall them for a few minutes."

We ran to a back room that had a door opening onto the western side of the facility, putting the administration building between ourselves and the inspectors. Once outside, Dr. Farid and I clambered up an embankment onto a single-lane road that overlooked our compound on one side and the Tigris River on the other. I could see the four UN vehicles in the parking lot but no inspectors, so I assumed they had been let inside. We hurried along the road on the ridge of the dam, not daring to look back in case the inspectors could see us through a window. Two well-dressed scientists walking quickly along the road away from the facility would have seemed a little out of place in that rural setting. After about a hundred yards, a bend in the road and some foliage blocked us from the compound's view. I figured we had made a clean getaway, and we slowed our pace, perspiring heavily despite the cool weather.

We walked along a row of date palm trees for about an hour, discussing the possible reasons the inspectors had come for a second inspection. They must have received some form of intelligence, but it was impossible to tell whether they had been tipped off by a person, images from spy satellites, or some other source. One of the engineers at the compound was well briefed on the official story to tell the inspectors, but I couldn't guess what new information the inspectors might confront him with. After an hour, unable to stand the suspense, I walked back along the road toward our compound. As I drew near, I dropped down to an agricultural field to approach the facility from the north. I tiptoed through the soft mud and crouched behind a low wall overlooking the driveway. The UN vehicles were still parked in front. I waited for two hours, peering over the wall at intervals, until the door opened and I heard voices speaking English. I ducked down and listened for the sound of the inspectors driving off. When they had gone, I hopped over the wall and went inside.

My staff informed me that everything had gone well at first. The inspectors had looked around and listened respectfully as the head engineer fed them the story that the facility was dedicated to water treatment and industrial projects and denied that any nuclear-related work had ever taken place there. But then the inspectors took samples from the walls of several buildings and the soil outside them. That was bad news. I knew the samples from the former centrifuge building would test positive for abnormally high traces of radioactive uranium. The orders from the Oversight Committee had been unequivocal. We were to disguise past nuclear work at the Rashdiya site.

I figured it would take at least a week for the inspectors to analyze the sample, after which they would certainly return to take further samples to prove their case. We had to act quickly. If the inspectors returned and dug deeply enough, uranium particles would be found in every shred of material present during our centrifuge work.

The same afternoon, I called a staff meeting and ordered the former centrifuge laboratory stripped of its walls and roof, right down to its frame, as well as the excavation of a foot and a half of topsoil from underneath and around the building, extending a hundred feet on the downwind side where traces of uranium might have blown.

"Within a week," I said, as if it were no big task, "we will fill in the hole with fresh soil and build an exact replica of the facility out of new materials."

My subordinates looked at me aghast, because the order seemed impossible. But they quickly realized the only other option would be to take responsibility for breaching the concealment plan. The consequences for our lives and those of our families didn't bear thinking about. My staff furiously set to work, bringing in crews and equipment day and night. It was probably one of history's fastest demolition and construction projects. I stayed on-site for seven days, worried that the inspectors might return to catch us at it, putting the regime in an uncomfortable position indeed.

When the inspectors returned unannounced about two weeks later, everything appeared as they had last seen it, down to the placement of the drafting tables and machines and the coffeemaker. I stayed away, but my staff later told me the inspectors had arrived with a triumphant and slightly accusatory attitude. They took dozens of samples from the walls, floor, insulation, and ground soil, and then left to send them to Vienna for confirmation. They must have been truly puzzled when the material later tested negative for abnormal uranium levels. I imagine they remain puzzled about it to this day.

I returned my attention to the brass scrap factory project until an unseasonably warm morning in February 1992, when I received an order to report to Qusay Hussein on the remaining potential of the centrifuge program. It surprised me that Qusay wanted a briefing independent from Hussein Kamel. No doubt there were political maneuverings within Saddam's vicious inner circle, where knowledge and the ability to advise the dictator were the keys to power.

Qusay was in his early twenties then and had not yet acquired the reputation for depravity of his older brother Uday, whose taste for drunken parties, firearms, and rape was already infamous in Iraq. Qusay was seen as more quietly sinister than his flamboyant older brother, and Saddam was already grooming him for a larger role in the regime. The idea of meeting him privately made me nervous because the entire family was temperamental, poorly educated, and well-known for throwing people in prison when they didn't get the answers they wanted. I had briefly met Qusay before at a meeting of the Oversight Committee. I thought of him as a young snake, still unsure of his power but with a potent venom that could kill instantly.

I drove to a rendezvous point near the Republican Palace, where a special security officer picked me up in a four-door pickup truck with tinted windows and chauffeured me onto the palace grounds. The officer led me to a one-story building, frisked me, and then waited outside the door as I entered. Qusay sat alone on an L-shaped sofa wearing a well-tailored suit. He motioned me to sit opposite him, without standing up or offering his hand in greeting. His soft face, dull eyes, and impatient demeanor spoke of a spoiled child who had never been denied anything in his life. We sat in silence for a few moments while he studied me, using a theatrical trick borrowed from his father. He dispensed with the polite banter that usually opens a conversation between two Iraqis and went directly to the issue at hand.

"Tell me what remains of the centrifuge program," he said.

I summarized what he already knew from his position on the Oversight Committee: the prototypes of the centrifuges had been handed over to the inspectors, who had smashed the carbon fiber tubes on the spot and taken the rest to the IAEA headquarters in Vienna for study. As far as I knew, most of the components, raw materials, and machines to produce them had been destroyed or were in the hands of inspectors. So far, the UN was unaware of many of the European companies that had manufactured components and of the identities of all of the German scientists who assisted us.

"Is that all?" he asked.

I told Qusay that I had a personal copy of the complete set of designs for each part of the centrifuge, along with a few of the most important components. Qusay took out a pen and notepad and scribbled a few notes as I described them.

"What about these documents?" he asked. "How important are they?"

"They are the instruction book," I said, "and more important even than the components."

"Who else has these documents? Some of your colleagues?"

His question revealed how amazingly little he had been involved, at least so far, in the details of the concealment effort. I explained that all other centrifuge blueprints and other papers had been turned over to the Iraqi security services the year before.

"Who else knows about the copies in your possession?" he asked.

"As far as I know, only Hussein Kamel," I said.

"Keep them out of sight," he said.

Qusay's face betrayed nothing of what he was thinking at that moment. I worried that I might find myself caught in the middle of a power struggle between Saddam's son and his son-in-law. Qusay did not have to tell me not to mention our conversation to Hussein Kamel. In the atmosphere of deception that surrounded Saddam's inner circle, everything was confidential unless stated otherwise. Opening one's mouth could only lead to trouble.

"Will we be able to begin the program again?" Qusay asked, interrupting my thoughts.

Again I was startled at such an inappropriate question. The country was crawling with weapons inspectors, whose sole purpose was to prevent Iraq from restarting its WMD programs. It reminded me of the simplistic question his father had asked me about the diffusion barrier several years earlier.

"That depends on the developments to come," I said, choosing my words carefully, "and, of course, on your orders."

Qusay made a few more notes and dismissed me. I considered the significance of our encounter as the security officer drove me back to my car. Qusay was certainly becoming more involved in his father's intelligence and security operations. And he had specific ambitions. The only conclusion was that, however vague and impractical, the long-term intention was to wait out the inspections process and try to build a bomb later, when the world was no longer watching.

I drove home thinking that I must find a safer place to stow my cache, somewhere no one would ever look. Then it occurred to me to bury them. Men have hidden their treasures underground since the beginning of history. After I parked my car in our garage, I went straight to my toolshed and found a fifty-gallon green plastic barrel. It was the perfect size, and with its lid fastened tightly it would protect the papers and delicate components from moisture in the soil. I went inside the house to check the whereabouts of my wife and children. I had decided not to tell them what I was about to do, because knowing what was buried in our garden would only cause them worry, and possibly even put them in danger. My son Zaid was out. Layla and the girls were busy indoors.

"I'm going to do a bit of gardening," I called to Layla as I made my way to the front door.

"It's the middle of the afternoon," she said. "Why don't you wait until it cools down?"

"I just want to do a bit of pruning," I said. "It won't take long. If anyone calls for me, just take a message."

I looked back and saw Layla standing in the kitchen doorway with a quizzical expression on her face. She saw that I was behaving strangely, but said nothing more. She knew that whenever I felt under pressure, I liked to unwind by working in our garden. Once outside, I took the plastic drum and a shovel into our outer yard, which was hidden from our house by a brick wall. The sun beat down fiercely, as I cast about for a discreet location. In the shade of a lotus tree, I found a soft spot in the earth and dug a hole about four feet deep. I wrapped the components and the two-foot-tall stack of centrifuge documents in separate plastic trash bags to further protect them. Then I packed everything in the plastic drum, sealed it tightly, and lowered it into the hole. As I shoveled dirt over the barrel, I felt strangely sentimental, almost as though I were burying a favorite pet that had died. The centrifuge program, which I had conceived and directed, was now reduced to an underground plot in my backyard. When I finished, I leaned exhaustedly on my shovel, realizing that I had buried a part of myself with those designs. I was the only person who knew exactly where they were. It was to be the only secret I have ever kept from Layla, my wife and my best friend. But it was a burden I knew I had to bear alone, for her safety and for the protection of our children. If Saddam's intelligence services wanted to find the keys to the nuclear program, the path led to a lotus tree a few steps from our bedrooms.

Even then I had a hunch that these secrets would not rest in peace, and that they would one day be resurrected under circumstances beyond my control. During the coming years, nightmares plagued my sleep. I often dreamt of Saddam's security men coming to my home to demand the centrifuge documents. In this recurring nightmare I would lead them into my garden to the *lote* tree. But every time, when I tried to point out the place where I had buried the plastic drum, there was nothing but an empty hole.

Throughout the years of weapons inspections in Iraq, a joke was often told on the streets of Baghdad. It involved a popular Iraqi dish known as *dulaymia*, in which pieces of lamb are covered by a mountain of rice and then baked so that the rice absorbs the meat juice. The joke went like this: One day, the weapons inspectors order *dulaymia* for lunch at a restaurant. Aiming to please, the owner places a heaping platter in front of them. Later, when he asks if they've enjoyed the meal, they apologize for not finishing the dish, saying they are full.

"That was delicious rice," says one inspector.

"And how did you enjoy the meat?" the owner asks.

"The meat?" the inspectors ask in surprise. "We didn't know there was any meat."

The owner scolds them: "But you haven't looked underneath the rice! If you want to find the meat, you have to dig deep!"

No one could appreciate this joke on quite the same level as I, who had buried the centrifuge secrets with his own shovel. But although it provoked many laughs at the inspectors' expense in the cafes and on the street corners of Baghdad, the joke poorly reflected reality. Most of the inspectors were competent professionals who worked methodically and, slowly but surely, eventually discovered and dismantled Iraq's nuclear capabilities.

In mid-1991 evidence provided by inspectors compelled the Oversight Committee to divulge the al-Atheer facility in the sleepy town of Musayyib, forty miles south of Baghdad, where Dr. Sa'id had directed the weaponization effort. The telltale equipment and design of the buildings finally gave inspectors what they felt was proof that Iraq had attempted to enrich uranium for bombs, not future reactors. When Dr. Kay's team confronted the Oversight Committee with this conclusion, it flatly denied the weapons program without offering any other credible explanation. In April 1992 the inspectors demanded the destruction of all eight buildings at al-Atheer unless Iraq provided better answers. Saddam still wouldn't budge. Rather than concede his intentions to produce nuclear weapons, he granted permission to destroy al-Atheer. As international monitors looked on, Iraqi crews dynamited the structures and bulldozed the foundations into the ground.

The inspectors persisted. They destroyed two of Dr. Jaffar's EMIS facilities, disabled the other sites used in the nuclear program, and installed surveillance cameras in buildings that had been converted to civilian use. They shipped the enriched uranium that had been stored at Tuwaitha out of Iraq for safekeeping and placed the stockpile of unenriched uranium under seal, to be monitored in future inspections. They confiscated or destroyed most of the rest of the material and components from our centrifuge program, and catalogued the flow-forming machine, electron beam welders, lathes, and other expensive equipment we had used to produce centrifuge parts. Concealing our procurement methods had been a top priority all along, and the committee continued its diplomatic chess match with the inspectors on this issue. It supplied an incomplete list of suppliers and then, when inspectors demanded more information, responded with letters alternately claiming ignorance and stalling for more time. Special care was taken to avoid revealing the extent to which the Germans had aided us. In its correspondence with inspectors, the Oversight Committee consistently failed to mention the roles of Hinze, Stemmler, Busse, and Schaab. The government must have considered them essential assets of the Iraqi centrifuge program.

Other investigations were afoot, however. German authorities had been tracking H&H Metalform, and in late 1992 they arrested Hinze, his partner, and two of his managers on charges of supporting Iraq's missile and nuclear programs in violation of German export laws. The indictment focused on the sale of the flow-forming machines that inspectors had discovered in Iraq and managed to trace back to Hinze's company. Hinze pleaded guilty in the summer of 1993 but avoided a long jail sentence. His lawyer successfully argued that German export laws had been so lax that helping the Iraqi nuclear program was only a minor crime. Busse fell ill and died around the same time, and was never prosecuted. Stemmler suffered a debilitating stroke and was also spared. Schaab, for the time being, was convicted only of violating German export laws by providing our carbon fiber centrifuge rotors.

Saddam monitored international politics hoping for signs of weakness in the resolve against him. When U.S. president George Bush lost the 1992 election to Bill Clinton, the state-controlled Iraqi media declared victory. On January 13, shortly before the end of Bush's presidency, U.S. aircraft attacked targets in northern Iraq, in response to alleged Iraqi violations of a no-fly zone imposed as part of the cease-fire agreement. Four days later, U.S. warships fired forty cruise missiles at a suspected Iraqi military complex in Baghdad, as punishment for Iraq's refusal to allow weapons inspectors to enter Iraq by air. Saddam hoped that a better relationship with incoming president Clinton might lead to the lifting of the sanctions and oil embargo imposed after the 1991 war. But the relationship with the new American administration quickly soured. In April of 1993 Kuwait claimed it had uncovered an Iraqi plot to assassinate former president Bush as he made a private visit to the emirate. President Clinton launched a missile strike on Saddam's intelligence head-quarters in Baghdad.

Negotiations with inspectors provoked another crisis in July, when Iraq denied permission to install surveillance cameras at several former weapons sites. Although Saddam eventually relented on the cameras, the ongoing climate of mutual suspicion dashed any hope of the sanctions' being lifted.

By 1994 the inspectors had largely dismantled Iraq's nuclear capabilities. But they had not discovered key ingredients of the centrifuge program. In addition to hiding elements of our procure-ment network, the Oversight Committee had avoided turning over any blueprints or documents related to detailed design. The inspect-ors were unaware of our plans for a longer and more advanced centrifuge. They still knew nothing of the crash program before the 1991 war or how close we had come to producing a nuclear weapon. The government continued to claim that the centrifuge program was conceived and developed at Tuwaitha and to deny the true purpose of the Engineering Design Center. The organizational structure of our centrifuge team was still in question. The inspectors had not been able to confirm my role or interview me as the program's supervisor.

Although my work for the past three years had been on civilian projects, the pressure remained intense. Hussein Kamel was still my boss, and he was as hot-tempered as ever. Perhaps keeping me under his thumb was part of a larger strategy to closely monitor me. After we completed the brass factory that had been halted by the war, Hussein Kamel commissioned me to look into ways of manufacturing black carbon, which makes up roughly half of the material needed for the production of automobile tires.

Iraq's tire-making industry relied on imported black carbon, most of which came from neighboring Iran, a fact that must have greatly irritated Saddam. At a meeting of government officials who oversaw the tire industry, I was asked to estimate how long it would take to build a black carbon factory. I said it would take two years to design and construct a pilot plant, and then another two or three years to build a full-scale industrial factory. I felt these were terms that any responsible project manager would give.

The next day Hussein Kamel called me into his office. His hawkish eyes fixed on me as he spewed a stream of rebukes.

"What is this I hear about five years to build a factory?" he asked. "Are you trying to make us kiss the hands of Iran?"

"No, sir," I said. "Of course not."

"Then I suggest you revise your plans," he said. "We are not going to continue to eat from the hands of our enemies."

"Respectfully, sir, may I suggest that doing this project in the correct way will save us time and money in the long run?" I said. "This is a normal time frame for projects in the industrialized world."

Hussein Kamel seemed enraged by my inference that Iraq should follow the same standards applied in other countries.

"I will give you six months to complete the job," he said. "If you fail to meet this schedule, you will be confined. Am I making myself clear?"

There was little I could say. The deadline was impossible, but there was no arguing with Hussein Kamel. He applied the same threatening pressure he had used years earlier during the centrifuge program. I was back on the dangerous treadmill. I set to work on the black carbon project, fearing that I would be imprisoned after six months. I worked from early morning until late at night, turning the drawings produced by my engineers into a workable facility. Instead of dividing the project into stages, we simultaneously undertook the pilot phase and production at the factory level. Six months later we had built four giant buildings at Baiji, about 120 miles north of Baghdad, with dozens of furnaces, chimneys, conveyor belts, piping, and electronics. It was a remarkable achievement in such a short period of time, but the facility was still not ready to produce black carbon. Hussein Kamel was on a trip to Jordan when the deadline came and went, but when he returned, he called me into his office once again.

"I hear there is a delay in producing the black carbon," he said when I had seated myself in front of his desk.

"We have made great progress," I said, hoping for a reprieve.

"That does not erase the fact that you have failed to follow my instructions," he said. "You will return to your building site and stay there until the project is completed. You will eat there, you will sleep there. You will not see your family until your job is done."

I followed his orders to the letter, knowing that I was only one step away from imprisonment. Layla was beside herself when I told her I would be kept at the work site. I tried to console her with the thought that if I succeeded with the black carbon project, we might be rewarded. But my upcoming confinement deeply troubled me. I wondered whether my value as Saddam's living and breathing nuclear secret had somehow also made me a target for Hussein Kamel's ongoing wrath.

I felt terrible breaking the news to the subordinates who would have to be confined along with me in order to finish the project. Many of them had been on my staff since the centrifuge program and were dear to me. The next day, about twenty of us packed our suitcases and went to Baiji for a long spell away from our homes and families. We worked for as long as we could stay awake every day, and slept on cots at our plant and in an oil refinery building next door to it. As we rebuilt conveyor belts and made other improvements, my staff grew increasingly jittery. I tried to lighten their spirits as best I could, but as the months wore on, I grew despondent, too. During exhausted hours of sleep, I dreamt of my children being taken to school by strangers. Every night I called Layla, unable to say when I would be allowed to come home, and after we hung up, I imagined her running our household as if she were a widow.

After six months we had a black carbon factory. I was invited to a meeting in Baghdad in which Hussein Kamel was discussing a number of projects with his senior staff. The meeting lasted four hours before Hussein Kamel finally turned to me.

"And how is the black carbon project, Dr. Mahdi?" he asked.

"Excellent, sir," I said.

"Excellent," he repeated, turning to his senior staff. "He says it is excellent."

I tried to control my rage at his sarcastic tone. Inside I was literally trembling.

"Why shouldn't it be, sir?" I asked. "We have spent six months in confinement. Now the specifications meet the standard set by Pirelli, and the output meets the demands of the Iraqi industry. What else do you want before it is declared excellent?"

Hussein Kamel seemed taken aback by my sharp tone and unexpected answer. He changed the subject and finished his discussions with his staff. Five minutes later he closed the meeting and rose to leave with the rest of them. Just before he reached the door, he stopped and looked back at me.

"Okay, Dr. Mahdi," he said. "You and your men are free to go home."

CHAPTER 8

The Dark Years

I was overjoyed to be home again. After six months of confinement
in the black carbon factory, I found new pleasure in the small
rhythms of family life that are too easily taken for granted. I
rose every morning at six thirty, performed my ablutions, and set
out a small carpet on the living room floor for my morning prayers.
In the quiet moments before the children awoke, Layla and I ate
our breakfast of bread, cheese, and tea in the kitchen and shared
our concerns for the day ahead. Before leaving for work, I looked in
on each of the children as they rose. At dinner those first few
evenings, they asked countless questions about my confinement,
and I described the loneliness I felt at being separated from them.
Gradually our conversation returned to its old form, in which we
would take turns analyzing everything from schoolwork to the
behavior of our neighbors. At the end of every meal, as was our
custom, we praised Layla's hands for preparing such delicious food.
We were happy to be together again, but we also realized from the
recent episode how quickly the whim of Saddam's men could shatter
our fragile sense of security.

Back at my office at GEET in Rashdiya, I began a new project overseeing the renovation of an iron-casting plant in Basra and a rolling-mill plant in Baghdad. To my great relief it was less challenging than the black carbon factory, and after a few months, I began to breathe easier. Then, late in the afternoon of August 7, 1995, as I was reviewing plans for the Basra plant, an assistant came into my office and said, "Hussein Kamel wants to see you right away."

I leapt to my feet, dreading what new torture my boss could have in store for me. I called Layla and told her that she and the children should plan to eat dinner without me.

"What do you think he wants at this hour?" Layla asked. I could hear the concern in her voice.

"I'm sure it is nothing," I said, trying to calm her.

I sped across town to Hussein Kamel's office near MIC headquarters. His young male secretary asked me to wait in the anteroom while he finished some business with another visitor. Through the door to his office I could hear muffled voices. The minutes turned into hours, and I couldn't imagine what Hussein Kamel, known for his abruptness, could be discussing for so long. I tried to work out why he might want to see me so urgently. My current project did not seem to warrant an evening meeting, but one never knew. Maybe he had a new assignment for me. I prayed this was not the case. I wasn't ready to endure another high-pressure job from this brutal taskmaster.

When the secretary finally ushered me into Hussein Kamel's office, I had to suppress a gasp. I barely recognized the man before me. Hussein Kamel appeared disheveled, as if he had not slept in days. He slumped forward in his chair with his arms resting so heavily on his desk it looked as though he might collapse onto it. He seemed preoccupied, and his usually fierce demeanor was gone.

"Sit down," he said, without acknowledging the four-hour wait.

He raised his face, and as we made eye contact, I saw that his normally hawklike eyes were completely bloodshot. His pupils barely focused on me for a moment before he turned away as though distracted by some pressing thought.

"How are things with you, Dr. Mahdi? How is your family? Are they well?"

Although these are habitual questions that open most Iraqi conversations, they seemed strange coming from the mouth of Hussein Kamel, whose lips were more accustomed to terse pronouncements. He spoke with something almost approaching gentleness. Although it was entirely out of character, I wondered whether, simply by mentioning my family, he was extending an indirect apology for my confinement the year before. I assured him that I and my family were in good health, and inquired about the welfare of his own family. He responded with a vague sigh. "I want to talk about the centrifuge program," he said. "Explain to me again the advantages of the centrifuge technique."

At first I was at a loss for words. Hussein Kamel had known the pros and cons of the centrifuge program as well as anyone on my staff. It was he who had jumped at the centrifuge idea during our midnight meeting at the Republican Palace eight years earlier. He had overseen its every step. Surely he could not have forgotten its most basic elements in the four and a half years since the war. For a moment I became suspicious that there might be some veiled purpose behind his question. Perhaps he was trying to trap me into giving a wrong answer that would land me in trouble again. But that didn't square with the appearance of the man in front of me. This colossus of Saddam's regime, whose words made everyone tremble, seemed himself deeply shaken. I wondered whether he was cracking under some pressure inside Saddam's inner circle. I had heard rumors of a power struggle between Hussein Kamel and Saddam's eldest son, Uday, and it was possible that the rivalry had reached a breaking point. This did not explain his current line of questioning, though.

I hid my bewilderment and reminded him that centrifuges require far less electricity than other techniques for uranium enrichment; they are relatively small, efficient, and easy to hide in a compact space. He absentmindedly jotted down a few notes.

"Tell me again about the equipment required for a centrifuge plant," he said. "And the things the inspectors have not yet discovered."

As he said this, Hussein Kamel unscrewed the lid of a medicine bottle, dumped two pills into his hand, and swallowed them with a gulp of orange juice, then replaced the bottle in a desk drawer. I had never seen Hussein Kamel take pills before, and I wondered whether they were the cause of, or a treatment for, his befuddled state of mind. I had also heard that Hussein Kamel underwent a brain operation in 1992, but until now his knifelike powers of perception had seemed unaltered.

I had sat across from him at this desk dozens of times over the years, terrorized by his threats and unreasonable demands. But this encounter was beginning to border on the surreal, because his questions were within his own areas of oversight. Only one thing was certain to me as I observed him with new eyes: the reins of clear thinking had slipped from his hand.

I walked Hussein Kamel through the centrifuge program as though explaining it for the first time, including the installation of all the equipment at the Engineering Design Center, our foreign contacts and procurements, and the crash program after the invasion of Kuwait. He took a few more notes and, at one point, interrupted me.

"Exactly how many centrifuges can fit into a small building?" he asked.

It was another odd question. I replied that a small warehouse could house a few hundred centrifuges.

"Why do you ask?" I ventured.

Hussein Kamel eyed me suspiciously, and for a moment I wished I had not asked. Then he shrugged.

"We suspect that the Russians may be supplying Iran with centrifuge technology," he said, "and I want to convince them not to go ahead with it."

This was plausible, but it didn't explain Hussein Kamel's muddled state of mind. He offered no other explanation and, with a wave of his hand, indicated that I was free to go. As I rose from my chair, he made another uncharacteristic gesture. Rather than simply dismissing me in his imperious way, he stood up, reached across his desk, and shook my hand. His grip was firm, but his palm felt damp with sweat. He momentarily held my gaze, and I saw in his eyes, for the briefest split second, an unexpected flicker of emotion. Later, reflecting on it with the benefit of hindsight, I would say it seemed earnest, almost wistful, as though he wanted to say something but couldn't.

I left his office utterly puzzled. It was nearly midnight.

I was scheduled to attend a social gathering of MIC officials and company directors the next afternoon. I drove to it still mulling over Hussein Kamel's strange behavior. I normally attended such events reluctantly, because they involve a great deal of social posturing, but on this afternoon I was anxious to see what state of mind my boss would be in and how he would conduct himself among his managers. As head of MIC, he would play the role of master of ceremonies. I wondered whether he would be able to pull it off. Whatever was ailing him, it seemed unlikely that he could have fully recovered. I tried to imagine the looks on the faces of the other officials when they saw Saddam's fearsome son-in-law in such wretched shape.

About two hundred managers were already gathered when I arrived at the MIC meeting hall. Hussein Kamel was nowhere in sight. As I headed in to greet some of my colleagues, the crowd seemed abuzz with gossip. Before long a manager I knew quite well took me by the elbow and, in a low voice, delivered the incredible piece of news.

"They are saying that Hussein Kamel defected to Jordan early this morning," he said. "It appears he took his entire family with him."

Details were sketchy at first, but during the following days a clearer picture emerged. In the early hours of August 8, as most of Baghdad slept, Hussein Kamel and his brother, Saddam Kamel, drove their families several hundred miles west through the desert to the Jordanian capital, Amman. Nearly thirty members of the Majid clan went with them, including Saddam's eldest two daughters, Raghad and Rana, who were married to Hussein Kamel and his brother. Enraged, Saddam denounced Hussein Kamel and demanded his extradition to Iraq, but Jordan's King Hussein granted asylum to the entire branch of the family. A few days after arriving in Jordan, Hussein Kamel made a fruitless speech calling on Iraqis to rise up in rebellion against the regime.

The astonishing escape caused a great stir in Baghdad, where it instantly became the topic of whispered rumors on street corners and in private homes. Speculation centered on Hussein Kamel's presumed rivalry with Saddam's elder son, Uday, who had recently encroached on some of his black-market business dealings. It was said that Hussein Kamel and his brother, who had headed the presidential security forces, had reached a point of irreconcilable differences with Saddam's sons. They were bound to lose that confrontation. I avoided talking about the matter as much as possible. I suspected I was the last person to see Hussein Kamel before his flight, and at first I told no one about our late-night meeting out of fear that I might become entangled in Saddam's net of suspicion. A few days later, however, I received a request to write a memo about our meeting from the Minister of Oil, Amir Rashid, an advisor to Saddam who must have found out about it from Hussein Kamel's secretary. I immediately took out a pen and paper and wrote him a full account of the strange meeting.

Hussein Kamel's defection had an almost instantaneous effect on my life, because it fundamentally changed the course of the weapons inspections. Within a week of arriving to Jordan, he began meeting with UN inspectors and western intelligence agents, who swarmed over him like bees to a newly opened flower. He detailed the programs to produce biological and chemical weapons that ended only with the 1991 war on Iraq, and Saddam's decision to destroy these toxins after the war in order to hide them from the outside world. He revealed that the centrifuge program had taken place at the Engineering Design Center in Rashdiya, and that we had attempted to build enough centrifuges for a single crude bomb in the months before the 1991 Gulf War. He disclosed more of our procurement network, including the extent of the assistance we had received from Schaab and the other Germans. And he confirmed that I was the leader of the centrifuge effort.

My final meeting with him made more sense now. Hussein Kamel apparently wanted to refresh his memory about the centrifuge program because those details would be currency in his negotiations with Jordanian and Western officials. His near-total lack of recall about some of its most basic facts still puzzled me, though. Either he was finally suffering from a brain affliction or else the stress of preparing to defect had scattered his wits.

At first, there was no way of knowing exactly what Hussein Kamel was divulging. But it was assumed the inspectors would thoroughly debrief him. Knowing that the game was up, the Oversight Committee moved to preempt the anticipated inquiries from the inspectors. They collected many documents from the WMD programs, along with remaining scattered materials such as a few tons of maraging steel and centrifuge jackets. They packed wooden and metal boxes full of microfiches, computer diskettes, videotapes, and photographs that had been kept hidden from inspectors throughout the early 1990s. Then they drove them to a chicken farm owned by Hussein Kamel in the Baghdad suburb of Haidar and locked all of the boxes in a henhouse.

On August 18, an SSO operative hinted to inspectors that they should investigate Hussein Kamel's chicken farm. They descended on the place, quickly found the cache of documents, and carted them off for examination. With this new information in hand, the UN inspectors pressed their case, and Saddam was forced to admit ambitions for a nuclear weapon. But the government made the incredible claim that Hussein Kamel had acted alone to initiate the crash program, and had stored these documents and materials at his farm unbeknownst to the government. Foreign Minister Tariq Aziz portrayed Hussein Kamel as a zealot who wanted to develop a shadow nuclear program without Saddam's knowledge and then depose the president. The inspectors quickly dismissed this claim, but it allowed Saddam's regime to officially deny responsibility for seeking a bomb.

Dr. Adil and I drove out to the Haidar farm soon after the weapons inspectors had been there. By the time we arrived, all the documents had been removed and little remained but the leftover maraging steel. It was clean and shiny and obviously had not been stored in Hussein Kamel's henhouse for long.

Around this time the Oversight Committee was renamed the National Monitoring Directorate (NMD), still under Tariq Aziz. I was able to see an NMD videotape showing exactly what had been uncovered at the chicken farm. As the camera panned across the pile of material, I was surprised to see a jumble of centrifuge parts. I figured they must have been the components separated out in 1991, when the SSO was trying to hide enough material for one hundred centrifuges. The fact that they were concealed for so long suggested an intent to restart the centrifuge program at some stage. But it was a ridiculous collection of parts that showed the lack of realistic thinking at the bureaucratic level.

Watching the video, I counted only seven crates of documents said to belong to the centrifuge program. I remembered that the SSO had taken about one hundred boxes of documents from Rashdiya in 1991. When I brought this discrepancy to the attention of the NMD, I was told that all of the other documents had been taken to another farm and burned. Inspectors later found evidence of this, when the NMD led them to the burning site and showed them the ashes and charred half sheets of paper. But they were never able to confirm that all of the centrifuge documents had been destroyed.

After Hussein Kamel's defection, the NMD was forced to admit that I was the leader of the centrifuge program. In mid-September, I received the order to meet inspectors in my acknowledged role. It was late morning as I waited for the English inspector, Garry Dillon, at my old workplace. I had arrived early, in order to spend some time looking around the compound. I walked around reminiscing about the centrifuge days. Although part of me was eager to finally unburden myself of the truth about our program at Rashdiya, I also felt nervous in anticipation of the inspectors' arrival. I need not have been. After three UN vehicles drove through the gate, Dillon stepped out and greeted me warmly, without a trace of accusation over the past years of deception. He was well aware of the fact that Iraqi scientists were not the decision makers behind the deception.

I toured Dillon and about a dozen of his colleagues around the former Engineering Design Center, pointing out the buildings where we had conducted experiments with the Beams centrifuge and made the separation test with the magnetic centrifuge. Dillon said the IAEA had suspected all along that Rashdiya was the nerve center of the program.

I had a crew remove debris piled high in the planned cascade hall, so that Dillon's team could see the footprint of the cascade design in the floor. Many of the structures had been changed, and I described them as they had appeared before. I told them about the frantic and heady days of 1990, when we tried to complete the program on a hopeless timetable. I felt a great sense of relief at finally being able to share these things.

"Why did you try to hide this facility for so long?" Dillon asked. "There are only structures here, with no equipment. So what was the point in denying its past purpose?"

I couldn't think of a strategic reason for disguising the true nature of the Rashdiya site for so long. In the year or two following the 1991 war, I felt that Saddam had hoped to reconstitute the nuclear program. But as the inspectors had effectively denuded Iraq's machinery for building nuclear weapons, the deceptions had become less of a measure to preserve the program and more of a reaction against foreign pressure.

"The orders were simply to hide it," I said. "The centrifuge program was always the top priority for concealment."

Analysis of what became known as the "chicken farm documents" required months of study at IAEA headquarters in Vienna. During this time I underwent dozens of interviews. At first the inspectors focused on the crash program, our foreign procurement network, and the history of how we developed centrifuges at Rashdiya.

It became clear from the inspectors' questions that the chicken farm documents included sketches of the centrifuges but not the actual design drawings used to manufacture the components. I expected to be confronted at any moment with testimony from Hussein Kamel that I had personally kept the master copy of our centrifuge blueprints. But the topic never arose. I began to wonder whether Hussein Kamel could have forgotten about my copies. It didn't seem possible, but as the months wore on, I could think of no other explanation.

The inspectors still had not seen the core knowledge behind the Iraqi centrifuge. They didn't know the measurements, the tolerances of the materials, or the calculations of hairy mathematics that had made possible our successful test of a prototype. I explained that the security forces had taken all of the papers from Rashdiya in 1991, and that my staff and I had been told they were destroyed on Saddam's order. But they asked again and again, "Where are the blueprints?" They couldn't accept that Iraq had burned all of these documents, and the NMD could provide no solid evidence that they had done so. This dynamic was apparently a problem in terms of biological and chemical weapons, too. The National Monitoring Directorate had declared that Iraq produced 8,500 liters of the bacterial agent anthrax during the 1980s but destroyed it all during the early 1990s. UN inspectors calculated that Iraq had the capacity to produce about three times that amount of anthrax, and they were unable to verify the amount destroyed. So their suspicions lingered.

From exile in Jordan, Hussein Kamel made overtures to Saddam begging forgiveness for his defection and asking permission to return to Iraq. It seemed suicidal. Later there were those who would whisper that Saddam had threatened to wipe out the entire branch of the family if the brothers didn't return. Others speculated that, robbed of his powerful position and abused by Western governments, Hussein Kamel had become disenchanted with life in Jordan and felt his life had no purpose there. With a smile on his face and a knife behind his back, Saddam sent a message to Hussein Kamel that all would be forgiven if he returned with his brother and their wives.

Inexplicably, the brothers took the bait. On February 20, 1996, they set off in a convoy from Amman toward Baghdad with Raghad and Rana. When they reached the Iraqi border, they met Uday Hussein and a retinue of armed men. What happened next is a matter of legend in Iraq. Uday put his sisters and their children in one helicopter and their husbands in another. Hussein Kamel and his brother were flown to Baghdad for interrogation and then allowed to return to their family estate in the al-Sayidiyah suburb west of Baghdad. On the morning of February 23, Saddam announced his daughters' divorces. That night, dozens of security officers supervised by Uday and Qusay Hussein surrounded the home at al-Sayidiyah. Another security team brought a busload of Hussein Kamel's relatives and friends to a nearby knoll, from which they would be forced to watch the terrible events that were about to unfold. At dawn, a fierce gun battle broke out. Hussein Kamel and his family tried to defend themselves by shooting at their attackers through the windows of their home. After several hours, most inside were dead, including Hussein Kamel's brother, his father, his sister, his nephew, and several bodyguards. The attackers stormed the mansion, dragged the wounded Hussein Kamel outside, and executed him in front of his relatives. It was rumored that they were told: "Let this be a lesson that no traitors will be allowed to live."

The defection of Hussein Kamel also had grave consequences for Karl Heinz Schaab. Inspectors learned that he not only manufactured the carbon-fiber rotors but also secretly provided the classified blueprints for the super-critical centrifuge and bellows. To escape treason charges by German authorities, Schaab fled in late 1995 to Brazil, followed by his wife, Brigitte. When German investigators finally tracked him to Brazil they demanded his extradition. Brazilian police arrested Schaab and put him in prison for nearly a year and a half, but he was later released under Brazilian law. He finally returned to Germany and pleaded guilty to treason in 1998. As part of the deal, he received a suspended sentence that took into account his time served in prison in Rio. The German media made a fuss over the light sentence, accusing the government of caving in to avoid a lengthy trial that might expose its lax security measures during the 1980s.

Throughout the second half of the 1990s, inspectors continued to grill me about the details of the centrifuge program and the possible whereabouts of the missing documents. For the most part, these encounters were extremely cordial and at times even bordered on the philosophical. In 1996 I brought the French inspector Jacques Baute to a site in al-Taji, about eighteen miles north of Baghdad, where early on in the program we had envisioned building a massive plant for four thousand oil centrifuges. It was a square-mile plot of farmland in the fertile region between the Euphrates and the Tigris rivers, obscured from view by rows of eucalyptus trees and set back nearly a half mile from the road. It would have been a perfect place to hide a nuclear facility. Baute and I parked by the side of the road and walked along a dirt path between furrowed soil thick with beautiful cucumber and tomato vines. The weather was agreeable, and we soon fell into pleasant conversation.

"Tell me, Mahdi," he said, "why did Iraq want to build a nuclear bomb?"

It was a question I had never been asked before. I reflected for a moment before I answered.

"You know, Jacques, almost every Iraqi house has protective bars on its windows, whereas there are hardly any on French homes. People in Iraq are afraid their houses will be broken into."

"Well, I never thought of that," he said. "But what are you getting at, exactly?"

"In Iraq there is a deep sense of insecurity. When you make people feel secure, they won't feel the need to protect their homes with window bars. The same thing goes for nations. As soon as they feel secure, they won't think of needing bombs. The question is how to achieve a feeling of security by some other means."

We discussed the Israeli bombing of Iraq's nuclear reactor in 1981 and the mutual distrust that may have fed a desire for nuclear weapons by both sides. Our conversation turned to the Cold War between the United States and the Soviet Union, and the fact that two superpowers spent nearly a half century in a game of atomic one-upmanship. We talked about the fact that France possessed nuclear weapons but that Germany, which had invaded his country twice during the past century, did not. Yet the two were now strategic part-ners in a newly united Europe. Surely this showed that cooperation could prevail over suspicion between nations. Dr. Baute and I contin-ued our chat as we walked back to the road where we had parked.

Other inspectors were more combative. In 1997 I butted heads with the American inspector Scott Ritter. Ritter had been exposing parts of the missile program still unaccounted for after Hussein Kamel defected. Although he had a limited technical background, as an ex-marine he exuded a competence that made many of the Iraqi scientists nervous. Because his work in Iraq had been related to the missile program, I was surprised when he wanted to speak to me about the centrifuge program. We met in a downstairs room at the National Monitoring Directorate headquarters, along with Dr. Jaffar and several inspectors I didn't recognize. After a number of insinuating questions, Dr. Jaffar called Mr. Ritter a stooge of the CIA and stormed out of the interview. Then Mr. Ritter turned his attention to me with a penetrating stare.

"We're onto you," he said. "I know you are hiding things."

He was looking for any inch of hesitation. The image of the documents and components buried in my garden flashed into my mind. I knew what could happen to me and my family if he were to get any hint that those secrets were hidden there. I went on the offensive as my best defense, using what I knew to be his weakness: his lack of technical knowledge in the nuclear field.

"Look here," I said. "A centrifuge program consists of the following: conceptual design, basic design, detailed design, manu-facturing, erection of buildings, construction of a prototype, and building a plant for production. Let me ask you a simple question. Which of these am I hiding?"

He balked at my antagonistic tone, so I continued in an effort to end the interview.

"Sir, I have been talking for many months to your colleagues who are competent and qualified technical people," I said. "I am a technical man myself. Discussions with your colleagues have been going well for the past few years. Now all of a sudden you appear accusing me of hiding something, yet you can't say what I am hiding. I feel that you do not possess the minimum credentials to discuss this with me."

He looked at me blankly, and then his face turned red. His hands fumbled here and there for his papers, and I felt he was looking for a way to get out of the room. The interview was over. I hadn't planned to be so aggressive with Ritter. But he had cut close to the bone. We never met again.

By 1998 inspectors had removed or incapacitated all of the machines, raw materials, and facilities of the centrifuge program. Saddam continued his defiant attitude, however, which fed suspicions that Iraq was hiding something. The UN demanded access to increasing numbers of sites, including presidential palaces, many of which had never been involved in Iraq's WMD programs. Saddam accused the United States of using the inspections as a way of spying on Iraq and denied access to the inspectors. This led to a confrontation that began in October 1998, when Saddam refused to allow any further inspections if sanctions were not lifted. United States president Clinton announced his intention to replace Saddam's regime with a more friendly government and threatened military action. Saddam agreed once again to cooperate with the inspectors. The UN teams complained about continued restrictions, however, and soon afterward they received orders to evacuate. On December 16 as President Clinton faced impeachment over his affair with an intern, the United States and Britain launched four days of intense air strikes, called Operation Desert Fox. Fighter jets and cruise missiles targeted more than one hundred Iraqi military and industrial sites.

Operation Desert Fox was intended to force Iraq's full cooperation with the UN inspections. But it had the opposite result. Saddam announced he would no longer allow weapons inspectors inside the country. They would not return until nearly four years later, in the months leading up to the 2003 war. The United States and its allies referred to the period beginning in December 1998 as "the dark years" because foreign intelligence about what was happening inside Iraq, which had relied on reports from inspectors, trickled to almost nothing.

Earlier that year, I had been made director general of the state engineering company Sa'ad, which gave me a broad view of the activities of the former nuclear scientists and engineers. Most worked under me or at other government-run engineering companies. As the world wondered what Saddam's WMD scientists were up to, we rehabilitated an ammunition factory in al-Qaaqaa, built a new one in Karbala, and worked to build six oil refineries across Iraq.

Although the IAEC lacked the resources or equipment to carry out practical work in the nuclear field, Saddam kept the nuclear commission alive rather than admit defeat, which was something he never did. This allowed him to preserve the fantasy that he had a nuclear program. He staffed it with younger scientists, most of whom had never been part of the enrichment programs. For the most part, they carried out research into rocket fuels and theory related to nuclear physics.

Saddam was reaping the rewards of an improved economy. In 1997 the United Nations had created a watered-down version of the sanctions known as the oil-for-food program, aiming to relieve the plight of ordinary Iraqis under the embargo. It allowed Iraq to sell oil abroad in exchange for food and medicine. Although the intention was humane, Saddam quickly found ways to exploit the program. The loosening of trade restrictions opened new black-market channels, and the government found many illicit ways to sell oil for cash. As much of the country wallowed in poverty, Saddam went on a spending spree. He erected many new palaces, which he lavishly filled with fine furniture and gold-plated fixtures.

Although many of my former colleagues and I worked on projects that could benefit our country, a survivalist approach had long ago replaced the spirit of scientific adventure. The smallest mistake on a mundane project could be met with severe punishments. My old friend and colleague, Dr. Farid, was promoted to a director-ship within the Ministry of Industry, a position he fully deserved. But the promotion only brought him closer to the unforgiving eye of Saddam's government. In 1998 he was assigned to construct a number of houses for government ministers and members of Saddam's inner circle. When his engineers failed to properly design the doors, Dr. Farid was confined to the building site, as I had been four years earlier at the black carbon plant. Soon afterward, I heard that he somehow arranged for his wife and children to be spirited out of Iraq while he was in confinement, and then he joined them in exile. He never came to say good-bye, of course, and we never learned where he had gone.

It was during this time that Layla begged me for a favor that I couldn't bear refusing her. For years she had yearned to make the hajj, or pilgrimage, to the holy city of Mecca in Saudi Arabia, which is the duty of every observant Muslim at least once in his or her lifetime. By this point in our lives both of us were feeling the tug of middle age, and it seemed that if we didn't make the hajj soon we might never see the birthplace of the Prophet Muhammad and the holy sites dear to our religion.

"Mahdi," she said one day, "can't you use your connections in the government to try to get visas?"

I knew there was absolutely no chance Saddam would let both of us out of the country at the same time, even if our children remained behind, serving as ransom for our return. I felt it would be dangerous even to apply because visa applications, especially those by prominent people, were reviewed by the intelligence services and it might raise suspicions that we planned to escape. The defections of Hussein Kamel and others had made Saddam even more watch-ful. And if news reached the ears of Qusay Hussein, who knew that I held Iraq's remaining nuclear secrets, that I had applied for foreign visas for myself and my wife, I feared it would only lead to trouble.

I motioned for Layla to follow me to the lawn of our garden, where I believed we were safe from listening devices.

"Layla," I said gently, "why don't I make an application for you to make the pilgrimage along with your brother? There is a much better chance of success that way."

She looked crestfallen. We had often dreamed of making the pilgrimage together, and I now had to concede that this dream was impossible. I toyed with the idea of telling her about the nuclear secrets buried only a few feet away so that she might understand my reasoning. But then I thought better of it. For the safety of her and the children, it was better if they knew nothing.

Layla became depressed for weeks. It devastated me to be unable to fully explain why I felt trapped. I begged her to understand that there were still very dangerous pressures on me. She finally reconciled to the idea of making the journey with her brother. I applied for her visa and asked for special consideration based on my years of service to the regime. For a few days I felt confident that the government would approve it, and I took heart that at least one member of our family would be able to make the journey. We received the response a week later flatly denying the application.

Iraq began to resemble a prison. I resigned myself to my captivity and tried to take solace in watching my children make their way into adulthood. My eldest daughter, Isra'a, married a fine young civil engineer named Ahmed. My son Zaid entered a mechanical engineering program at the University of Technology in Baghdad, and my youngest two daughters excelled in high school. I was proud of all of my children. Yet I couldn't shake the sense of guilt that my leadership of Saddam's centrifuge program, as well as the secrets buried beneath the lotus tree in our garden, might hinder their lives forever. Because of me, I thought, they might never be allowed to travel abroad and experience the same freedoms their father had enjoyed in his own youth.

My former boss, Hussein Kamel, was dead, but for me the snake grew another head in the form of the new MIC chief, Abdul Tawab Mullah Hwaish. Abdul Tawab rose quickly to the top of Iraqi politics during the late 1990s, amid rumors that he had pledged his daughter to Saddam as an extra wife. Like Hussein Kamel, he tended to fly into fits of rage. Abdul Tawab made my life difficult in many ways, and I resolved to try to escape the military-industrial world and his oversight.

In early 2000 I wrote to the Iraqi minister of oil, Amir Rashid, asking whether he could find a place for me in the industry where I had begun my career so many years earlier. He responded that the Ministry of Oil would consider it a privilege to offer me a good position. Full of hope, I wrote to Abdul Tawab that I believed I was unsuited to continue as director general of Sa'ad and requested a meeting to discuss my transfer to the Ministry of Oil. He didn't answer my letter, and I suddenly received assignments for extra paperwork on a completely unreasonable deadline. The next time I saw him was the following month, in April, at a large meeting of the MIC steering committee. The directors general for every MIC company gave progress reports. When it came time to discuss the Sa'ad company, Abdul Tawab turned and spoke to me for the first time in weeks.

"You have been late in your paperwork," he said. "This is unacceptable. Such lapses will surely land you in prison."

His intimidation tactics made my situation seem hopeless. I feared I would spend the rest of my life trapped in MIC. Although it risked provoking Abdul Tawab further, I wrote him three more letters during the next year and a half. I sent the last one in June 2001, just after finishing the design of an oil refinery. I wrote, politely and to the point:

> Since I have finished the tasks recently given to me, I find it opportune to reapply my request for transfer. I am fully convinced that I cannot continue at MIC. I greatly desire to practice my specialization in petroleum refining for what remains of my lifetime. I send my thanks and respects, hoping that you agree and accept my request so that we can do more for our homeland.

When I received no reply, I sent a second letter directly to the office of Saddam Hussein asking for the transfer. It was a desperate move that did not pay off. Abdul Tawab finally called me into his office to discuss the matter. I assume he heard about my correspondence with Saddam's office and wanted to nip this in the bud.

"You have written your last letter on the subject of moving to the Oil Ministry," he said. "That is an order."

"What if I simply wait a few months before writing anything further?" I asked. "The circumstances could change."

"The circumstances have changed," he said. "I have a new assignment for you."

He said I would be relieved of my position at Sa'ad and made director of projects for all of MIC. I would oversee budgets for the massive public and military works agency that was the largest organization in Iraq. This meant I would have to move into the MIC headquarters building. Rather than getting farther from Abdul Tawab, I was to be brought closer.

"What if I decline the transfer?" I asked.

"You cannot," he said. "If you try, there will be consequences. And you probably know what they are."

In Iraq, a veiled threat is always more dangerous than an explicit one. His public threat to imprison me during the steering committee meeting a year earlier was a way of putting me in my place. But I understood the coded message. Because he did not mention throwing me in a dungeon, I knew that Abdul Tawab was deadly serious this time. I wondered whether, by moving me into MIC, he simply intended to bring me closer to the fold. The regime had become so secretive that true intentions were almost impossible to detect. A colleague later bore out my suspicions when he told me he had heard MIC security were given explicit orders to keep an eye on me.

I moved into a corner office on the second floor of MIC headquarters, and soon settled into a routine. I arrived at work at eight every morning, after which my secretary brought me a Turkish coffee and the papers to be reviewed for the day. My staff of forty engineers, technicians, and accountants was responsible for about three hundred projects. We oversaw the planning, evaluation, and follow-up, so I got the widest possible view of the government's military-industrial works. Weapons of mass destruction programs were ancient history by then. The electronics group worked on radar and military communication, and the armaments division produced hardware such as artillery pieces, rifles, and rockets. The chemicals group handled refineries and the production of gunpowder, acids for making munitions, fuel for rockets, and the like. About a third of the projects were civilian in nature, such as refineries and water treatment plants.

During this period I came under increasing pressure to join the Baath Party. I had resisted joining the party since my early days at the IAEC in the 1970s. For me the Baath Party was devoid of meaning. Although it began as a movement for Arab unity in the mid-twentieth century, in Iraq it withered into an organism of loyalty to Saddam Hussein. It developed its own hollow jargon like that of the Communist Party in the Soviet Union. Although party membership was often a key to promotion, its meetings were full of mindless slogans and flattery of the president. If nothing else, I felt it was a colossal waste of time.

"I can't digest this sort of dogma," I told Layla. "It is nonsense. They speak of freedom when there is none. It makes me want to vomit."

Abdul Tawab sent one of his deputies to confront me about my indifference toward the party, around the time I sent my first letter requesting transfer.

"Do you know that you are the only director general who is not a Baath Party member?" the deputy asked. "This could prove hazardous, you know."

Under this duress, I half-relented. I agreed to become a party supporter. Far from membership in the party, this nevertheless would require me to attend meetings. I went to one. I found it ridiculous and vowed to myself never to attend another. In the following weeks, I received calls from junior Baath Party staff members asking why I had missed official gatherings. I apologized each time with the excuse that I was busy with important and time-consuming scientific work. Though disingenuous, this alibi worked every time and I never attended another meeting.

My new position allowed me not only to see the full scope of MIC's work, but also to experience firsthand the wastefulness and corruption that had spread to all corners of the government. Saddam increasingly demanded direct oversight of military-industrial programs, but he seemed so detached from reality that project leaders felt free to fabricate progress. This offended my sensibilities. When science becomes corrupt, it is no longer science. I saw many examples of trumped-up projects that had little basis in fact, but one especially sticks out in my memory. I reviewed a report by a project manager who had been allocated tens of millions of dollars worth of funds to develop a shoulder-launched antiaircraft rocket. His progress report stated that the project was more than 70 percent completed. When I asked to see the designs for the rocket, however, I saw that they had only a list of parameters. The whole thing smelled like a rotten fish. I brought this up to Abdul Tawab, who at first ordered me to conduct an investigation but then closed down my inquiry after I asked to interview Baghdad University researchers listed as consultants to the project.

Deception was spiraling out of control. Subordinates fed Saddam what he wanted to hear, and he had a loose grasp of details at best. When the MIC director general in charge of the al-Samoud missiles was called upon to give him a progress report, for example, he avoided the topic of his work altogether. Instead of giving a report, the director recited a poem he had written praising Saddam. Apparently moved by the reading, Saddam commended him for his literary efforts, and the details of the al-Samoud project were brushed aside.

Iraqi armament projects continued, though, despite internal corruption and external obstacles. The ongoing UN sanctions prohibited Iraq from purchasing so-called dual-use items that could be used for prohibited unconventional weapons programs or long-range missiles. A recurring problem was acquiring high-quality gyroscopes used for stabilizing rockets. Although UN sanctions allowed Iraq to produce short-range military rockets, the gyroscopes could also be used for rockets that exceeded the imposed ninety-three-mile limit. The restrictions were not airtight, however, and I noticed that the MIC apparatus had a number of channels for circumventing them. Whenever gyroscopes were needed, the Procurement Department went through Iraqi front companies in the private sector that had extensive black-market connections in countries like Russia and Belarus. Through these back channels, Iraq was able to smuggle many banned items into the country.

So why didn't Saddam restart his nuclear weapons program? If prohibited items could still be bought on the black market for conventional weapons, why not use these same methods to try again to develop unconventional weapons? No one can fully answer this question except for Saddam Hussein, of course. But from a logical standpoint, he had a few very practical reasons for not pursuing the bomb again. First of all, he was profiting handsomely from the oil-for-food program. The new palaces being constructed across Iraq were only one sign of this. Ironically, the oil-for-food program had also strengthened his hold on power. Most of the population, especially the rural poor, was now dependent on government rations for basic items, such as flour and cooking oil. This gave the regime a new lever of control over them. It is possible that Saddam was quite content with the status quo and felt he couldn't afford to risk jeopardizing this program. Smuggling a few gyroscopes was one thing, but if he reconstituted his WMD programs, and the UN found out about it, the international community would almost certainly pull the plug on the oil-for-food agreement.

Second, restarting the nuclear program would have been a massive undertaking. Throughout the 1990s the inspectors had decimated our programs so thoroughly that all we had left was the knowledge in our heads and the documents buried in my garden. They had removed Iraq's enriched uranium stockpiles. They had removed or incapacitated the machines to manufacture components indigenously. And the international network of parts suppliers and technical expertise, on which we had relied so heavily, had been exposed. The British government had closed down Matrix Churchill and Iraqi front companies in the United Kingdom. Although Swiss authorities had not prosecuted managers at

Schaublin or the other Swiss companies that supplied parts to us, one could assume that any trade with Iraq was closely watched. After the high-profile trials in Germany, our connections there were finished. Restarting the nuclear program would have required us to begin almost from scratch in terms of foreign procurement. And the whole world was watching.

Another factor may have been the absence of Hussein Kamel. The nuclear program really took root the moment he was named head of MIC in 1987. He ordered me to start the centrifuge program, and it was he who initiated the weaponization program led by Dr. Sa'id. He directed the talent of scientists into effective teams and motivated us through the promise of reward and, especially, punishments. It is possible that Hussein Kamel was the force that focused the weapons of mass destruction programs and that, without him, Saddam's nuclear ambitions slipped back into the realm of vague dreams.

The question remains whether Saddam intended to reconstitute the bomb program. Under his unpredictable rule, a vague dream could become an imperative at the snap of his fingers. He had clearly demonstrated his intentions in the past, from the uneven steps with the French reactor in the 1970s to the full-scale uranium enrichment efforts and crash program before the 1991 war. Until the defection of Hussein Kamel, he had hidden as much of the centrifuge program as possible.

Even during the dark years, there were signs of a lingering desire for nuclear weapons. The most obvious is the fact that Saddam kept funding the IAEC from 1991, when the programs ended, until the war in 2003. He may have wanted the world to believe that he had an ongoing nuclear program, and he may have wanted to believe it himself. It is easy to picture Saddam imagining that he was keeping the oven warm, at least on some level. This atmosphere may have led to individual flights of fancy—whispers, a theorem scratched on a slip of paper here and there, a discussion of equipment—by a scientist or two. These were not substantial efforts based on a strategy, but small hints of intentions. The desire for nuclear weapons seemed to remain long after the programs were dead, like a ghost dragging its chains around a haunted house.

Would Saddam have tried to build nuclear weapons again, if sanctions had been lifted and the conditions were right? One can only imagine he would have. For the time being, however, the core knowledge for rebuilding the centrifuge program lay buried in my garden, waiting for the order from Qusay Hussein or his father. And the order never came.

CHAPTER 9

The March to War

A different order landed on my desk in early December 2002, shortly after the arrival of UN weapons inspectors: "Move your documents from your offices to the basement."

As I sat at my desk reading the memo from Abdul Tawab to all MIC directors general, I couldn't help thinking that this was a strange and rash directive. I called my secretary into my office.

"Can you find out more about this?" I asked. "Which documents are they talking about? Current documents? Archived documents? Payroll? Inventory?"

The answer came soon enough: "All of them."

The regime had obviously panicked now that inspectors were fanning out across Iraq for the first time in four years. Mountains of paper quickly piled up in the basement of the MIC headquarters, as directors emptied their offices of files. The project was halted a few days later, however. A BBC news crew somehow learned that MIC officials were shifting large amounts of documents, and the network aired a story accusing Saddam of planning to destroy evidence. Abdul Tawab reversed his order and instructed department heads to retrieve everything from the basement. This happened so quickly that we had not even begun to move our Projects Department documents.

The episode underscored the state of confusion at the highest levels of the Iraqi government. Our documents contained nothing more damning than evidence of illegal procurements for conventional weapons; there was nothing pertaining to the weapons of mass destruction that preoccupied the United States and Britain. Saddam had needlessly reverted to concealment mode, as if by instinct. From inside the MIC hierarchy, I could see that this attitude was a strategic mistake. To the outside world, it only fueled doubts that Saddam had abandoned his chemical, biological, and nuclear programs.

The situation had been brewing since the terrorist attacks on the United States the year before. After U.S.-backed forces drove the Taliban from power in Afghanistan, the United States shifted the focus of its "war on terror" onto Iraq. The leaders of the United States and Britain accused Saddam of restarting his weapons of mass destruction programs and secretly dealing with al-Qaeda. Saddam reluctantly agreed to new rounds of weapons inspections only under the threat of large-scale military action. In this atmosphere of mistrust, the Iraqi government's protestations that it had no WMD fell on deaf ears.

The inspectors focused on accusations made in a dossier the British government produced in late September 2002 that claimed, among other things, that Iraq could produce a nuclear weapon within one or two years if it obtained enough uranium and components from abroad. The dossier fixed its allegations squarely on what it claimed was a renewed centrifuge program. It suggested that Iraq had attempted to build a magnet production facility and acquire thousands of aluminum tubes to use as centrifuge rotors. It also cited intelligence reports that Iraq had recently tried to purchase significant amounts of uranium in Africa.

After the IAEA inspectors presented these claims to the National Monitoring Directorate, Dr. Jaffar called a meeting of top scientists from the former nuclear program. He was now a presidential advisor on the topic of transfer of technology, with an office overlooking the Tigris River next to the former British embassy. In this elegant setting we discussed the three allegations one by one. The importance of supplying good explanations to the inspectors was clear. We took the task very seriously because so much could be riding on our answers.

Dr. Jaffar said that the NMD would investigate the claim that Iraq had tried to purchase uranium in Africa. It was an allegation beyond the expertise of scientists. It was agreed that Dr. Faris, my former Engineering Support Department head during the centrifuge program, would look into the aluminum tubes issue. Dr. Jaffar asked one of his former EMIS scientists to research the allegation about the planned magnet production facility, along with my assistance.

I knew about the plans for a magnet plant at al-Tahadi, about thirty kilometers east of Baghdad, because the proposal had crossed my desk at MIC. But I wasn't familiar with the intricate details of the project, which was still unrealized. Logic punched a hole in the notion that the designers of the magnet plant had secret ambitions to manufacture centrifuge components. Such a large-scale endeavor would imply that Iraq already had a production-scale centrifuge facility in the works. To satisfy the inspectors, however, I felt we needed to dig deeper. I called Dr. Widad Hattam, who had worked with centrifuge magnets in the UK during the 1980s, and asked her to investigate the plans for the facility, including the production schedule and the physics behind the plans for the magnets. She was an accomplished scientist, and after a couple of weeks of research, she was able to show convincingly that the planned magnets were intended for applications such as water pumps, large-scale industrial motors, and shoulder-fired rockets, but not centrifuges.

The aluminum tubes were another matter. My first reaction when I heard the allegation was that it defied logic. Why would Iraq stockpile tubes, allegedly for centrifuge rotors, when there was no infrastructure for the rest of a centrifuge program? The weapons inspectors seemed fixated on the issue, however.

The day before the meeting with Dr. Jaffar, I received a call from Saddam's advisor, Lieutenant General Amir al-Saadi, who said that inspectors had made an impromptu visit to a facility in Arraya, where Dr. Kadhim Mijbil was rehabilitating some of the tubes after they had been improperly stored. General al-Saadi put Dr. Kadhim on the phone. His tone of voice seemed almost plaintive. He said he had felt tricked by the inspectors who, when he told them the tubes were for artillery rockets, challenged him to explain why they couldn't also be used for centrifuge rotors.

"I told them that I didn't know anything about centrifuges," Dr. Khadim said. "But they treated me as though I were hiding the truth."

When General al-Saadi came back on the line, I informed him that we had experimented with aluminum rotors during our early efforts with the Beams-type centrifuge, but with a larger diameter than the tubes Iraq had recently ordered for rockets. I said that aluminum rotors could not be used for the magnetic type of centrifuge with which we succeeded in enriching uranium in 1990. After we hung up, I had second thoughts. I consulted with one of my junior engineers, Jamal, from the centrifuge days, who reminded me that Professor Zippe had used aluminum in early magnetic centrifuge work at the University of Virginia during the late 1950s. I called General Saadi back to correct myself. It was extremely important, I said, to give the inspectors the right arguments for the implausibility of the aluminum tubes allegation. We could not categorically state that aluminum tubes were unsuited for magnetic centrifuges. We needed to present a very detailed case. I knew that Dr. Faris was making a thorough investigation into the tolerances and specifications of the aluminum tubes, in order to show that they were indeed intended for artillery rockets. And I felt confident that we would be able to refute charges that Iraq had secretly restarted its nuclear program.

Meanwhile, under intense international pressure, Saddam was cooperating with weapons inspectors on an unprecedented scale. They received immediate access to any building including presidential sites and palaces. IAEA teams with advanced equipment for nuclear inspections visited carefully selected sites every day. They swooped down unannounced on cement factories, chemical plants, food-processing facilities, mineral plants, and centers dedicated to electronics and lasers, where they were given full cooperation by the Iraqi managers. They visited the former al-Furat facility, which had been renamed al-Milad and converted into a military research center. They repeatedly scoured the IAEC facility at Tuwaitha. At our former Engineering Design Center at Rashdiya, they conducted tests for uranium traces. They took samples of water, sediment, and vegetation around sites formerly associated with the nuclear program. They checked equipment at manufacturing sites. They took documents and downloaded computer files at trading companies, munitions factories, and banks. They performed radiometric surveys up and down Iraq's main waterways. They took aerosol samples in specially equipped vehicles that logged thousands of miles over the course of a few months. None of their efforts turned up any evidence of a revived nuclear program.

But as the National Monitoring Directorate scrambled to refute the allegations over the planned magnet factory, the aluminum tubes, and the supposed purchase of African uranium, other disputes arose. The UN pressed Saddam to accept surveillance flights by spy planes over Iraq and to adopt national legislation that would ban weapons of mass destruction. Saddam initially rejected both as affronts to Iraq's national sovereignty. Even more contentious was the inspectors' demand to meet with former WMD scientists privately, without government minders and free of restrictions. President Bush pressured Saddam to let leading scientists and their families out of Iraq where they could speak openly without fear of reprisals. Saddam might have been afraid that if given their freedom, the scientists would return the favor in exile by providing false information that could help justify war against Iraq. After weeks of negotiations, the Iraqi government finally agreed to allow some scientists to speak privately to inspectors. But the NMD stipulated that all interviews should be tape-recorded for later review by their superiors.

As the inspectors went about their work, officials at MIC simply ignored the growing threat of war. The sense of denial was so great that as late as December, I was overseeing a ten-year development plan. It was absurd. While the world's mightiest army was preparing to invade his nation, Saddam was blithely calling for military-industrial plans up to the year 2012. I did not voice my opinion that this was perhaps the wrong priority, given the circumstances. Instead, I gathered all the department heads and asked them to propose projects that both adhered to UN sanctions on Iraq's military procurements and advanced the country's defenses into the distant future.

Our plan addressed shortcomings in Iraq's antiaircraft systems. For years, U.S. and British bombers had intermittently struck air defenses in the northern and southern no-fly zones. The Iraqi radar sent out signals so detectable that they were easy targets. On the other hand, Iraqi surface-to-air missiles were limited in range and accuracy. They had not downed a single American or British airplane during more than a decade of hostilities, and U.S. missiles reached their targets in Iraq with impunity. Our plan included the development of more accurate missiles and a new radar system. They would be ready by 2008.

Meanwhile, a low-level confrontation had already begun. U.S. and British jets were flying daily raids to further weaken Saddam's outmatched air defenses. In late December, President Bush authorized the deployment of U.S. troops to the Gulf region. Cable news channels reported on the preparations at American military bases as soldiers mobilized for full-scale war. I saw a number of reports that U.S. Special Forces were already operating on the ground inside Iraq. I watched this news at home at night, and during the day I was busy at MIC headquarters putting the final touches on budgets for armament factories, a water purification plant, and oil refineries to be completed within the next decade.

In January 2003 IAEA director general Mohammed ElBaradei and Hans Blix, chief of the U.N. inspections in Iraq, declared to the U.N. Security Council that "open questions" remained regarding Iraq's former weapons of mass destruction programs. Under intense international pressure, and in a climate of continued suspicion, they called on Iraq to be more proactive in its cooperation.

In the public places of Baghdad, ordinary citizens warily discussed the events unfolding in the international arena that would soon determine their fates. Fear of government informers kept a tight rein on people's words. The consensus, at least in public, was that the Americans would not invade, but if they did, they would be routed by Iraqi forces.

Every night, Layla, the children, and I crowded around the television in our living room to watch the news on Al-Jazeera and the BBC. American troops streamed into Kuwait and set up massive bases in the desert not far from the Iraqi border. Reporters estimated before long they would number 200,000. Millions of people across the world took to the streets to protest the looming war. Western pundits engaged in heated debates about the fate of my country.

On February 5 we watched U.S. secretary of state Colin Powell present evidence to the UN Security Council that Iraq was still developing weapons of mass destruction, including a lengthy allegation over the aluminum tubes. Important nations such as France, Germany, and Russia seemed unimpressed by the presentation. We speculated about whether Saddam could rely on the support of these countries to prevent an invasion. I thought this was very unlikely. I sensed that an American invasion was inevitable. The U.S. troop buildup neared completion in northern Kuwait, with too many supplies and soldiers amassed to allow for a face-saving retreat.

Saddam reacted to the events swirling around him like a weary boxer in the twelfth round waiting for the knockout blow. He gave speeches full of bluster and defiance but was unable to respond to the terrible forces building against him. I heard rumors that, instead of preparing for war, he was working on a new novel. Saddam had "anonymously" published two other novels during the past two years. The first was *Zabibah and the King*, in which a kindly ruler, representing Saddam, defends a beautiful woman, representing the

Iraqi people, from her villainous husband, representing the United States. I had read a few pages of it and then tossed it aside as the sort of rubbish that could come only from a fully delusional mind. It was clear that Saddam was living in a world of pure fiction.

In a conciliatory move, he agreed to allow flights by U-2 spy planes over Iraqi territory, but the concession was brushed aside by the United States and Britain. Saddam seemed to have no real strategy for dealing with the military threat building at his doorstep. He divided Iraq into sectors for defense against an enemy whose strengths he did not fully comprehend. He began distributing extra rations among the population in a haphazard way, with no predictions as to how long the fighting might last. For the most part, it seemed the regime preferred to close its eyes to the threat in the hope that it would just go away. At MIC headquarters, officials held countless meetings about how to deal with inspectors but avoided planning for an imminent war.

Soon after Powell's speech, the National Monitoring Directorate notified me that I was to meet UN inspectors for what would turn out to be my last interview with them. A car from the Directorate picked me up at MIC headquarters the afternoon of February 12, 2003. On the way to the UN office, my escort, Mr. Shaker al-Rayis, handed me a cassette recorder and told me to tape the entire conversation with the inspectors. Saddam stated he wanted the interviews taped so that Western governments could not twist statements or add false information into the record.

Mr. Shaker escorted me to the cafeteria on the second floor of a Baghdad office building and remained in the hallway as I walked through the door. Five inspectors seated around a linoleum-topped table rose when I entered the room. I recognized a Canadian, George Healey, from inspections during the 1990s, but had never seen any of the others before. They included two women, from Holland and South Africa, and two men, from the United Kingdom and Egypt. We introduced ourselves and exchanged pleasantries. As we took our seats, Healey looked at the tape recorder.

"Is that really necessary?" he asked.

"It's only procedural," I said, knowing that there would be trouble if I returned without a recording of our session. "But I haven't turned it on yet, so if you would like to ask me something beforehand . . ."

This suggestion was somewhat reckless, but something in me wanted to hint that at least in my garden, there were still truths to be uncovered. The inspectors looked at each other and, perhaps realizing that it was best to stick to the rules set down by the NMD, agreed that the conversation should be recorded in full.

I switched on the tape recorder, and Healey and his colleagues took turns asking questions. At first they covered territory that had been fully explored during the 1990s. They asked about the division of responsibilities among the centrifuge scientists during the late 1980s, and where we worked after the 1991 war. I told them that our old centrifuge team was even more dispersed now than in 1998, which was another indication that we had no active program.

They asked about Iraq's attempted purchases of high-quality magnets and the scrapped plans to build a magnet production line. I explained our research into the matter and assured them that the magnets would have had many industrial uses and that if they had been meant for centrifuges, I would have known about it. Then they came to their main point. As Colin Powell had pointed out a week earlier, Iraq had in recent years ordered tens of thousands of high-grade aluminum tubes for military rockets, which were prohibited under UN sanctions. The inspectors wanted to know if these couldn't be a dual-use item intended for use as centrifuge rotors.

I explained the major flaws in this idea. The diameter of the tubes Iraq had ordered was eighty-one millimeters to meet the specifications of our artillery rockets. The centrifuge rotors we had worked with during the late 1980s were nearly twice this diameter. This major discrepancy alone would have rendered all of our designs and blueprints useless and required a complete redesign of the program.

"As you know, our centrifuge program was designed to use carbon fiber rotors," I said. "We were also prepared to use maraging steel. But aluminum is a far lower-grade material. We would have found it nearly impossible to work with aluminum rotors. We also had no designs or calculations that were appropriate for a smaller diameter."

I knew that Dr. Faris had already presented his findings about the mechanical tolerances of the suspect tubes and their application to artillery rockets. I went further to explain why they were unsuitable for a centrifuge program from a basic engineering point of view. With our designs borrowed from the German centrifuge, we had been able to build an exact replica. This is a process known as reverse engineering, by which one copies an already successful model. But any significant alteration of that model would have required a whole new level of science. The radical change in rotor diameter alone would have forced us to design from scratch a new ball bearing, along with its microscopic grooves, the magnet, caps, motor, and dozens of other components. It would have required us to go back to the drawing board to recalculate the hairy mathematics. One could compare us to a team of automobile engineers who knew how to manufacture a certain model of Mercedes-Benz, and whose designs, skills, and knowledge were geared to that model only. If someone were to give this team a part from another type of car—a piston from a Fiat, for example—they would have a very difficult time building a complete Fiat from it.

I wanted to scream at the inspectors: "You're barking up the wrong tree! Forget about the aluminum; think harder about the capabilities Iraq possesses!" But they were like racehorses wearing blinders, and it seemed they could run in only one direction. When they finally exhausted every possible question about aluminum tubes, they ended the session.

I wondered whether the inspectors might have toned down their suspicions if they had learned of my buried cache of documents and components, which would have been needed to restart the centrifuge program. I imagined bringing a UN team to my home and walking them through the rose garden to the foot of the lotus tree to begin digging. They would have seen how the earth covering the plastic drum was packed tight, hardened by more than a decade of changing seasons while the program remained dormant.

I turned off the tape recorder, but I was reluctant to leave the cafeteria just yet. It had been many years since I had met a group of foreign scientists, and even our two-hour confrontation invigorated me in a way. I felt a powerful urge to help these fellow scientists reach the truth. The threat posed by the centrifuge program was not in a secret facility somewhere in Iraq churning out enriched uranium that could be given to terrorists. The danger was latent, in the form of knowledge that could spread throughout the world. An ancient Chinese proverb says, "Give a man a fish and feed him for a day; teach a man to fish and feed him for a lifetime." What the inspectors had never found was the centrifuge knowledge that could enable Iraq, another country, or a well-funded group to jump-start a uranium enrichment program. Such knowledge was potentially as dangerous as, if not more than, an actual weapon. But this was a subject I could not raise with Healey or the other UN inspectors.

About a week after this meeting, a few other Iraqi scientists and I met with a group of counterparts from South Africa's former nuclear weapons program in a last-ditch effort to help Iraq clear up its misunderstandings with the UN. The South Africans had a history of transparent dealings with inspectors. In 1990, as we mounted our crash program for a single bomb, South Africa became the first nation to voluntarily renounce its nuclear ambitions, and afterward its scientists began cooperating closely with international monitors to dismantle the nuclear equipment and provide documentation.

The seminar lasted only a few hours. Dr. Rihab Taha, the woman known outside Iraq as Dr. Germ, talked about the past Iraqi work on biological weapons. Dr. Faris presented the aluminum tubes analysis he had made for the IAEA inspectors. It was the first time I had heard his arguments in detail. He showed that the dimensions of the aluminum tubes fitted artillery rocket requirements. The tolerances of the metal also matched, Dr. Faris explained, with the help of an overhead projector.

The most important tolerance in a cylindrical object is its eccentricity, or the tiny distance between two axes around which it may rotate. In a rocket, eccentricity helps determine the flight path. It was true that the eccentricity of the aluminum tubes Iraq had ordered was infinitesimally small. The South Africans asked Dr. Faris why Iraq would need such high-quality rocket tubes. The specifications seemed much higher than one would expect for Iraqi military use.

I began to understand how the British and Americans had arrived at the conclusion that the aluminum tubes must have been for some use other than artillery rockets. They had followed a classic false syllogism of logic. Because Iraq would need high-quality tubes for a centrifuge program, they assumed that their purchase was proof of such a program. But they failed to take into consideration, among other things, the cultural differences in Iraq, where standardization was extremely rare and the quality of materials varied widely from project to project. I imagined some young Iraqi engineer designing artillery rockets on his drafting board and requesting the highest specifications, careful to avoid any design error that could get him in trouble, unaware that his request would eventually raise the suspicions of the international community.

The same week that we met the South Africans, inspectors found Iraqi al-Samoud 2 and al-Fatah missiles capable of exceeding by a few miles the ninety-three-mile limit. The difference in range was strategically insignificant, but the UN said the missiles must be destroyed for Iraq to meet its obligations. At first Saddam refused unless the UN lifted sanctions on Iraq, which only fueled tensions. Inspectors also destroyed ten artillery shells filled with lethal mustard gas, which they discovered during the 1990s and which had remained under UN seal throughout "the dark years." Both incidents seemed to feed an international perception that the inspectors had only scratched the surface, and that Iraq must still possess banned weapons. President Bush made a series of speeches preparing his nation for battle. In late February Saddam challenged him to a debate, which was quickly rejected by the U.S. administration.

American commanders in the Gulf region said they were ready for an invasion.

At MIC headquarters we received a new desperate order: the equipment at MIC facilities was to be moved or dismantled and stored elsewhere. For weeks before the war, workers scurried around taking apart expensive machines for milling and welding and storing them where they were less likely to be bombed. Then, near the end of February, a nervous-looking deputy marched into my office with a new order from Abdul Tawab.

"Destroy all documents," he said.

I looked up from my desk, taken aback by the sudden and sweeping nature of the order. It was another sign of confusion and panic within the bureaucracy.

"In which manner shall we destroy them?" I asked. "Shredding or burning?"

The deputy was not prepared to answer this one.

"Prepare all documents to be destroyed. The manner will be made clear forthwith."

The next day I was called into a security meeting at MIC, where the order was changed. We should now scan all paper documents and transfer computer files onto CDs, which could be easily hidden. Then the paper documents and computer hard drives would be collected for destruction.

Saddam must have foreseen that the Americans might seize control of the entire country and go though the files of every ministry. Yet he obviously envisioned a return to power. Otherwise, why order the creation of CDs? It was a chaotic process, in which file transfers were done in such a haphazard manner that even if the CDs were recovered, they would be hopelessly out of order.

With his back against the wall, Saddam agreed to destroy the al-Samoud 2 and al-Fatah missiles that exceeded their allowed range. In early March, Iraqi workers began the humiliating task of cutting apart the missiles and the casting chambers used to produce them. The National Monitoring Directorate drafted a letter reaffirming earlier claims that Iraq had destroyed its stores of anthrax and the deadly VX nerve agent. The Bush administration rejected these concessions as too little, too late.

Nuclear inspectors continued their radiation surveys. They searched trading companies, medical centers, and industrial facilities, including the Sa'ad Company where I had been director general. On March 7 IAEA director general Mohammed ElBaradei went before the United Nations Security Council to summarize the inspectors' findings so far. Apparently convinced by our well-researched arguments, he concluded that there was no indication that Iraq's efforts to either import aluminum tubes or produce magnets were related to centrifuges. He said the allegations that Iraq sought to buy uranium in Africa were unfounded. He also stated that inspectors should continue and urged Saddam to step up the pace of cooperation. He repeated his request to interview scientists outside Iraq. But after three months of intrusive inspections, he said, the IAEA had found no evidence or plausible indication of the revival of a nuclear weapons program.

During the following week, the world's most powerful nations continued to argue about invading Iraq. The United States, Britain, and Spain supported military action unless Saddam provided immediate proof that he had no weapons of mass destruction. On the other side, France, Germany, Russia, and China argued that inspectors should be given more time to carry out their work. By March 15, when the United States rejected a Chilean proposal to give Saddam a last chance, the case was closed. The moment of truth had arrived.

On March 17 President Bush issued an ultimatum that Saddam and his sons leave Iraq within forty-eight hours or face a full military onslaught. Saddam refused. The next day, the UN evacuated its weapons inspectors on the advice of the U.S. government. In Baghdad, schoolteachers canceled classes. My daughters stayed at home, too frightened to study anyway. Shopkeepers shuttered their doors and boarded up their windows. We waited for hell to rain down from the skies.

The night of March 19, American warplanes bombed three

buildings in Baghdad, including a restaurant where Saddam was thought to be hiding, in an unsuccessful attempt to assassinate him before war broke out. The "shock and awe" attacks that followed were inadequately named. They should have been called "shock and terrorize" attacks. The scream of incoming bombs, the crack of explosions, the shaking of the earth struck in us a fear that life would end with the next incoming missile. Every night my heart raced until I thought it would burst as I prayed for the deliverance of my family. The horizon glowed with fire in every direction. Tracers from antiaircraft fire streaked upward through the sky. Air raid sirens wailed almost constantly, drowned out by explosions that sent out concussive waves. If the blasts were far enough away, we would see the flash of light of the explosion a second or two before the wave of sound and energy passed through our bodies. They fell without warning, leaving no time to steady the heart beforehand.

In the mornings, clouds of black smoke from burning buildings and dozens of oil fires darkened the sky as I drove to the improvised MIC headquarters at the kindergarten in Jumhuriya. MIC officials clung to their habits and schedules, arriving at eight every morning, maintaining the illusion that it was all a nightmare that would pass.

The week after the bombing started, a sandstorm blew into Baghdad on a gale force wind, extinguishing the light of the sun. The orange haze of dust mixed with the foul smoke and the fog of war. It became hard to see, literally and figuratively. They say that truth is the first casualty of battle, and this was especially true in Baghdad. Parallel versions of the conflict unfolded on the ground and on satellite TV at home. On March 26, international news channels reported that American and British forces had taken Iraq's port of Umm-Qasr. Saddam's Minister of Information, Muhammed al-Sahhaf, claimed that the port was still safely under Iraqi control. He also stated that Iraqi troops had repulsed the American attack at the Kuwaiti border. Within hours missiles slammed into Baghdad's television tower, extinguishing state broadcasts. At the temporary MIC headquarters, officials kept to the party line that Iraq was on the threshold of a great victory. That evening I received a phone call from a friend in the southern town of Nasiriyah, shortly before U.S. bombs cut off telephone service across the country.

"I'm looking out my window, and there is an American tank parked on the street in front of my house!" he said in an urgent voice. "I thought the Americans were still fighting at the border."

"I know," I said, momentarily forgetting my fear that my phone was tapped. "I'm watching it via satellite."

When I related this phone call to a MIC official the next day, he muttered that my friend should be condemned for his treasonous lying. But I could hear the hollowness of his accusation; and I could see the hypocrisy in his eyes giving way to something like resignation. But he could not openly express what his eyes said.

The propaganda war was in full swing on both sides. A few days after the invasion began, a snowstorm of paper leaflets fluttered down from the skies above our home. They skittered along the ground, propelled by gusts of wind, coming to rest against residential fences and shrubbery. Two of them landed in my garden. They were written in flawless Arabic.

One of the fliers showed photographs of a normal Iraqi family on one side, and on the other side one of Saddam's high-ranking officers, along with the message: "Who needs you more, your families or the system? Go back to your homes and your families!" The other flier bore a stranger statement. It stated, "Iraq: we can see everything. Do not use nuclear, biological or chemical weapons."

One of my final orders from Saddam's regime was to check on the MIC gasoline inventory in Taji, about fifteen miles north of Baghdad. I set off in the late morning with the assistant director of the FAO Engineering Establishment. The streets were unnervingly desolate, and as soon as we reached the outskirts of Baghdad, ours was the only car on the road. The air raid sirens faded behind us. We raced northward on the highway toward Tikrit, terrified that on the open road our car would be targeted by the American jets overhead.

About half a mile from the gasoline depot, we passed a telephone exchange complex. The perimeter walls were ripped open with bomb holes. Smoke still rose from the wreckage inside. We pulled into the depot and saw about fifteen panicked residents of local towns who had been press-ganged by Saddam's security men into trying to sandbag the massive gasoline tanks to hide them from air attacks. The hopelessness of the project was stunning. It would have required at least a hundred men. Rows of sixteen white tanks, three yards wide and fifteen yards long with hundreds of thousands of gallons of gasoline inside, dwarfed the poor workers. As they struggled to fill sandbags from mounds of bulldozed earth, their eyes filled with fear. They knew that if a bomb hit the tanks they would be instantly consumed in a firestorm. I wished I could authorize them to leave their posts and go home to their families, but I could not. It was still Saddam's Iraq.

Under orders, I returned with Zaid to see about their progress two days later. The same fifteen workers were on-site, still terrified of being bombed but even more afraid of reprisals from the security forces if they were found to have abandoned the job. They had covered only two of the sixteen tanks with sand bags. Zaid and I hurriedly left that dangerous scene. As we drove away, I said a prayer for the safety of those men.

We drove through Baghdad to the southern suburb of Zafaraniya, where I grew up, to check on a group engineers from the Electrical Department of the Sa'ad Company, who were holed up next to one of their facilities. They had built a bunker like the one at the kindergarten headquarters, with a shipping container half-buried in the ground. The engineers huddled inside, under orders not to leave their post, waiting for death. They said antiaircraft batteries had been set up nearby, hidden in the orange groves heavy with fruit. In the distance we could hear the thud of artillery rounds. The Americans were approaching. They would soon be at the gates of Baghdad, then rolling into the city in an invasion my family and I would barely survive.

CHAPTER 10

The Time Capsule

A week into the occupation, soon after Captain Butler and his army engineers disentangled the American bomb from my tool rack and drove off with it, I walked back to look at the place where the missile had come to rest a few feet from my daughters' bedroom. The collapsed metal shelving retained the curled shape of the bomb, and I shuddered as I thought about how death's shadow had nearly fallen over my family several times during the battle for Baghdad. Overcome with emotion, I sank to my knees and said a silent prayer of thanks to Allah for sparing us.

The sun beat down on my neck, and when I stood up, I felt lightheaded for a few moments. When I regained my bearings, I walked over to the foot of the *lote* tree. I was about to make decisions that would affect the lives of me and my family in ways I could not predict. I had passed through many trials in my life, but I foresaw that dealing with the ticking time bomb below my feet would be a very difficult test. I looked down at the innocuous-seeming patch of earth and tried to fathom a situation well beyond my depth.

There were many people who would like to get their hands on the centrifuge secrets, if they knew about them. The tyrant had been pushed out of office, but those who favored tyranny still lurked in Iraq, waiting in the wings, exerting their power wherever they could. If Saddam, his sons, or his loyalists wanted these documents, they would come for me. The centrifuge knowledge was valuable for anyone interested in building a nuclear bomb or selling the secrets on the black market. It could easily proliferate. What if agents from a foreign country or a terrorist group paid me a visit and coerced me into spilling my secrets? They might covet the materials buried under my tree. They might even force me to assist in a clandestine centrifuge program in a foreign country, as the Soviets did to Gernot Zippe at the end of World War II. I tried to tell myself these were only paranoid thoughts. Yet the fear persisted.

I imagined that the Americans would also be interested to learn of my centrifuge cache. Now that the occupation had spread to all corners of Iraq, U.S. soldiers were hunting for weapons of mass destruction and arresting leading figures in Saddam's government. My predicament would get even murkier if I were on a blacklist. Rumors swirled around Baghdad that the Americans had developed a "deck of cards" list of the fifty-five Iraqis most wanted for arrest. In those early days, we didn't know who was on it. I feared I might be included. Already, troops were arresting some of my former bosses.

I weighed my options. I could leave the centrifuge designs and components buried in my garden and tell no one about them. Unless Qusay Hussein or one of his confidants said something, no one would ever know of their existence. I tried to imagine the consequences in Iraq's distant future but kept drawing a blank. The past held my mind on a leash. My dream as a young man had been to see my beloved country bloom. But tyranny perverted my ambitions, as Saddam forced me to use my knowledge and capabilities for his aggressive purposes. No one could promise that the past would not repeat itself, that Iraq would not one day be ruled by another dictator willing to develop bombs that could annihilate humanity. There was no guarantee that I would not be forced to bring out my secrets once again, only to be ground up again in a new mincer.

If I unearthed the documents and components, I could try to sell them for a tremendous amount of money. But the penalty would be heavy if I were caught, and the idea of assisting another covert nuclear program was repugnant to me. The only other option left was to give them to the Americans. Deep inside, I yearned to reveal the truth about the capabilities leftover from the Iraqi centrifuge program and finally rid myself of this liability.

But by approaching the Americans, I could completely lose control of my destiny. There was no way of knowing how they would treat any of Iraq's former WMD scientists. And I was still holding evidence. I feared they would imprison me. They had just waged a war to find Iraq's alleged weapons of mass destruction. They might see me as a culprit in their investigation. Another consequence of approaching them was potentially more lethal. I was afraid of forces still loyal to Saddam and his sons. Saddam surely had a well-organized network of hard-core followers still in the streets. If they found out that I had voluntarily handed over his last nuclear secrets, my family and I could easily become targets for retribution. These were trained assassins who thought nothing of killing civilians. How could the Americans guarantee my safety in this case?

I brought my wife and children home from my eldest daughter Isra'a's house. After we had settled in again, I revealed to Layla and Zaid that I had buried the centrifuge items in our garden. I explained that I had kept this from them all these years out of fear for their safety, and they quickly grasped the gravity of the matter.

Soon after the fall of Baghdad, an American radio broadcast called for all Iraqi WMD scientists to turn themselves in. It didn't say where or to whom. I had heard rumors that a thousand or more American-sponsored weapons investigators would be coming to Iraq to try to substantiate its prewar claims. But they were weeks away, at least. All telephone service was cut, so I sent Zaid to ask my former department heads, Dr. Adil and Dr. Faris, to come to my house so we could discuss the best way of approaching the Americans. We sat in my garden trying to predict how they would treat us.

"Do you think they will arrest us and lock us up?" Dr. Faris asked.

"No, it doesn't make sense for them to arrest us," I said, trying to disguise my lack of confidence.

I was only guessing. We agreed that one of us should approach the Americans as an emissary, which would discourage them from detaining one scientist and frightening the others into hiding. The next day Dr. Faris went to the Republican Palace, Saddam's former center of power, where the U.S. military was setting up its head-quarters. He returned to my house late in the afternoon and said a U.S. Army official had told him to go home and that U.S. investigators would find him when they were ready.

"Was that all?" I asked.

"They asked me if I knew the whereabouts of Saddam," he said, "or weapons of mass destruction."

Dr. Faris and Dr. Adil had no new information to give regarding the nuclear program, and this is where our paths parted ways. After Dr. Faris left, I felt I needed to take a more proactive approach. But Baghdad was in a state of total chaos. Constant skull-splitting explosions, mostly from American forces detonating unexploded bombs, rattled our nerves. A sense of permissiveness and fear ruled the streets. Law-abiding people kept mostly to their homes. Simply driving across town could be hazardous. Random crimes went unpunished, and no one went out after dark. In the total absence of law and order, I wondered what forces, domestic or foreign, might be roaming the city in pursuit of their own agendas.

I reread the *Washington Post* article downloaded from the Inter-net, which named me as one of the Iraqi scientists inspectors had most wanted to interview outside Iraq before the war. The article quoted a former inspector named David Albright, who was based in Washington. I had met Albright a few times after the defection of Hussein Kamel in 1995. It occurred to me to try to contact him. Someone like him would understand the significance of what I had to offer, which I figured was of a nature too technical for the U.S. troops hunting for actual weapons in Iraq. Because he was in Washington, I thought, he could gauge the intentions of the U.S. government toward the scientists and perhaps offer desperately needed advice. The trouble was that I didn't have a telephone number for Albright, and even if I did, there was no phone service in Iraq. We were completely cut off from the world.

Zaid and I drove across town to the Palestine Hotel, where the international press corps and some U.S. government officers were based. U.S. marines had cordoned off a perimeter around the hotel with barbed wire. Inside the barricade, several tanks and dozens of soldiers protected the foreigners staying at the Palestine and the Sheraton Hotel next door. The tanks faced Firdos Square, where the remnants of Saddam's statue lay at the foot of its pedestal. A huge demonstration was in progress. Thousands of Iraqis thronged outside the barbed wire cordon. Zaid and I parked and moved through the outer edge of the crowd for a closer look. We found ourselves in a mob organized by a mosque in one of Baghdad's poorer areas. They were demanding the release of two clerics arrested by U.S. forces earlier in the day. "Down, down, America!" they chanted in Arabic. "No to occupation!" On the other side of the barbed wire, American marines, wearing bulletproof vests and helmets, fingered the triggers of their assault rifles. I could see that they could understand neither the words nor the intentions of the demonstrators a few feet away. I jostled through the crowd until I had reached the cordon, where I tried to catch the attention of one of the marines.

"I am trying to get inside the hotel," I shouted.

"Nobody goes in without a pass," he said.

"I am a scientist," I said. "A radio broadcast said we should turn ourselves in."

The chanting around me grew deafening, and the marine looked fidgety.

"You're not coming in here!" he shouted. "What do you want me to do? Do you want me to handcuff you and take you to prison?"

Zaid and I backed away to a street corner, between the demonstrators and Firdos Square, to watch the confrontation. It seemed there was no way for us to enter the hotel. Then, in the middle of the melee, I spotted a blond-haired woman with two cameras slung over her shoulders, accompanied by an Iraqi-looking man I assumed was her translator. I approached her and spoke in English.

"Excuse me, are you a journalist?"

She stopped and seemed to take note of the fact that I was dressed in a coat and tie, differentiating me from the rest of the crowd.

"I am Dr. Mahdi Obeidi, one of Saddam's nuclear scientists," I said. "I would like to speak to a journalist."

The woman introduced herself as Molly. I showed her a worn printout of the *Washington Post* article, to identify who I was. She said she would put me in touch with a colleague inside the Palestine Hotel. I waited on a street corner, until her colleague came out. He ushered Zaid and me through the hotel cordon by telling the tense-looking U.S. soldiers at the checkpoint that we were his translator and driver. After a short discussion, he agreed to help me locate Albright. We stood on the balcony of his hotel suite overlooking the growing demonstration and the increasingly nervous U.S. soldiers below, and discussed whether the Americans knew what they were getting themselves into.

The next day the journalist brought his satellite phone to my home and said Albright was waiting for my call. We sat on plastic chairs on my lawn as I nervously dialed Washington.

"It has been a long time," Albright said. His voice faded in and out as the signal bounced off a satellite in the heavens and reached me after a short delay.

"Seven years, David," I said. "It is good to speak to you again."

Albright asked several technical questions straightaway, leading to whether there had been any recent centrifuge work. He must have known I would not contact him without something to reveal.

"No," I said, "we have not worked on the centrifuge program since 1991."

I took a deep breath. Even by hinting at the nature of my secrets, I was opening the door to unknown consequences.

"David," I said, "there is something I want to discuss that has so far been hidden."

I could feel his attention snap into focus thousands of miles away.

"Yes?" he said. "What is it, and where?"

I was afraid of giving too much information all at once. If someone in Iraq found out I had nuclear secrets in my garden, they might come for me. I took another breath and said the telltale words.

"We are speaking of documents, and of components."

"That haven't been seen before?" he asked.

"That is right," I said. "But before I say anything more about them, I want to discuss the safety of my family. There is no law and order here. The situation is very unstable. I am afraid that coming forward might have a very dangerous effect on us."

Albright seemed to understand my predicament. He advised me not to approach U.S. troops with anything until proper arrangements could be made.

"Be careful what you say," he said. "This line is probably not secure."

I had thought of this. With their sophisticated equipment, the Americans could listen to any telephone or radio communication in Iraq. "The people on the ground are desperate to find evidence of weapons. Has anyone come to your home?"

"Not yet," I said. "Do you think they might detain me?"

"They might."

"I want it to be known that I am coming forward on my own, in good faith," I said.

Albright agreed to contact some people he knew, and we arranged to speak by satellite phone again the next day.

Several days later, I saw some of the boys in our neighborhood reading a paper distributed by American forces that listed the fifty-five most-wanted Iraqis on the deck of cards. I scanned the sheet from top to bottom. Saddam and his sons were at the top of the list, followed by presidential advisors, government ministers, military top brass, and regional Baath Party chairmen. Oil Minister Amir Rashid Mohammad, who had invited me to take a position in the Oil Ministry, was the six of spades. The ten of hearts, Abdul Tawab, had been my boss until two weeks earlier. The head of the National Monitoring Directorate, Husam Mohammed Amin, was the six of clubs. The chestnut-haired Dr. Humam Abd al-Khaliq, the four of hearts, had coached me before my interview with Perricos back in 1991. To my great relief, my name was not on the list.

During the next couple of weeks, Albright and I spoke almost daily. He urged me to be patient. Then, on a late afternoon in mid-May, I was startled by a loud banging on the metal front gate of our driveway. Zaid was out, so I told Layla and the girls to stay inside the house and went out to see who it was. When I slid open the narrow viewing slit, I saw a tall, bearded man wearing baggy pants of the style favored in northern Iraq.

"Is this the home of Dr. Mahdi?" he asked in a Kurdish accent.

"Who is inquiring?" I asked, suspicious that a stranger would come to my house and ask for me by name. The Kurd didn't answer at first. He searched my face as he groped for an answer.

"I am looking for a dentist," he said. "The pharmacy told me I would find a Dr. Mahdi here."

This was a clumsy cover story. The Kurd was obviously trying to confirm my place of residence.

"I'm sorry, there are no dentists or even medical doctors on this block," I said. "I'm afraid you must look elsewhere."

"Thank you very much," he said, as though satisfied with my answer. "Sorry to have disturbed you."

I slid shut the eyehole of my gate anxiously. Who was this man, and who or what group was behind his visit? I reassured myself that as a Kurd, he was almost certainly not working with Saddam's resistance. He could be affiliated with the Americans. But what was the meaning of his deceitful approach? He could just as easily be a bounty hunter for some other group. The situation in Baghdad bred nothing but suspicion.

Zaid maintained his nighttime guard position on the living room sofa with a Kalashnikov rifle within reach. I began meeting the journalist with the satellite phone away from our house as much as possible. We met in the courtyards and living rooms of acquaintances' homes, often by lamplight due to the lack of electricity in Baghdad. Albright said the situation seemed chaotic from his perspective in Washington, too. American troops throughout Iraq were hunting for weapons of mass destruction, but there was no consensus yet in the U.S. capital about how to deal with scientists. The United States had started to assemble a team of more than a thousand inspectors to coordinate the search, called the Iraq Survey Group, but still no one knew how many weeks would elapse before they would arrive in Iraq. Meanwhile, he said, intelligence operatives from different agencies were on the ground in Iraq, competing to find the WMD evidence that would justify the invasion.

I grew increasingly anxious that events would overtake me. As my trust in Albright grew, I began to reveal the general nature of my buried items without mentioning specifics or where I kept them. Over the satellite phone, I told him I had access to several prototype components and detailed drawings for the centrifuge.

"The component drawings?" he asked. "The German centrifuge documents?"

"Yes," I said. "The ones the inspectors never saw."

The short silence on the other end of the line told me that Albright was struck by the significance of what I was saying. He said, however, that soldiers in Iraq might not be able to appreciate the importance of my documents, which weren't exactly the smoking gun the Americans were looking for. They could be interpreted as evidence that Saddam had intended to reconstitute the nuclear program, because the seeds of the centrifuge had been kept hidden all along. But by the same token, the fact that they were buried for more than a decade was evidence that Iraq's nuclear ambitions had lain dormant for just as long. It was important, Albright said, that I speak to experts with proper knowledge.

The intelligence agencies seemed to descend all at once. On an afternoon not long after the mysterious visit from the Kurd, Albright told me that the following morning an American agent would be waiting for me at one of Saddam's lesser-used palaces south of Baghdad. I drove home and Layla told me that, while I was out, two American men had come to the house, identified themselves as Army intelligence agents, and requested that I meet them at their new office in central Baghdad at the same time as the meeting Albright had just arranged. I also received a message from one of my junior scientists who had been approached by a British woman, who he assumed was an agent from MI6, wanting to know the whereabouts of the former centrifuge scientists.

At about seven A.M. the next morning, Zaid and I set out for the place Albright had indicated. As we drove along the Abu Ghraib Expressway, I looked back and noticed that we were being followed by several Korean cars of the Kia make. My heart froze. This was the same model of car used by Saddam's enforcers. The three-lane highway was nearly deserted, and I told Zaid to keep driving normally. The drivers of the Kias pulled up alongside our car and slowed down. I looked over and saw the driver to our right staring at us menacingly. As we approached an intersection manned by U.S. troops, the Kia drivers sped up and dispersed. The old fear jumped back into my stomach. Zaid and I wondered whether these men were assassins, leftover security men, or just looters in vehicles stolen from the former government. As we continued on to our meeting with the American intelligence agents, the long arm of Saddam's tyranny seemed to have come close to grabbing us.

Iraqi guards wearing sweat suits and carrying automatic weapons ushered us through the gates of the palace driveway. A young, clean-cut American was waiting just inside the gates. He introduced himself as Gary. As we drove up a hill to the palace grounds, he spoke very respectfully and seemed to choose his words carefully. We sat in an office adjacent to the main palace building on fine Iraqi-style sofas that had until recently belonged to Saddam. It seemed that the Americans had only just moved into this palace because they still had no generator for electricity. Without air conditioning the office was already stiflingly hot in the midmorning. A soldier sat dozing off in the corner with a rifle across his knees.

From Gary's first questions it was apparent he did not possess a deep knowledge of the Iraqi WMD programs, so I gave him a brief history of the centrifuge program and the dismantling of it after the 1991 Gulf War. He was especially interested in the work of the Sa'ad Company during the 1990s, and I told him about the refineries and other civil projects, as well as the ammunition plant we had worked on.

He asked if I knew anything about Saddam's alleged mobile biological labs, which U.S. soldiers had recently found. I didn't, except for what I had heard on the news. Gary showed me photographs of several trailers that were being inspected to determine whether their purpose was to manufacture biological agents. I studied the pictures. Although I knew nothing of the use of the trucks, I pointed out to him that the piping was uneven and shoddily welded together, as if they were put together in a haphazard way. They were almost certainly not manufactured by Sa'ad or any of the other engineering companies, where the quality of work was very high. He took some notes and said the input was valuable.

The oppressive heat began to weigh on our interview. Rather listlessly, Gary asked about the centrifuge program and the work undertaken by myself and other scientists since 1991. He expressed interest in meeting some of the managers at Sa'ad, which was far from the topic I had hoped to discuss. I chose my words carefully to steer his interest in the right direction.

"We are talking about history, but I wanted to discuss something more current," I said. "As you know, the UN inspectors were here before the war. There were some significant points that they were unable to see. I am hoping to speak to someone in this context, but I also have some concerns about my safety."

Gary perked up at this hint. He seemed intelligent enough to quickly grasp that I needed to meet with someone with a deeper knowledge of our programs and more power over how I would be treated. We agreed that rather than meeting with managers from Sa'ad, he would arrange for me to speak with some of his colleagues in the days to come.

When Zaid and I returned home we found Layla in a distressed state. One of the Army men who had come the day before, named John, arrived in the early afternoon with an Iraqi interpreter. Layla recounted his intimidating tone.

"How dare your husband miss our meeting?" he had asked. "Don't you know that we could throw him in prison? If he doesn't come tomorrow, there could be trouble."

Layla said these words had shaken her. But she is a strong woman. I couldn't help feeling proud of her when she told me her response to the Iraqi interpreter.

"We have been oppressed and threatened with imprisonment for more than twenty years under Saddam," she told him in Arabic. "Are we to be similarly oppressed under this new regime?"

This apparently took John aback. After the interpreter translated it to him, he left shaking his head. I knew the threat was serious, however, so Zaid and I drove to the office John had specified. Adjacent to the Hunting Club, formerly a popular haunt for Saddam's inner circle, the whole area was now guarded by armed Iraqis working for the Americans and the Iraqi National Congress, a party led by the long-exiled businessman Ahmed Chalabi. A group of large-bellied Iraqi men sat partially blocking the entrance to the army intelligence office in a gun-happy way. Zaid and I politely excused ourselves but were forced to squeeze past them as they refused to budge. Once inside, we were led to a large, shabby room with unpainted brick walls, cheap tables, and the atmosphere of an Iraqi police station. I could hear the hum of a generator outside, and at least the place was cooled by air conditioning.

After about ten minutes, the agent John arrived and introduced himself and two of his colleagues. In his early sixties, with a crew cut and receding hairline, John wore the face of a man who has had a hard life. I apologized for being unable to meet him earlier and explained that I had been meeting some of his compatriots at another location. He became suspicious.

"Who were they?" he asked. "Who else are you talking to?"

"They didn't reveal to me exactly who they were," I said.

John exchanged a look with one of his fellow Americans.

"The CIA is trying to intrude," the colleague said to him. "As if they don't have enough on their plate."

"We have to settle this matter of who you are talking to," he said, turning back to me. "You should be talking to us and not them."

I was surprised that agents of one American intelligence agency would feel it was appropriate to take issue with another, especially in front of me, a stranger and a foreigner. I tried to come up with diplomatic words for this unusual situation.

"To me, an American is an American," I said. "It makes no difference in my eyes. I am ready to answer your questions."

We were joined by an Army scientist, David, with a broad Asiatic face and a friendly demeanor. John sat next to me at a table with an assistant next to him to take notes. David sat across from me and asked most of the questions. He was respectful and clearly understood nuclear science, but he didn't seem well versed in the Iraqi nuclear weapons program either. I walked him through the history. David asked whether the program had been restarted after 1991. He barely hid his disappointment when I said it had not.

"Were there any machines purchased for the centrifuge program?" he asked. "Were you seeking materials? Any procurements at all?"

"Just keep writing, 'No,'" I said to the assistant taking notes as David's questions continued.

David eventually changed the subject to the achievements of the centrifuge program in the 1980s. We spoke in technical terms about the small amount of uranium we had enriched with the prototype in 1990 and other issues that had been covered with UN weapons inspectors during the past twelve years. Despite the cordial dialogue with David, I could tell that John was getting restless.

"Do you know that you are on the most-wanted list?" he asked at one point.

I blanched at this. What most-wanted list?

"I have seen the deck-of-cards list," I said. "I understand that I am not on it."

John said there was an extended list. He led me over to another table and showed me an official-looking paper. I recognized it as a list of the fifty-five most-wanted Iraqis. Then he unfolded a supplementary page and cupped his hands over most of the names so that I could not read them.

"Here you are," he said.

I bent down to peer between his fingers and saw my own name and the number next to it. Sixty-six. I tried to hide my sense of alarm. I had no idea who had drawn up this list, but it implied that I could be put in the same category as Saddam's cronies who were slowly but surely being locked up by the Americans. I couldn't imagine what to make of this thinly veiled threat. John left the room without explaining anything more. Zaid and I exchanged courteous words with David and the assistant, and nervously left for home.

My fears hardened into something real. There was no question now that I was on a blacklist, and prison loomed as a possibility. Everything seemed so cluttered in my head. The suspicions piled up at my door: I was apparently suspected of running an ongoing centrifuge program, as well as leading the Sa'ad Company, which was accused of producing biological weapons. I was being torn between these agencies that seemed to agree only that I was important. The Kurd asking for a dentist named Obeidi aggravated my anxiety further. Who would come next to my home, I wondered, to subject me to an unknown agenda?

During the following weeks I met several times with Gary's colleagues. They said they understood that I was potentially putting myself and my family at risk by approaching them. But I didn't know how far I could trust them. I didn't know whether to trust anyone. I felt I had to do something to put myself in the clear, so I offered to show a sample of what I was offering. One blazingly hot afternoon in early May, I disentangled a shovel from my wrecked tool rack and started digging at the foot of the lotus tree. The earth was hard-packed and dry, but soon I had uncovered the rim of the green plastic drum. I dug a wide hole to loosen the dirt around its outsides. Then I pulled the container out of the ground and set it beside me. It was like digging up a time capsule. I unsealed the top and found the plastic bags with the documents and components just as I had packed them more than a decade earlier. I took them into my back bedroom and removed a sample for the Americans: the centrifuge ball bearing along with a sheaf that contained the detailed drawings and specifications for manufacturing it.

When I gave these specimens to Gary's colleagues, they seemed excited to have something tangible that related to Iraq's weapons of mass destruction programs and that the United Nations had never seen. They also seemed impressed when I told them I had access to several more components and designs for the rest of the centrifuge, which I handed over the next day. I began to feel hopeful that the Americans would value my contribution enough to secure the safety of my family and bring us out of Iraq. I phoned Washington to speak with Albright, who said he was lobbying on my behalf. He had received no indications about how I would be treated.

About eight in the morning on June 3, as my children still slept, Layla and I were eating breakfast at our kitchen table. I heard the diesel engines of American military vehicles in the alley next to our home, coming closer. At first I was not alarmed, because the American military regularly patrolled the streets of Baghdad and I figured perhaps they were lost. Layla and I continued eating our bread and cheese and drinking our small cups of tea. Suddenly, a voice outside our garden wall started shouting, "Go! Go! Go!" I looked out the window and saw commandos leaping over the wall into my bed of gardenia flowers. They ran toward our front door. A second later, they kicked it in with a loud crash. I dropped my tea and hurried in the direction of the shouting: the living room, where Zaid usually slept on a sofa with a Kalashnikov rifle to protect the family.

I gasped when I saw half a dozen American soldiers aiming their automatic weapons at my son, shouting, "Don't move! Don't move!" Zaid looked terrified. I glanced around for the Kalashnikov.

He had not slept with it this night, a stroke of luck that almost certainly saved his life. When the soldiers saw me, two of them pointed their weapons at my chest.

"You, on the ground!" they shouted. My heart pounded as I raised my hands in the air and knelt down next to the coffee table.

"There must be some mistake," I said. But the soldiers seemed on edge and didn't listen.

"On the ground!" they shouted. "Now!"

As I lay face down on my floor, about two dozen more soldiers filed into our home and spread out into the different rooms. I raised my head and saw that Layla had hurried in from the kitchen. She cried out loud when she saw Zaid and me on our stomachs surrounded by gunmen. The soldiers told her to lie facedown near us. Other soldiers brought my two teenage daughters, Amne and Ayat, and told them to lie down, too. We were all shivering with fear. With my face against the floor, I struggled to regain my poise.

"What do you want of us?" I asked. "We don't mean you any harm."

A man who seemed to be the commanding officer asked for my identification papers. I was still wearing my pajamas, and I told him my papers were in my bedroom with my clothing.

"Get up," he said. "Let's go."

I walked down the corridor followed by the commanding officer and his Iraqi translator. My hands shook as I handed them my ID card. The translator looked at my name written in Arabic and my picture and then looked into my face.

"That's him," he said. "This is the one you want. This is Dr. Mahdi Obeidi."

The officer and a group of his soldiers led me past the worried faces of my family and out my front door. When we reached my garden, I felt a chill in my spine as one of the soldiers told me to put my hands behind my back and handcuffed me. I had seen such a thing happen to outlaws and criminals. It never occurred to me that someday my own hands would be tied behind my back. The soldiers escorted me through my front gate, and I saw the wife of my friend and neighbor. She shrieked when she saw me in handcuffs being led to an American Humvee, surrounded by armed guards. The commanding officer ordered one of his soldiers to re-handcuff me with my hands in front because I was being cooperative. They helped me into the back seat of the Humvee next to the commanding officer. We rolled down the alley toward the main road.

"I believe there must be a misunderstanding," I said. "I have already been interviewed many times by your intelligence services during the past days."

"I'm afraid I don't know anything about that," he said. "I only have orders to bring you in."

About a mile away, our convoy stopped at another home. A group of the commandos disappeared through the front gate but returned a few minutes later alone, apparently having made a mistake. I was the only captive being taken to an unknown fate that morning. As we sped off in the direction of the international airport at more than fifty miles per hour, a hot wind blew in through the windows of the Humvee. We passed groves of date palms and the wrecks of Iraqi tanks on both sides of the road. I began to feel my heart beating more slowly, so I tried to strike up a conversation with the American officer. He seemed more relaxed now. As we drew closer to the airport, we discussed the battle between the American and Iraqi forces there during the invasion weeks before. I was surprised when he said there had been no real battle, and that the Americans had taken the airport in a few hours. I told the officer that my superiors at the MIC had claimed that Iraqi forces had defended the airport so fiercely that it had been littered with the corpses of American soldiers. He found this amusing.

The Humvee rolled across the tarmac toward the main compound and stopped at a hangar where the entrance was surrounded by barbed wire. A hand-painted sign read "EPW." Enemy Prisoner of War. My heart filled with dread. Was I now a prisoner of war? The officer kept me at a distance as he spoke to another officer. Then he took me for a medical check to the holding pen surrounded by more barbed wire. He freed my hands and I found a cardboard box to sit on. A young officer came and asked me questions about my health. Then he asked me if I knew the whereabouts of Saddam Hussein. The question revealed how little he understood about Iraq.

"I am a scientist," I said. "How would I know where he is?"

The officer shrugged and left. I looked around at the other prisoners sitting on the ground on blankets or the bare concrete. Many of them appeared to be common criminals and thugs. A young female American soldier stood guard at the entrance to the enclosure, listening to pop music on a portable stereo. She seemed carried away by one of the songs and started moving her hips in time to the music. One of the Iraqi inmates, a dirty, deranged-looking fellow, stood up from the concrete floor and began to dance with her from a distance. The soldier laughed and obliged the prisoner with a dance for a few moments. It seemed awfully sordid. I sat there feeling dispirited and humiliated.

Time seemed to pass very slowly. Across the tarmac I could see a bungalow where I imagined the Americans might be keeping celebrity war prisoners such as Tariq Aziz, Sa'adon Hummadi, the head of Saddam's Iraqi National Parliament, and Abdul Tawab. I despaired at the thought that the Americans might lock me away in that place, away from my family. I feared what could become of them. My only small consolation was that if I were put in prison with top figures in Saddam's regime, they would probably be safe from his loyalists.

There are times in a man's life when a line the width of a hair can separate truth from falsehood, trust from mistrust. I felt I was balancing on such a fateful line. Only days earlier American agents had seemed pleased that I would provide them with a three-foot stack of centrifuge documents and designs. I had unearthed the potentially lethal secrets from under my lotus tree and was prepared to turn over the lot. I had opened my heart and mind and finally, after all the years of deceptions, been able to reveal the truth without leaving anything untold. I had made my intentions clear and had approached the Americans in good faith. What was this, then? Was my reward to be made a prisoner of war? Would the Americans double-cross me with such ruthlessness? As I felt such dark ideas poisoning my mind, I resorted, as I often do in times of crisis and doubt, to prayer. I began to recite to myself the sura from the Koran known as the Verse of the Throne:

> *God! There is no god*
> *But He, the Living,*
> *The Self-Subsisting, Eternal.*
> *No slumber can seize him*
> *Nor sleep. His are all things*
> *In the heavens and on earth.*
> *Who is there that can intercede*
> *In his presence except*
> *As he permitteth?*

These words comforted me somewhat and I tried to resign myself to my fate, whatever it might be. I took solace from the lifting of the weight that had held me down for the past twelve years as I had withheld the truth. Strangely, at the very moment I found myself facing the possibility of prison, I felt freer than I had in years. It reminded me of a scientific phenomenon known as threshold energy, in which energy must reach a critical level before settling into a lower state of equilibrium. Digging up the truth was my destiny in the end, and this gave me a feeling of being closer to myself as a scientist and as a person.

I lost track of the passage of time as I sat immersed in these thoughts. At some point, an army officer entered the enclosure and came over to me. He greeted me courteously and gave me a chair to sit on in place of the cardboard box. I was slightly baffled by the gesture. After he left, I looked around at my fellow detainees, who were all sitting on the ground.

"That's a nice chair you have there," the female guard said.

"Please take it for yourself," I said, standing up.

"No, no, I'm just kidding," she said, apparently sensing that I was not an ordinary prisoner.

At about three o'clock in the afternoon, I received a visit from an officer with plenty of stripes on his uniform and a tall man in civilian clothes. They introduced themselves, and we shook hands, as the other Iraqi prisoners and the guard looked on. The civilian did the talking.

"Dr. Obeidi, my name is Carl," he said. "I'm afraid there has been a terrible mistake. I hope you will be kind enough to forgive us. It seems our right hand doesn't know what our left hand is doing."

"I was hoping that this was the case," I said, sighing with relief. "But thank you."

"I will take you home whenever you are ready," he said.

As Carl drove me home, I thought of the beginning of the sura that follows the Verse of the Throne. It seemed oddly fitting:

Let there be no compulsion in religion,
Truth stands out clear from Error . . .

My family wept with joy when Carl delivered me home late in the afternoon. They had expected the worst, and for most of that day it had seemed inconceivable to them that I could be back so soon. A couple of hours earlier one of the intelligence agents to whom I gave the ball bearing prototype and designs had come to the house looking for me. Layla said he was very upset when he heard that the army had arrested me.

"Damn them!" he had told Layla. "How could they do such a thing?"

He had tried to comfort my wife and daughters, who were in tears, and promised them he would do something about it. But after the traumatic morning, Layla said, she didn't know what to believe.

From then on events moved very quickly. Despite the fact that I had turned over the rest of the documents and components to the Americans, my wife and daughters were nervous about staying in our house because they feared U.S. soldiers could barge in on them at any minute and take me away again. I was more concerned about reprisals from Saddam's loyalists. Word was bound to leak out. Too many Americans had been seen coming and going from our home.

We started sleeping at the homes of my daughter Isra'a and other family members. After some difficult negotiations I finally received word that my family of nine—my wife, my children, my son-in-law, and my two grandchildren—should prepare to leave Iraq. We returned to our house during the daytime to gather our belongings. Knowing that we would not be coming back anytime soon, Layla packed boxes of dishes, bedding, books, and clothes. My children filled their suitcases, knowing that they could not tell their friends that they were about to disappear. The day before our departure, I watered my garden for the last time. As I gave the fruit trees an extra soaking, I saw a young mango hanging from a low branch of its small tree. Slender and green, it was the first mango of the year. The sight of it struck in me a melancholy chord, as I realized I would not have a chance to watch it mature into a sweet yellow-red fruit. I was sad to be leaving my homeland, which had given me so many wonderful, as well as terrifying, memories. Looking at the unripe mango reminded me that I would not be able to take part in the reconstruction of Iraq either, at least not directly, until I felt it was safe to return.

The next morning, on June 20, Americans in two sport utility vehicles arrived to collect my family and me for the trip to Kuwait. Curious neighbors peered out from cracks in their front gates as we gathered our belongings at the edge of our driveway. Although the sun was still low in the sky, it beat down fiercely. We loaded our bags into the American vehicles as though in a trance. In the back seat, I put my arms around my two youngest daughters, who were still numb with fear. There was no telling what the future had in store for us. I assumed we would be brought to the United States, but even this was still unclear. As we pulled away from our home, my family and I instinctively turned our heads around for a final look at our front gate. No one said a word. We were too exhausted for conversation, overwhelmed by conflicting feelings as we left behind one uncertain place and set out for another. Although I was thankful that my family would be safer once removed from the chaos and insecurity in Iraq, we were all devastated by a sense of loss. In many ways we were leaving ourselves behind, along with our friends, our extended family, and our past.

EPILOGUE

My family and I now live in a suburban housing complex in an undisclosed location in the United States. Our three apartments are clean and comfortable, with automatic dishwashers, cable TV, and an indoor swimming pool nearby. Although we sometimes find our new circumstances bewildering, my family and I are trying to adjust to an American way of life as best we can. My young grandchildren have started to pick up English as though it were their native tongue. Zaid, Amne, and Ayat are studying the language to prepare to enter American schools. My daughters are still huge fans of Arabic pop music, but they have recently been listening to Western singers such as Mariah Carey and Britney Spears. Zaid works out at the gym in our building to counter the effects of his newfound love of American junk food. He is reading the works of Ernest Hemingway to widen his vocabulary, and is pre-enrolled in an engineering program at a respected university.

Layla anchors our home and our social life as she always did, organizing get-togethers with Iraqi friends and distant relatives who live in the United States. To the repertoire of Iraqi meals she manages to cook with ingredients from the American supermarket she has added Western dishes, such as shepherd's pie and fried chicken. Her English is improving too, although we shared a laugh the day she came home from her shopping without raisins because she couldn't remember the word for them and was unable to describe them to the clerk.

The cinema and the shopping mall that are within walking distance of our apartment have become Amne's and Ayat's favorite haunts which, after many months of homesickness, is perhaps a sign that they are beginning to assimilate. We often go to the mall on family outings to look into the brightly lit shops and eat at the food court, which offers takeout fare from around the world. As we dine on pita sandwiches, tacos, or sushi, the bustle of families and groups of teenagers around us seems as lively as an Arabic bazaar. The center of the mall is surrounded by young palm trees that reach toward the glass skylight in the ceiling. Sitting in this strange indoor garden, I am often reminded of the groves of majestic date palms in Iraq—and of my own garden. My garden is one of the things I miss most from home. I long for the peace and solitude I used to find while tending to my flower beds and fruit trees, and I worry that they will die in my absence, even though some friends in Baghdad have promised to look after our home for us.

Soon after arriving to the United States in August 2003, I took my family to Washington, D.C., to see the monuments and buildings of the capital, including the Jefferson Memorial where I had first stood forty years earlier as a soon-to-be college freshman. I led Layla and Zaid to the center of the rotunda and pointed out the quotation on the inside of the dome, in which Jefferson swears "eternal hostility against every form of tyranny over the mind of man." As we stood under the bronze likeness of the former president, I thought of the nightmare of tyranny that seemed to have ended with the fall of Saddam's statue in Baghdad. But tyranny does not let go of the mind so easily.

These days, when strangers strike up conversations with me on the elevator or at the post office, I am friendly but still careful not to reveal too much about my background. Decades of fear and mistrust have left their mark on me. My mind knows that I am now living in relative safety, but my nerves cannot completely shake free of the conditioning of a quarter century in Saddam's grip. I catch myself looking over my shoulder at times. There are nights when I wake up disoriented, terrified that Saddam's security services still have me under surveillance. I would like to think that I will be able to banish this fear. But in some ways I probably never will.

As I try to make sense of my past and put it into perspective, one thing is clear. Although Saddam never had nuclear weapons at his disposal, the story of how close Iraq came to developing them should serve as a red flag to the international community. The nuclear threat is not going away. Other countries are trying to develop nuclear weapons, and one may assume that many more will attempt to do so in the future. The centrifuge is the single most dangerous piece of nuclear technology. Because it is the most efficient and easiest method to hide, the centrifuge will continue to be the preferred method for illicitly producing bomb-grade uranium. With advances in centrifuge technology, it is now possible to conceal a uranium enrichment program inside a single warehouse.

I hope my tale can serve as a warning about how this happens and will help the general public understand the danger. I also hope it illustrates the best way to combat this danger. Illicit nuclear programs share a common weak spot: they need international complicity. The Pakistanis developed the bomb because their scientists tapped expertise from the Netherlands, for example. The Iraqi centrifuge program could never have succeeded if we hadn't benefited from German, British, Swiss, and U.S. assistance.

The avenues I pursued in these and other countries have been closed down, partly because the Iraqi case made their governments more vigilant. Since the UN discovered our dealings with former M.A.N. New Technology scientists, for example, Germany and other Western countries have become leaders in export control laws.

The most powerful nations of the West are by now probably the worst place on earth to shop for illegal nuclear components. Regulations on dual-use items, and the companies that produce them, are forbidding. But it is nearly impossible to close every loophole worldwide. Many other nations are becoming advanced enough to produce centrifuge components. Companies in places such as Singapore, Indonesia, or Finland, which have high-tech infrastructure but no nuclear programs of their own, might be enlisted to manufacture components without setting off alarm bells.

Iraq is still central to stopping the threat of proliferation. Hundreds of nuclear scientists with expertise needed to enrich uranium and build bombs remain in Baghdad. Some of my former colleagues may have left the country before and after the invasion, and this poses an ongoing danger that the know-how to produce weapons of mass destruction might proliferate beyond Iraq's borders. Long after Saddam's nuclear program ended, its scientists remain walking encyclopedias of centrifuge technology. They could be very valuable to a foreign weapons program.

As my story shows, scientists are often recruited for their knowledge and then placed in situations over which they have little control. Despite the brave words imprinted on the Jefferson Memorial, tyranny can put a man in an untenable position if he wants to protect his family. Understanding this pressure is a key to stopping the proliferation of nuclear weapons. I do not believe that my former colleagues are actively trying to sell their nuclear knowledge on the black market. But Iraq is a dangerous and unstable place to live now, and some former WMD scientists may be out of work. They could easily become targets for anyone wanting to tap into the skills they learned at Saddam's bidding.

As the uncovering of the Libyan nuclear program demonstrated in 2004, there still exists an international black market hungry for nuclear technology and expertise. The world was shocked to learn how centrifuge secrets from Pakistan had spread to Libya, Iran, and North Korea, and perhaps beyond. The lesson is simple: knowledge is the first and most important ingredient for a covert weapons program, and once nuclear know-how goes underground it is difficult to control.

Former nuclear scientists in Baghdad need good jobs that give them an incentive to stay in Iraq. Steps should be taken to ensure their safety, so that the possibility never arises that they might be coerced into serving a clandestine nuclear program for another country or terrorist group. Perhaps some of the top-tier scientists could be brought out of Iraq for the time being. It is crucial that one consequence of the liberation of Iraq is to lessen the risk of proliferation rather than increasing it.

Every night my family and I watch the news on Al Jazeera and CNN in an attempt to understand what is happening in our homeland. The future is so uncertain, and it is frustrating to be so far removed from these developments about which I care so much. I know it is not yet safe for me to return to Iraq, but I plan to do so someday, at least to be buried in my birthplace. As for my children, I cannot begin to imagine what paths their lives will take, just as I could not have imagined my own fate when I was their age. I can only pray that tyranny will never shape their careers as it did mine.

Zaid recently told me that if the situation in Iraq becomes more stable, he wants to return to Baghdad after he earns his university degree to help in the reconstruction of the country. When he said this, I saw a spark of passion in his eye that rekindled something in me. I suddenly saw myself at his age, idealistic and dreaming that I could help my fertile country bloom once again. I would like to think that, unlike me, he will be able to use his engineering skills toward more peaceful ends.

ACKNOWLEDGMENTS

I want to acknowledge the sacrifices and suffering of a generation of Iraqis who lived through the Saddam Hussein era. For the sake of those who did not survive and of those who were left scarred, we must never forget the oppression of his regime lest it be repeated.

The authors would like to give special thanks to David Albright whose assistance made this book possible. Many thanks also to Molly Bingham, Corey Hinderstein, Jamal Salman, Jacques Baute, Garry Dillon, Alice Martell, Danelle Morton, Seamus Conlan, Christiane Jory, Eric Nelson, Laura Cusack, Lori Sayde-Mehrtens, and Devra K. Nelson. We would also like to thank the Obeidi and Pitzer families, for their love and support through difficult times.

INDEX

Abdullah, Dr., 126–128
Afghanistan, 186
airline transport, of radioactive
    material, 112
al-Atheer facility, destruction of,
    154–155
Albright, David, 206–207,
    208–209, 210, 211–212
al-Furat facility
    centrifuges, 129
    UN weapons inspectors,
    146–147, 189
algebra, 116
Ali, Ali Mutalib, 87–88, 99, 101,
    105, 109, 122, 133
Al-Jazeera television network, ix,
    22, 191, 229
Almelo (Netherlands), 87–88
al-Qaeda, 186
aluminum tubes
    centrifuge program, x
    rocket technology, 195–196

UN weapons inspectors,
    187–188, 193–194
    See also Iraqi nuclear program
Amin, Husam Mohammed, 210
anthrax, 198
antiaircraft rocket, shoulder-
    launched, 181
antiaircraft system, of Iraq, 190
Austria, magnet procurement,
    109–111, 112
Aziz, Faris Abdul, 67, 126,
    144–145, 187, 194, 195–196,
    205–206
Aziz, Tariq, 144, 168, 220

Baath Party
    coup d'état of 1963, 36
    coup d'état of 1968, 36
    formation of, 33
    Military Industrialization Com-
    mission (MIC, Iraq), 13, 15
    Obeidi, Mahdi, 180